D1882695

REVISED TRANSLATION OF THE
CHAHAR MAQALA

REVISED TRANSLATION OF THE

CHAHAR MAQALA

(" FOUR DISCOURSES")

OF

NIZAMI-I-'ARUDI

OF SAMARQAND,

FOLLOWED BY AN ABRIDGED TRANSLATION OF MIRZA MUHAMMAD'S NOTES TO THE PERSIAN TEXT

BY

EDWARD G. BROWNE,

M.A., M.B., F.B.A., F.R.C.P.

GYAN

Published by

Gyan Publishing House
5, Ansari Road
Daryaganj, New Delhi-110002
Phone: 011-47034999, 9811692060
E-mail: books@gyanbooks.com

Distribution Network
gyanbooks.com
India, USA, Canada, UK, Australia, France

© Publisher

All rights reserved. No part of this work may be reproduced, stored, adapted, or transmitted in any form or by any means, electronic, mechanical, photocopying, micro-filming, recording or otherwise, or translated in any language, without the prior written permission of the copyright owner and the publisher.

ISBN : 978-81-212-6362-7 (PB)
First Published, 1921

2nd Impression 2022

Printed at: Gyan Press, Delhi.

The book is sold subject to the condition that it shall not, by way of trade or otherwise, be lent, resold, hired out, or otherwise circulated without the prior publisher's written consent.

REVISED TRANSLATION OF THE CHAHAR MAQALA
Author: EDWARD G. BROWNE

REVISED TRANSLATION
OF THE
CHAHÁR MAQÁLA

("FOUR DISCOURSES")

OF

NIẒÁMÍ-I-'ARÚḌÍ

OF SAMARQAND,

FOLLOWED BY AN ABRIDGED TRANSLATION OF MÍRZÁ MUḤAMMAD'S NOTES TO THE PERSIAN TEXT

BY

EDWARD G. BROWNE,
M.A., M.B., F.B.A., F.R.C.P.

1921

"E. J. W. GIBB MEMORIAL" PUBLICATIONS.

OLD SERIES. (25 works, 37 published volumes.)

I. **Bábur-náma** (Turkí text, fac-simile), ed. Beveridge, 1905. *Out of print.*

II. **History of Ṭabaristán** of Ibn Isfandiyár, abridged transl. Browne, 1905, 8*s.*

III, 1-5. **History of Rasúlí dynasty of Yaman** by al-Khazrají; 1, 2 transl. of Sir James Redhouse, 1907–8, 7*s.* each; 3, Annotations by the same, 1908, 5*s.*; 4, 5, Arabic text ed. Muḥammad 'Asal, 1908–1913, 8*s.* each.

IV. **Omayyads and 'Abbásids,** transl. Margoliouth from the Arabic of G. Zaidán, 1907, 5*s.*

V. **Travels of Ibn Jubayr,** Arabic text, ed. de Goeje, 1907, 10*s.*

VI, 1, 2, 3, 5, 6. **Yáqút's Dict. of learned men** (*Irshádu-'l-Aríb*), Arabic text, ed. Margoliouth, 1908–1913; 20*s.*, 12*s.*, 10*s.*, 15*s.*, 15*s.* respectively.

VII, 1, 5, 6. **Tajáribu'l-Umam of Miskawayhi** (Arabic text, fac-simile), ed. le Strange and others, 1909–1917, 7*s.* each vol.

VIII. **Marzubán-náma** (Persian text), ed. Mírzá Muḥammad, 1909, 12*s.*

IX. **Textes Ḥouroûfîs** (French and Persian), by Huart and Riẓá Tevfíq, 1909, 10*s.*

X. **Mu'jam,** an old Persian system of prosody, by Shams-i-Qays, ed. Mírzá Muḥammad, 1909, 15*s.*

XI, 1, 2. **Chahár Maqála**; 1, Persian text, ed. and annotated by Mírzá Muḥammad, 1910, 12*s.*; 2, English transl. and notes by Browne, 1921, 15*s.*

XII. **Introduction à l'Histoire des Mongols,** by Blochet, 1910, 10*s.*

XIII. **Díwán of Ḥassán b. Thábit** (Arabic text), ed. Hirschfeld, 1910, 7*s.* 6*d.*

XIV, 1, 2. **Ta'ríkh-i-Guzída** of Ḥamdu'lláh Mustawfí; 1, Persian text, fac-simile, 1911, 15*s.*; 2, Abridged translation and Indices by Browne, 1914, 10*s.*

XV. **Nuqtatu'l-Káf** (History of the Bábís) by Mírzá Jání (Persian text), ed. Browne, 1911, 12*s.*

XVI, 1, 2, 3. **Ta'ríkh-i-Jahán-gusháy** of Juwayní, Persian text, ed. Mírzá Muḥammad; 1, Mongols, 1913, 15*s.*; 2, Khwárazmsháhs, 1917, 15*s.*; 3, Assassins, in preparation.

XVII. **Kashfu'l-Maḥjúb** (Ṣúfí doctrine), transl. Nicholson, 1911, 15*s.*

XVIII, 2 (all hitherto published), **Jámi'u't-Tawáríkh** of Rashídu'd-Dín Faḍlu'lláh (Persian text), ed. and annotated by Blochet, 1912, 15*s.*

XIX. **Kitábu'l-Wulát** of al-Kindí (Arabic text), ed. Guest, 1912, 15*s*.

XX. **Kitábu'l-Ansáb** of as-Sam'ání (Arabic text, fac-simile), 1913, 20*s*.

XXI. **Díwáns of 'Ámir b. aṭ-Ṭufayl and 'Abíd b. al-Abraṣ** (Arabic text and transl. by Sir Charles J. Lyall), 1914, 12*s*.

XXII. **Kitábu'l-Lum'a** (Arabic text), ed. Nicholson, 1915, 15*s*.

XXIII, 1, 2. **Nuzhatu-'l-Qulúb** of Ḥamdu'lláh Mustawfí; 1, Persian text, ed. le Strange, 1915, 8*s*.; 2, English transl. le Strange, 1918, 8*s*.

XXIV. **Shamsu'l-'Ulúm** of Nashwán al-Ḥimyarí, extracts from the Arabic text with German Introduction and Notes by 'Aẓímu'd-Dín Aḥmad, 1917, 5*s*.

[XXV. **Díwáns of aṭ-Ṭufayl b. 'Awf and aṭ-Ṭirimmáḥ b. Ḥakím** (Arabic text), ed. Krenkow, in preparation.]

NEW SERIES.

Ráḥatu'ṣ-Ṣudúr (History of Saljúqs) of ar-Ráwandí, Persian text, ed. Muḥammad Iqbál (in the Press).

Fárs-náma of Ibnu'l-Balkhí, Persian text, ed. le Strange and Nicholson (in the Press).

Letters of Rashídu'd-Dín Faḍlu'lláh, abridged English transl. by Muḥammad Shafí', followed by transl. of **Tansúq-náma** (on Precious stones) by the late Sir A. Houtum-Schindler (in preparation).

Mázandarán, topography of, and travels in, by H. L. Rabino, with Map.

This Volume is one
of a Series
published by the Trustees of the

"E. J. W. GIBB MEMORIAL."

The Funds of this Memorial are derived from the Interest accruing from a Sum of money given by the late MRS GIBB of Glasgow, to perpetuate the Memory of her beloved son

ELIAS JOHN WILKINSON GIBB,

and to promote those researches into the History, Literature, Philosophy and Religion of the Turks, Persians and Arabs, to which, from his Youth upwards, until his premature and deeply lamented Death in his forty-fifth year, on December 5, 1901, his life was devoted.

تِلْكَ آثَارُنَا تَدُلُّ عَلَيْنَا * فَانْظُرُوا بَعْدَنَا إِلَى الآثَارِ

"These are our works, these works our souls display;
Behold our works when we have passed away."

"*E. J. W. GIBB MEMORIAL*":

ORIGINAL TRUSTEES.

[*JANE GIBB, died November 26, 1904.*]

E. G. BROWNE,

G. LE STRANGE,

[*H. F. AMEDROZ, died March 17, 1917.*]

A. G. ELLIS,

R. A. NICHOLSON,

SIR E. DENISON ROSS,

ADDITIONAL TRUSTEE.

IDA W. E. OGILVY GREGORY, appointed 1905.

CLERK OF THE TRUST.

W. L. RAYNES,

15, Sidney Street,

CAMBRIDGE.

PUBLISHER FOR THE TRUSTEES.

MESSRS LUZAC & Co.,

46, Great Russell Street,

LONDON, W.C.

PREFACE

TWO reasons have led me to publish this revised translation of the *Chahár Maqála*, or "Four Discourses," of Niẓámí-i-'Arúḍí of Samarqand. The first is that the translation which I originally published in the July and October numbers of the *Journal of the Royal Asiatic Society* for 1899, and which also appeared as a separate reprint, is exhausted, and is now hardly obtainable. The second is that that translation contains many defects and errors which it is now possible to amend and correct, partly through the learning and critical acumen brought to bear on the text by Mírzá Muḥammad of Qazwín, whose admirable edition, accompanied by copious critical and historical notes in Persian, was published in this Series (xi, 1) in 1910; and partly from the fact that the most ancient and correct MS. of the work at present discovered[1], that preserved in the Library of 'Áshir Efendi at Constantinople (No. 285), was not available when I made my original translation, while it has served as the basis for Mírzá Muḥammad's text. Hence my old translation is not only practically unobtainable, but, apart from the defects inherent in a first attempt of this sort, no longer entirely corresponds with what is now the accepted Persian text, so that it is at times liable to confuse and puzzle, rather than to help, the student. The old translation has been carefully revised throughout, and the proofs have all been read by Mírzá Muḥammad, who supplied many valuable criticisms, together with a good deal of new material in the notes. They have also been diligently read by Muḥammad Iqbál, one of the Government of India Research Students at Cambridge, who has made many useful suggestions and saved me from numerous small errors. To these and to other friends who have helped me in a lesser degree I am deeply indebted, but special thanks are due to Mr Ralph Shirley, editor

[1] It was copied in Herát in 835/1431–2.

of the *Occult Review*, and to Mr W. Gornold for the valuable astrological notes with which they have been kind enough to supply me[1]. To facilitate comparison, the points in the translation corresponding with the beginning of each page of the Persian text are indicated by the appropriate Arabic numbers. Mírzá Muḥammad's notes, which in the original partake of the nature of a running commentary on the text, though materially separated from it, and occupy 200 pages (٩٠—٢٨٩), I have, from considerations of space, rearranged and greatly compressed. The shorter ones appear as foot-notes on the pages to which they refer, while the substance of the longer ones, reduced to a minimum, and shorn of many of the *pièces justificatives* which serve to illustrate them in the original, has been divided according to subject-matter under thirty-two headings, fully enumerated in the following Table of Contents. But although the English notes embody the more important results of Mírzá Muḥammad's researches, it has been necessary, in order to effect the required condensation, to omit many interesting details and quotations of texts accessible only in rare manuscripts, so that those who read Persian with any facility are strongly recommended to study the original commentary.

A full account of this work and its author is given both in the Persian and English Prefaces to the companion volume containing the text, and it will be sufficient here to summarize the facts set forth more fully in that place.

The Author.

Aḥmad ibn 'Umar ibn 'Alí of Samarqand, poetically named Niẓámí and further entitled 'Arúḍí (the "Prosodist") flourished in the first half of the sixth century of the *hijra* (twelfth of the Christian era), and seems to have spent most of his life in Khurásán and Transoxiana. What we know of him is chiefly derived

[1] See Notes XXIV and XXXII, pp. 130–4 and 164–7.

from this book, which contains a good deal of autobiographical material. The events in his life to which he refers lie between the years 504/1110–1111 and 547/1152–3, and we find him successively at Samarqand, Balkh, Herát, Ṭús and Níshápúr. He was primarily a poet and courtier, but, as we learn from Anecdotes XXXI (p. 74) and XLIII (p. 96), he also practised Astrology and Medicine when occasion arose. His poetry, in spite of the complacency displayed by him in Anecdote XXI (pp. 59–61), was not, if we may judge by the comparatively scanty fragments which have survived, of the highest order, and is far inferior to his prose, which is admirable, and, in my opinion, almost unequalled in Persian. It is by virtue of the *Chahár Maqála*, and that alone, that Niẓámí-i-'Arúḍí of Samarqand deserves to be reckoned amongst the great names of Persian literature.

The Book.

At the present day, apart from the text printed eleven years ago in this series and the rare and bad lithographed edition[1] published at Tihrán in 1305/1887–8, the *Chahár Maqála*, so far as at present known, is represented only by three or four MSS., two in the British Museum (Or. 2955, dated 1274/1857–8, and Or. 3507, dated 1017/1608–9), and one in Constantinople transcribed at Herát in 835/1431–2, while a fourth, of which no particulars are available to me, is said to exist in India. During the thirteenth, fourteenth and fifteenth centuries of our era it seems to have been better known than during the four succeeding centuries, for it is mentioned or cited in the thirteenth century by 'Awfí (in the *Lubábu'l-Albáb*) and Ibn Isfandiyár (in his History of Ṭabaristán); in the fourteenth century by Ḥamdu'lláh Mustawfí of Qazwín (in the *Ta'ríkh-i-Guzída*); in the fifteenth century by Dawlatsháh and Jámí (in the *Silsilatu'dh-Dhahab*); and in the sixteenth by the Qáḍí Aḥmad-i-Ghaffárí (*Nigáristán*). It is often referred to as the *Majma'u'n-Nawádir* ("Collection of Rarities"), which the

[1] Indicated by the letter L in a few of the foot-notes.

Turkish bibliographer Ḥájji Khalífa supposes to be distinct from the *Chahár Maqála*, though, as Mírzá Muḥammad has conclusively proved, these are but two different names for the same book.

Not less remarkable than the style of the *Chahár Maqála* is the interest of its contents, for it contains the only contemporary account of 'Umar Khayyám, and the oldest known account of Firdawsí, while many of the anecdotes are derived from the author's own experience, or were orally communicated to him by persons who had direct knowledge of the facts. The book is therefore one of the most important original sources for our knowledge of the literary and scientific conditions which prevailed in Persia for the two or three centuries preceding its composition, which may be placed with certainty between the years 547/1152 and 552/1157, and with great probability in the year 551/1156[1]. Against this twofold excellence, however, must be set the extraordinary historical inaccuracies of which in several places the author has been guilty, even in respect to events in which he claims to have participated in person. Fifteen such blunders, some of them of the grossest character, have been enumerated by Mírzá Muḥammad in the Preface to the text[2], and some of these are fully discussed in Notes IV, V, VIII and XXI at the end of this volume. Nor can all these blunders be charitably ascribed to a careless or officious copyist, since the point of the story is in several cases dependent on the error.

Here at all events is the translation of the book, of the value and interest of which the reader, aided if necessary by the notes, can form his own judgement.

[1] See p. xvi of the English Preface to the text.
[2] Pp. xx–xxiii of the English Preface.

EDWARD G. BROWNE.

April 11, 1921.

TABLE OF CONTENTS

NOTES.

In the name of God the Merciful the Clement.

PRAISE, thanks and gratitude to that King who, by the intervention[1] of the Cherubic and Angelic Spirits, brought into being the World of Return and Restoration, and, by means of that World, created and adorned the World of Growth and Decay, maintaining it by the commands and prohibitions of the Prophets and Saints, and restraining it by the swords and pens of Kings and Ministers. And blessings upon [Muḥammad] the Lord of both worlds, who was the most perfect of the Prophets; and invocations of grace upon his Family and Companions, who were the most excellent of Saints. And honour to the King of this time, that learned, just, divinely-strengthened, heaven-aided and ever-victorious monarch *Ḥusámu'd-Dawla wa'd-Dín*, Help of Islám and the Muslims, Exterminator of the infidels and polytheists, Subduer of the heretical and the froward, Chief of hosts in the worlds, Pride of Kings and Emperors, Succourer of these days, Protector of mankind, Arm of the Caliphate, Beauty of the Faith and Glory of the Nation, Controller of the Arabs and the Persians, noblest of mankind, *Shamsu'l-Ma'álí, Maliku'l-Umará*, Abu'l-Ḥasan 'Alí ibn Mas'úd[2], Helper of the Prince of Believers, may his life be according to his desires, may the greater part of the world be assigned to his name, and may the orderly government of the human race be directed by his care! For to-day he is the most excellent of the kings of the age in nobility, pedigree, judgement, statesmanship, justice, equity, valour and generosity, as well as in the enriching of his territory, the embellishment of his realms, the maintenance of his friends, the subjugation of his foes, the raising of armies, the safe-guarding of the people, the securing of the roads, and the tranquillizing of the realms[3], by virtue of upright judgement, clear understanding, strong resolve and firm determination; by whose excellence the concatenation of the House of Shansab[4] is held together and maintained in order, and by whose perfection the strong arm of that Dynasty's fortune is strengthened and recognized. May God Almighty

[1] L. has بلا توسّط "without the intervention."

[2] *I.e.* Ḥusámu'd-Dín Abu'l-Ḥasan 'Alí ibn Fakhru'd-Dín Mas'úd. See Note I at the end.

[3] L. has از مهالك "from perils," instead of ممالك.

[4] See Note I at the end, and the *Ṭabaqát-i-Náṣirí* (ed. Nassau Lees), pp. 101 *et seqq.* Instead of *Shansab*, the correct reading, B. has الساتيت and L. آل شيب.

vouchsafe to him and to the other kings of that line a full portion of dominion and domain, throne and fortune, fame and success, command and prohibition, by His Favour and universal Grace!

SECTION I.

It is an old custom and ancient convention, which custom is maintained and observed, that an author (٢) or compiler, in the introduction to his discourse and preface of his book, should commemorate somewhat of his patron's praise, and record some prayer on behalf of the object of his eulogy. But I, a loyal servant, instead of praise and prayer for this prince, will make mention in this book of the favours ordained and vouchsafed by God Most High and Most Holy to this King of kingly parentage, that, these being submitted to his world-illuminating judgement, he may betake himself to the expression of his thanks for them. For in the uncreated Scripture and unmade Word God says, "*Verily if ye be thankful I will give you increase*[1]"; for the gratitude of the servant is an alchemy for the favours of the Munificent Lord. Briefly, then, it behoves this great King and puissant Lord to know that to-day, upon the whole of this globe of dust, and within the circle of this green parasol[2], there is no king in more ample circumstances than this monarch, nor any potentate enjoying more abundant good than this sovereign. He hath the gift of youth and the blessing of constant health; his father and mother are alive; congenial brothers are on his right hand and on his left. And what father is like his sire, the mighty, divinely-strengthened, ever-victorious and heaven-aided *Fakhru'd-Dawla wa'd-Dín*[3], Lord of Írán, King of the Mountains (may God prolong his existence and continue to the heights his exaltation!), who is the most puissant Lord of the age and the most excellent Prince of the time in judgement, statecraft, knowledge, courtesy, swordsmanship, strength of arm, treasure and equipment! Supported by ten thousand men bearing spears and handling reins he hath made himself a shield before his sons, so that not even the zephyr may blow roughly on one of his servants. In her chaste seclusion and unassailable abode is a prayerful lady (may God perpetuate her exaltation!) whose every invocation, breathed upwards at earliest dawn to the Court of God, works with the far-flung host and wheeling army. Where again is a brother like the royal Prince *Shamsu'd-Dawla wa'd-Dín*[4], Light of Islám and the Muslims (may his victories be

[1] *Qur'án*, xiv, 7.

[2] The variant چرخ (wheel, firmament), though more attractive than چتر (parasol, umbrella), rests on weaker manuscript authority.

[3] Fakhru'd-Dín Mas'úd ibn 'Izzu'd-Dín Ḥasan. See Note I at the end.

[4] Shamsu'd-Dín Muḥammad ibn Fakhru'd-Dín Mas'úd. See Note I at the end.

glorious!), who reaches the extreme term and limit in the service of this my Lord (whose exaltation may God perpetuate!)? Praise be to God that this my Lord falls short neither in reward nor retribution; yea, by his face the world enjoys clear vision, and life passes sweetly by his beauty! And a blessing yet greater is this, that the All-Perfect Benefactor and Unfailing Giver hath bestowed on him an uncle like the Lord of the World and Sovereign of the East, *'Alá'u'd-Dunyá wa'd-Dín* Abú 'Alí al-Ḥusayn ibnu'l-Ḥusayn[1], *Ikhtiyáru Amíri'l-Mú'minín* (may God prolong his life and cause his kingdom to endure!), who, with fifty thousand mail-clad men, strenuous in endeavour, hurled back all the hosts of the world (٣) and set in a corner all the kings of the age. May God (blessed and exalted is He!) long vouchsafe all to one another, grant to all abundant enjoyment of one another's company, and fill the world with light by their achievements, by His Favour, and Bounty, and Grace!

BEGINNING OF THE BOOK.

This loyal servant and favoured retainer Aḥmad ibn 'Umar ibn 'Alí an-Niẓámí al-'Arúḍí as-Samarqandí, who for forty-five years hath been devoted to the service of this House and inscribed in the register of service of this Dynasty, desireth to dedicate to the Supreme Imperial Court (may God exalt it!) some work equipped according to the canons of Philosophy with decisive proofs and trenchant arguments, and to set forth therein what kingship truly is, who is truly king, whence is derived this honourable office, to whom rightly appertaineth this favour, and in what manner such an one should shew his gratitude for, and after what fashion accept, this privilege, so that he may become second to the Lord of the sons of men[2] and third to the Creator of the Universe. For even so hath God, in His Incontrovertible Scripture and Eternal Word, co-ordinated on one thread and shewn forth on one string the pearls represented by these three exalted titles. "*Obey God*," saith He, "*and obey the Apostle, and such as possess authority amongst yourselves*[3]."

For in the grades of existences and the ranks of the intelligibles, after the Prophetic Function, which is the supreme limit of man's attainment, there is no rank higher than kingship, which is naught else than a Divine gift. God, glorious and exalted is He, hath accorded this position to the King of this age, and bestowed on him this degree, so that he may walk after the way of former kings and maintain the people after the manner of bygone ages.

1 'Alá'u'd-Dín Ḥusayn, called *Jahán-súz*, "the world-consumer," A.H. 544–556 (A.D. 1149–1161). See Notes I and XV at the end, and p. 31, n. 1 *ad calc.*

2 *I.e.* to the Prophet, who is subordinate only to God, as the king is to him.

3 *Qur'án*, iv, 62.

SECTION II.

The Royal Mind (may God exalt it!) should deign to know that all existing beings fall necessarily into one of two categories. Such being is either self-existent, or it exists through some other. That Being which is self-existent is called "*the Necessarily Existent,*" which is God most High and most Holy, who existeth by virtue of Himself, and who, therefore, hath always existed, since He awaiteth none other; and who (1) will always exist, since He subsisteth by Himself, not by another. But that existence whose being is through another is called "*Contingent Being,*" and this is such as we are, since our being is from the seed, and the seed is from the blood, and the blood is from food, and food is from the water, the earth and the sun, whose existence is in turn derived from something else; and all these are such as yesterday were not, and to-morrow will not be. And on profound reflection [it appeareth that] this causal nexus reacheth upwards to a Cause which deriveth not its being from another, but existeth necessarily in itself; which is the Creator of all, from Whom all derive their existence and subsistence. So He is the Creator of all these things, and all come into being through Him and subsist through Him. And a little reflection on this matter will make it clear that all Phenomena consist of Being tinctured with Not-being, while He is Being characterized by a continuance reaching from Eternity past to Eternity to come. And since the origin of all creatures lies in Not-being, they must inevitably return again to nothing, and the most clear-sighted amongst the human race have said, "*Everything shall return unto its Origin,*" more especially in this world of Growth and Decay. Therefore we, who are contingent in our being, have our origin in Not-being; while He, who existeth necessarily, is in His Essence Being, even as He (glorious is His Praise and high His Splendour) saith in the Perspicuous Word and Firm Hand-hold, "*All things perish save His Countenance*[1]."

Now you must know that this world, which lies in the hollow of the Heaven of the Moon[2] and within the circle of this first Sphere, is called "the World of Growth and Decay." And you must thus conceive it, that within the concavity of the Heaven of the Moon lies the Fire, surrounded by the Heaven of the Moon; and that within the Sphere of the Fire is the Air, surrounded by the Fire; and within the Air is the Water, surrounded by the Air, while within the Water is the Earth, with the Water round about it. And in the middle of the earth is an imaginary point, from

[1] *Qur'án*, xxviii, 88.

[2] This is the lowest or innermost of the nine celestial spheres which environ the earth. Concerning the Muslim Cosmogony, see Dieterici's *Makrokosmos*, pp. 178 *et seqq.*

which all straight lines drawn to the Heaven of the Moon are equal; and when we speak of "down," we mean this point or what lies nearest to it; and when we speak of "up," we mean the remotest heaven, or what lies nearest to it, this being a heaven[1] above the Zodiacal Heaven, having naught beyond it, for with it the material world terminates, or comes to an end[2].

Now when God most Blessed and most High, by His effective Wisdom, desired to produce in this world minerals, plants, animals and men, He created the stars, and in particular the sun and moon, whereon He made the growth and decay of these to depend. And the special property of the sun is that (•) by its reflection it warms all things when it stands opposite to them, and draws them up, that is attracts them, by the medium of heat. So, by its opposition, it warmed the water; and, by means of the warmth, attracted it for a long while, until one quarter of the earth's surface was laid bare, by reason of the much vapour which ascended and rose up therefrom. Now it is of the nature of water to be capable of becoming stone, as it is admitted to do in certain places, and as may be actually witnessed[3]. So mountains were produced from the water by the glow of the sun; and thereby the earth became somewhat elevated above what it had been, while the water retreated from it and dried up, according to that fashion which is witnessed. This portion, therefore, is called the "Uncovered Quarter," for the reason above stated; and is also called the "Inhabited Quarter," because animals dwell therein.

SECTION III.

When the influences of these stars had acted on the peripheries of these elements, and had been reflected back from that imaginary [central] point, there were produced from the midst of the earth and water, by the aid of the wind and the fire, the products of the inorganic world, such as mountains, mines, clouds, snow, rain, thunder, lightning, shooting stars, comets, meteors, thunder-bolts, halos, conflagrations, fulminations, earthquakes, and springs of all kinds, as has been fully explained in its proper place when discussing the effects of the celestial bodies, but for the explanation and amplification of which there is no room in this brief manual. But when time began, and the cycles of heaven became continuous, and the constitution of this lower world matured, and the time was come for the fertilisation of

[1] This outermost, or ninth, celestial sphere is the *Primum mobile* of the Ptolemaic system, called *al-Falaku'l-Aṭlas* or *Falaku'l-Aflák* by the Muslim philosophers.

[2] That the material universe is finite and bounded by the Empyrean, or *Falaku'l-Aflák*, is generally accepted by Persian philosophers. See my *Year amongst the Persians*, pp. 143–144.

[3] The author apparently alludes to petrifaction and the formation of stalactytes.

that interspace which lies between the water and the air, the vegetable kingdom was manifested. Then God, blessed and exalted is He, created for that substance wherefrom the plants were made manifest four subservient forces and three faculties. Of these four subservient forces one is that which draws to itself whatever is suitable for its purpose, and this is called "the Force Attractive" (*Jádhiba*). Another retains what the first may have attracted, and this is called "the Force Retentive" (*Másika*). The third is that which assimilates what has been attracted, and transmutes it from its former state until it becomes like unto itself, and this is called "the Force Assimilative" (*Háḍima*). The fourth is that which rejects what is not appropriate, and it is called "the Force Expulsive" (*Dáfi'a*). And of its three faculties one is that which increaseth it (۱) by diffusing throughout it nutritious matters with a proportionate and equable diffusion. The second is that which accompanies this nutriment until it reaches the extremities. The third is that which, when the organism has attained perfection and begins to tend towards decline, appears and produces ova, in order that, if destruction overtake the parent in this world, this substitute may take its place, so that the order of the world may be immune from injury, and the species may not become extinct. This is called "the Reproductive Faculty" (*Quwwat-i-Muwallida*).

So this Kingdom rose superior to the inorganic world in these several ways which have been mentioned; and the far-reaching Wisdom of the Creator so ordained that these Kingdoms should be connected one with another successively and continuously, so that in the inorganic world the first material, which was clay, underwent a process of evolution and became higher in organisation until it grew to coral (*marján, bussad*), which is the ultimate term of the inorganic world[1] and is connected with the most primitive stage of plant-life. And the most primitive thing in the vegetable kingdom is the thorn, and the most highly developed the date-palm and the grape, which resemble the animal kingdom in that the former needs the male to fertilise it so that it may bear fruit[2], while the latter flees from its foe. For the vine flees from the bind-weed[3], a plant which, when it twists round the vine, causes it to shrivel up, wherefore the vine flees from it. In the vegetable kingdom, therefore, there is nothing higher than the date-palm and the vine, inasmuch as they have assimilated themselves to that which is superior to their own kingdom, and have subtly overstepped the limits of their own world, and evolved themselves in a higher direction.

[1] The Pearl, however, seems generally to be placed higher. See Dieterici's *Mikrokosmos*, p. 11.

[2] See Dieterici's *Mikrokosmos*, p. 25.

[3] *'Ashaqa*, a species of *Dolichos*. See Lane's Arabic Lexicon, *s.v.*

SECTION IV. *The Five External Senses.*

Now when this kingdom had attained perfection, and the influence of the "Fathers" of the upper world had reacted on the "Mothers[1]" below, and the interspace between the air and the fire in its turn became involved[2], a finer offspring resulted and the manifestation of the animal world took place. This, bringing with it the faculties already possessed by the vegetable kingdom, added thereunto two others, one the faculty of discovery, which is called the "Perceptive Faculty" (*Mudrika*), whereby the animal discerns things; the second the power of voluntary movement, by the help of which the animal moves, approaching that which is congenial to it and retreating from that which is offensive, which is called the "Motor Faculty" (*Muḥarrika*).

Now the "Perceptive Faculty" is subdivided into ten branches, five of which are called the "External Senses," and five the "Internal Senses." The former are "Touch" (v), "Taste," "Sight," "Hearing," and "Smell." Now Touch is a sense distributed throughout the skin and flesh of the animal, so that the nerves perceive and discern anything which comes in contact with them, such as dryness and moisture, heat and cold, roughness and smoothness, harshness and softness. Taste is a sense located in that nerve which is distributed over the surface of the tongue, which detects soluble nutriments in those bodies which come in contact with it; and it is this sense which discriminates between sweet and bitter, sharp and sour, and the like of these. Hearing is a sense located in the nerve which is distributed about the auditory meatus, so that it detects any sound which is discharged against it by undulations of the air compressed between two impinging bodies, that is to say two bodies striking against one another, by the impact of which the air is thrown into waves and becomes the cause of sound, in that it imparts movement to the air which is stationary in the auditory meatus, comes into contact with it, reaches this nerve, and gives rise to the sensation of hearing. Sight is a faculty, located in the optic nerve which discerns images projected on the crystalline humour, whether of figures or solid bodies, variously coloured, through the medium of a translucent substance which extends from it to the surfaces of reflecting bodies. Smell is a faculty located in a protuberance situated in the fore part of the brain and resembling the nipple of the female breast, which apprehends

[1] By the "Seven Fathers above" and the "Four Mothers below," the seven planets and the four elements are intended.

[2] The four elemental spheres (terrestrial, aqueous, aerial and igneous) present three interspaces (*furja*), in the first of which is produced the mineral kingdom, in the second the vegetable, and in the third the animal. These three are called the "threefold offspring."

what the air inhaled brings to it of odours mingled with the vapours wafted by air-currents, or impressed upon it by diffusion from the odorific body.

SECTION V. *The Five Internal Senses*[1].

Now as to the Internal Senses, some are such as perceive the forms of things sensible, while others are such as apprehend their meanings. The first is the "Composite Sense" (*Ḥiss-i-mushtarik*), which is a faculty located in the anterior ventricles of the brain, and in its nature receptive of all images perceived by the external senses and impressed upon them to be communicated to it, such perception being apprehended only when received by it. The second is the Imagination (*Khayál*), a faculty located (٨) in the posterior portion of the anterior ventricle of the brain, which preserves what the "Composite Sense" has apprehended from the external senses, so that this remains in it after the subsidence of the sense-impressions. The third is the "Imaginative Faculty" (*Mutakhayyila*), thus called when animals are under discussion, but, in the case of the human soul, named the "Cogitative Faculty" (*Mutafakkira*). This is a faculty located in the middle ventricle of the brain, whose function it is to combine or separate, as the mind may elect, those particular percepts which are stored in the Imagination. The fourth is the "Apprehensive Faculty" (*Wahm*), which is a faculty located in the posterior portion of the middle ventricle of the brain, whose function is to discover the supra-sensual ideas existing in particular percepts, such as that faculty whereby the kid distinguishes between its dam and a wolf, and the child between a spotted rope and a serpent. The fifth is the "Retentive Faculty" (*Ḥáfiza*), also called the "Memory" (*Dhákira*), which is a faculty located in the posterior ventricle of the brain. It preserves those supra-sensual ideas discovered by the "Apprehension"; between which and itself the same relation subsists as between the "Imagination" and the "Composite Sense," though the latter preserves forms, and the former ideas.

Now all these are the servants of the "Animal Soul," a substance having its well-spring in the heart, which, when it acts in the heart, is called the "Animal Spirit," but when in the brain, the "Psychic Spirit," and when in the liver, the "Natural Spirit." It is a subtle vapour which rises from the blood, diffuses itself to the remotest arteries, and resembles the sun in luminosity. Every animal which possesses these two faculties, the Perceptive and the Motor, and these ten subordinate faculties derived therefrom, is called a perfect animal; but if any faculty is lacking in it, defective. Thus the ant has no eyes, and the snake, which is

[1] See my *Year amongst the Persians*, pp. 144–145.

called the deaf adder, no ears; but none is more defective than the maggot, which is a red worm found in the mud of streams[1], called therefore *gil-khwára* ("mud-eater"), but in Transoxiana *ghák-kirma*[2]. This is the lowest animal, while the highest is the satyr (*nasnás*)[3], a creature inhabiting the plains of Turkistán, of erect carriage and vertical stature, with wide flat nails. It cherishes a great affection for men; wherever it sees men, it halts on their path and examines them attentively; and when it finds a solitary man, it carries him off, and it is even said that it will conceive from him. This, after (٩) mankind, is the highest of animals, inasmuch as in several respects it resembles man; first in its erect stature; secondly in the breadth of its nails; and thirdly in the hair of its head.

ANECDOTE I.

I heard as follows from Abú Riḍá ibn 'Abdu's-Salám of Níshápúr in the Great Mosque at Níshápúr, in the year 510/1116–1117:—"We were travelling towards Tamgháj[4], and in our caravan were several thousand camels. One day, when we were marching in the mid-day heat, we saw on a sand-hill a woman, bare-headed and quite naked, extremely beautiful in form, with a figure like a cypress, a face like the moon, and long hair, standing and looking at us. Although we spoke to her, she made no reply; and when we approached her, she fled, running so swiftly in her flight that probably no horse could have overtaken her. Our muleteers, who were Turks, said that this was a wild man, such as they call *nasnás*." And you must know that this is the noblest of animals in these three respects which have been mentioned.

So when, in the course of long ages and by lapse of time, equilibrium became more delicately adjusted, and the turn came of the interspace which is between the elements and the heavens[5], man came into being, bringing with him all that existed in the mineral, vegetable and animal kingdoms, and adding thereunto the capacity for abstract concepts. So by reason of in-

[1] Cf. Dieterici's *Mikrokosmos*, p. 43.

[2] The correct reading of this word, which appears in a different form in each MS., is doubtful, and it is probably a local term only. Mírzá Muḥammad takes *ghák-kirma* as equivalent to *kirm-i-khák*, "earthworm."

[3] The term *nasnás* either denotes a real animal or a fabulous monster. In the first sense it is used of various kinds of monkeys, *e.g.* the orang-outang and marmoset; in the latter it is equivalent to the *Shiqq* or Half-man (which resembles a man cut in two vertically) of the Arabs, and the *Dív-mardum* of the Persians. See Qazwíní's *'Ajá'ibu'l-Makhlúqát*, p. 449; and my *Year amongst the Persians*, pp. 165, 267.

[4] See Qazwíní's *Átháru'l-Bilád*, p. 275. China or Chinese Turkistán appears to be meant. See Note II at the end.

[5] See n. 2 at the foot of p. 7 *supra*. This fourth interspace (*furja*) lies outside the "Igneous Sphere" and inside the "Heaven of the Moon."

telligence he became king over all animals, and brought all things under his control. Thus from the mineral world he made jewels, gold and silver his adornment; from iron, zinc, copper, lead and tin he fashioned his utensils and vessels; from the vegetable kingdom he made his food, raiment and bedding; and from the animal world he obtained for himself steeds and beasts of burden. And from all three kingdoms he chose out medicaments wherewith to heal himself. Whereby did there accrue to him such pre-eminence? By this, that he understood abstract ideas, and, by means of these, recognized God. And whereby did he know God? By knowing himself; for "*He who knoweth himself, knoweth his Lord.*"

So this kingdom [of man] became divided into three classes. The first is that which is proximate to the Animal Kingdom, such as the wild men of the waste and the mountain, whose aspiration doth not more than suffice to secure their own livelihood by seeking what is to their advantage and warding off what is to their detriment. The second class compriseth the inhabitants of towns and cities, who possess civilisation, power of co-operation, (١٠) and aptitude to discover crafts and arts; but whose scientific attainments are limited to the organisation of such association as subsists between them, in order that the different classes[1] may continue to exist. The third class compriseth such as are independent of these things, and whose occupation, by night and by day, in secret and in public, is to reflect, "Who are we, for what reason did we come into existence, and Who hath brought us into being?" In other words, they hold debate concerning the real essences of things, reflect on their coming, and anxiously consider their departure, saying, "How have we come? Whither shall we go?"

This class, again, is subdivided into two sorts; first, those who reach the essence of this object by the help of masters and by laborious toil, voracious study, reading and writing; and such are called "Philosophers." But there is yet another sort who, without master or book, reach the extreme limit of this problem, and these are called "Prophets."

Now the peculiar virtues of the Prophet are three:—first, that, without instruction, he knows all knowledges[2]; secondly, that he gives information concerning yesterday and to-morrow otherwise than by analogical reasoning; and thirdly, that he hath such psychical power that from whatever body he will he taketh the form and produceth another form, which thing none can do save such as are conformed to the Angelic World. Therefore in the Human World none is above him, and his command

[1] Or perhaps "races." The word is انواع, plural of نوع, "species."

[2] This is what is called *'Ilm-i-Ladunní*, or knowledge directly derived from God.

is effective for the well-being of the world; for whatever others have, he has, while possessing also an additional qualification which they have not, that is to say communication with the Angelic World. This additional qualification is in brief termed the "Prophetic Function," and is in detail such as we have explained.

Now so long as such a man lives, he points out to his people what things conduce to well-being in both worlds, by the Command of God, glorious is His Name, communicated to him by means of the Angels. But when, by natural dissolution, he turns his face towards the other world, he leaves behind him as his representative a Code derived from the indications of God Almighty and his own sayings[1]. And assuredly he requires, to maintain his Law and Practice, a vice-gerent who must needs be the most excellent of that community and the most perfect product of that age, in order that he may maintain this Law and give effect to this Code; and such an one is called an "Imám." But this Imám cannot reach the horizons of the East, the West, the North and the South in such wise that the effects of his care may extend alike to the most remote and the nearest, and his command and prohibition may reach at once the intelligent and the ignorant. Therefore must he needs have vicars to act for him in distant parts of the world, and not every one of these will have such power that all mankind shall be compelled to acknowledge it. Hence there must be an administrator and compeller, which administrator and compeller is called a "Monarch," that is to say, a king; and his vicarious function "Sovereignty." The king, therefore, is the lieutenant of the Imám, the Imám of the Prophet, and the Prophet of God (mighty and glorious is He!). Well has Firdawsí said on this subject:—(۱۱)

چنان دان که شاهیّ و پیغمبری ٬ دو گوهر بود در یك انگشتری ٬

"*Then learn that the functions of Prophet and King*
Are set side by side like two stones in one ring."

The Lord of the sons of men[2] himself hath said, "*Church and State are twins,*" since in form and essence neither differs from the other, either as regards increase or defect. So, by virtue of this decree, no burden, after the Prophetic Office, is weightier than Sovereignty, nor any function more laborious than that of governing. Hence a king needs round about him, as men on whose counsel, judgement and deliberations depend the loosing and binding of the world, and the well-being and ill-being of the servants of God Almighty, such as are in every respect the most excellent and most perfect of their time.

[1] *I.e.* the Scripture and the Traditions, in the case of the Prophet Muḥammad the *Qur'án* and the *Ḥadíth*.

[2] *I.e.* the Prophet Muḥammad.

Now of the servants essential to kings are the Secretary, the Poet, the Astrologer and the Physician, with whom he can in no wise dispense. For the maintenance of the administration is by the Secretary; the perpetuation of immortal renown by the Poet; the ordering of affairs by the Astrologer; and the health of the body by the Physician. These four arduous functions and noble arts are amongst the branches of the Science of Philosophy; the functions of the Scribe and the Poet being brancnes of the Science of Logic; that of the Astrologer, one of the principal subdivisions of Mathematics; while the Physician's Art is amongst the branches of Natural Science. This book, therefore, comprises *Four Discourses*, to wit:—

First Discourse, on the essence of the Secretarial Art, and the nature of the eloquent and perfect Secretary.

Second Discorrse, on the essence of the Poetic Art, and the aptitude of the Poet.

Third Discourse, on the essence of the Science of Astrology, and the competence of the Astrologer in that Science.

Fourth Discourse, on the essence of the Science of Medicine, and the direction and disposition of the Physician.

Such philosophical considerations as are germane to this Book will therefore be advanced at the beginning of each Discourse; and thereafter ten pleasing anecdotes, of the choicest connected with that subject and the rarest appropriate to that topic, of what hath befallen persons of the class under discussion, will be adduced, in order that it may become plainly known to the King that the Secretarial Office is not a trivial matter; that the Poetic Calling is no mean occupation; that Astrology is a necessary Science; that Medicine is an indispensable Art; and that the wise King cannot do without these four persons, the Secretary, the Poet, the Astrologer, and the Physician.

(۱۴) FIRST DISCOURSE.

On the essence of the Secretarial Art, and the nature of the perfect Secretary and what is connected therewith.

The Secretarial Function is an art comprising analogical methods of rhetoric and communication, and teaching the forms of address employed amongst men in correspondence, consultation, contention, eulogy, condemnation, diplomacy, conciliation and provocation, as well as in magnifying matters or minimising them; contriving means of excuse or censure; imposing covenants; recording precedents; and displaying in every case orderly arrangement of the subject matter, so that all may be enunciated in the best and most suitable manner.

Hence the Secretary must be of gentle birth, of refined honour, of penetrating discernment, of profound reflection, and of piercing judgement; and the amplest portion and fullest share of literary culture and its fruits must be his. Neither must he be remote from, or unacquainted with, logical analogies; and he must know the ranks of his contemporaries, and be familiar with the dignities of the leading men of his time. Moreover he should not be absorbed in the wealth and perishable goods of this world; nor concern himself with the approval or condemnation of persons prejudiced in his favour or against him, or be misled by them; and he should, when exercising his secretarial functions, guard the honour of his master from degrading situations and humiliating usages. And in the course of his letter and tenour of his correspondence he should not quarrel with honourable and powerful personages; and, even though enmity subsist between his master and the person whom he is addressing, he should restrain his pen, and not attack his honour, save in the case of one who may have overstepped his own proper limit, or advanced his foot beyond the circle of respect, for they say:—"*One for one, and he who begins is most in the wrong*[1]."

Moreover in his forms of address he should observe moderation, writing to each person that which his family pedigree, kingdom, domain, army, and treasure indicate; save in the case of one who may himself have fallen short in this matter, or made display of undue pride, or neglected some point of courtesy, or manifested a familiarity which reason cannot regard otherwise than as misplaced in such correspondence, and unsuitable to epistolary communications. In such cases it is permitted and allowed to the Secretary to take up his pen, set his best foot forward, (۱۳) and in this pass go to the extreme limit and utmost bound, for the most perfect of mankind and the most excellent of them (upon him be the Blessings of God and His Peace) says:—"*Haughtiness towards the haughty is a good work*[2]." But in no case must he suffer any dust from the atmosphere of recrimination in this arena of correspondence to alight on the skirt of his master's honour; and in the setting forth of his message he must adopt that method whereby the words shall subserve the ideas and the matter be briefly expressed; for the orators of the Arabs have said, "*The best speech is that which is brief and significant*, [*not long and wearisome*][3]." For if the ideas be subordinated to the

[1] ‘واحدةٌ بواحدةٍ و البادئ اظلم’ *i.e.* "Tit for tat, and the aggressor is most to blame."

[2] ‘التكبّر مع المتكبّر صدقة’ .

[3] ‘خَيرُ الكلام ما قلّ و دلّ و لم يطل فيملّ’ The printed text omits the last words.

words, the discussion will be protracted, and the writer will be stigmatised as prolix, and "*He who is prolix is a babbler*[1]."

Now the words of the Secretary will not attain to this elevation until he acquires some knowledge of every science, obtains some hint from every master, hears some aphorism from every philosopher, and borrows some elegance from every man of letters. Therefore he must accustom himself to peruse the Scripture of the Lord of Glory, the Traditions of Muḥammad the Chosen One, the Memoirs of the Companions, the proverbial sayings of the Arabs, and the wise words of the Persians; and to read the books of the ancients, and to study the writings of their successors, such as the *Correspondence* of the Ṣáḥib [Isma'íl, ibn 'Abbád][2], Ṣábí and Qábús[3]; the compositions of Ḥamádí, Imámí and Qudáma[4] ibn Ja'far; the *Gests* of Badí'[u'z-Zamán al-Hamadání][5], al-Ḥarírí[5] and al-Ḥamídí[6]; the *Rescripts* of al-Bal'amí[7], Aḥmad-i-Ḥasan[8] and Abú Naṣr Kundurí[9]; the *Letters* of Muḥammad 'Abduh, 'Abdu'l-Ḥamíd, and the Sayyidu'r-Ru'asá; the *Séances* of Muḥammad-i-Manṣúr[10], Ibn 'Abbádí[11] and Ibnu'n-Nassába the descendant of 'Alí; and, of the poetical works of the Arabs, the *Díwáns* of Mutanabbí[12], Abíwardí[13] and Ghazzí[14]; and, amongst the Persian poets, the poems of Rúdagí[15], the Epic of Firdawsí[16], and the panegyrics of 'Unṣurí[17]; since each one of these works which I have enumerated was, after its kind, the incomparable and unique product of its time; and every writer who hath these books and doth not fail to read them, stimulates his mind

[1] المكثار مهذار.

[2] See the *Yatímatu'd-Dahr* (ed. Damascus), vol. iii, pp. 31–112; de Slane's *Ibn Khallikán*, vol. i, pp. 212–217, and Note III at the end. L. omits Ṣábí.

[3] The *Tarassul*, or Correspondence, of Qábús ibn Washmgír, the Ziyárid Prince of Ṭabaristán, who was killed in 403/1012–13. See p. 95 of the Persian notes.

[4] See von Kremer's *Culturgesch.*, i, pp. 269–270.

[5] See von Kremer's *Culturgesch.*, ii, pp. 470–476; Brockelmann's *Gesch. d. Arab. Litt.*, i, pp. 93–94 and 276–278.

[6] See Rieu's *Persian Catalogue*, vol. ii, pp. 747–748, where a very fine old MS. of the *Maqámát-i-Ḥamídí* is described, written in the 13th cent. of our era.

[7] Abú 'Alí Muḥammad al-Bal'amí (d. 386/996).

[8] The Ghaznawí minister, Aḥmad ibn Ḥasan of Maymand (d. 424/1033).

[9] See de Slane's *Ibn Khallikán*, vol. iii, pp. 290–295.

[10] Probably Muḥammad ibn Manṣúr al-Ḥaddád. See *Ḥ. Kh.*, No. 1729.

[11] Abú 'Áṣim Muḥammad ibn Aḥmad al-'Abbádí (see Rieu's *Arabic Suppl.*, p. 755), who died in 458/1066, is probably intended.

[12] See von Kremer's *Culturgesch.*, ii, pp. 380–381; Brockelmann's *Gesch. d. Arab. Litt.*, i, pp. 86–89.

[13] See Brockelmann's *Gesch. d. Arab. Litt.*, i, p. 253; and the *Yatíma*, vol. iv, pp. 25 and 62–64, where mention is made of this well-known Abíwardí (whose *Díwán* has been printed at Beyrout) and another.

[14] Brockelmann, *op. cit.*, i, p. 253. A., however, reads عزّي.

[15] See Ethé's monograph and also his article *s.v.* in the *Encyclopaedia Britannica.*

[16] See especially Nöldeke's *Das Iranische Nationalepos* in vol. ii (pp. 130–211) of Geiger and Kuhn's *Grundriss der Iranischen Philologie.*

[17] See Ethé in the same *Grundriss*, pp. 224–225.

polishes his wit, enkindles his fancy, and ever raises the level of his diction, whereby a Secretary becomes famous.

Now if he be well acquainted with the *Qur'án*, with one verse therefrom he may discharge his obligation to a whole realm, as did Iskáfí[1].

ANECDOTE II.

Iskáfí[1] was one of the secretaries of the House of Sámán (may God have mercy on him), and knew his craft right well, so that he could cunningly traverse the heights, and emerge triumphant from the most difficult passes. He discharged the duties of secretary in the Chancellery of Núḥ ibn Manṣúr[2], but they did not properly recognize his worth, or bestow on him favours commensurate with his pre-eminence (١٤). He therefore fled from Bukhárá to Alptagín at Herát. Alptagín, a Turk, wise and discerning, made much of him, and confided to him the Chancellery, and his affairs prospered. Now because there had sprung up at the court a new nobility who made light of the old nobles, Alptagín, though he patiently bore their presumption [for a while], was finally forced into rebellion, by reason of some slight put upon him at the instigation of a party of these new nobles. Then Amír Núḥ wrote from Bukhárá to Zábulistán that Subuktigín should come with that army, and the sons of Símjúr[3] from Níshápúr, and should oppose and make war on Alptagín. And this war is very celebrated, and this momentous battle most famous.

So when these armies reached Herát, the Amír Núḥ sent 'Alí ibn Muḥtáj[4] al-Kashání, who was the Chief Chamberlain (*Ḥájibu'l-Báb*), to Alptagín with a letter [fluent] like water and [scathing] like fire, all filled with threats and fraught with menaces which left no room for peace and no way for conciliation, such as an angry master might write from a distance to his disobedient servants on such an occasion and in such a crisis, the whole letter filled with such expressions as "I will come," "I will take," "I will slay." When the Chamberlain Abu'l-Ḥasan 'Alí ibn Muḥtáj al-Kashání submitted this letter and delivered this message, withholding nothing, Alptagín, who was already vexed,

[1] Abu'l-Qásim 'Alí ibn Muḥammad al-Iskáfí. See *Yatíma*, vol. iv, pp. 29–33, and iii, 4.

[2] This seems to be an error (though it stands thus in all three copies) for Manṣúr ibn Núḥ (Manṣúr I), who reigned A.H. 350–366; for Núḥ ibn Manṣúr (Núḥ II) reigned A.H. 366–387, and Alptagín died in A.H. 352 or 354. Concerning the *Díwánu'r-Rasá'il* see von Kremer's *Culturgesch.*, i, pp. 174, 200; and A. de B. Kazimirski's *Menoutchehri*, pp. 36 and 43. According to Ibnu'l-Athír (Buláq ed. of A.H. 1303, vol. viii, p. 179), Alptagín's revolt took place in A.H. 351, when Iskáfí was already dead. See p. ١٠٤ of the Persian notes and Note IV at end of this volume.

[3] See Defrémery's *Hist. des Samanides*, pp 260–261.

[4] Concerning this general, see Defrémery's *Hist. des Samanides*, pp. 247–248.

grew more vexed, and broke out in anger, saying, "I was his father's servant, but when my master passed from this transitory to that eternal abode, he entrusted him to me, not me to him. Although, to outward seeming, I should obey him, when you closely examine this matter a contrary conclusion results, seeing that I am in the last stages of old age, and he in the first stages of youth. Those who have impelled him to act thus are destroyers of this Dynasty, not counsellors, and are overthrowers of this House, not supporters."

Then in extreme ill-temper he instructed Iskáfí saying, "When thou answerest this letter omit no detail of disrespect; and I desire that thou shouldst write the answer on the back of the letter." So Iskáfí answered it on the spur of the moment, and first wrote as follows:

"*In the Name of God the Merciful the Clement. O Núḥ, thou hast contended with us and made great the contention with us. Produce, then, that wherewith thou threatenest us, if thou art of those who speak truly*[1]."

When this letter reached Núḥ ibn Manṣúr the Amír of Khurásán, he read it, and was astonished; and all the gentlemen of the Court were filled with amaze, and the scribes bit their fingers [in wonder]. And when the affair of Alptagín was disposed of, Iskáfí fled away privily, for he was fearful and terrified; until suddenly Núḥ sent a messenger to summon him to his presence, and conferred on him the post of Secretary (١٠). So his affairs prospered, and he became honoured and famous amongst the votaries of the Pen. Had he not known the *Qur'án* well, he would not have hit upon this verse on that occasion, nor would his position have risen from that degree to this limit.

ANECDOTE III.

When Iskáfí's affairs waxed thus prosperous, and he became established in the service of the Amír Núḥ ibn Manṣúr, Mákán son of Kákúy[2] rebelled at Ray and in Kúhistán, withdrew his neck from the yoke of obedience, sent his agents to Khwár and Simnak, captured several of the towns of Kúmish[3], and paid no heed to the Sámánids. Núḥ ibn Manṣúr was afraid, because this was a formidable and able man, and set himself to deal with this matter. He therefore ordered Tásh, the Commander-in-chief, to

[1] *Qur'án*, xi, 34.

[2] The chronological difficulties involved in these two stories are considerable, for the rebellion of Mákán ibn Kákúy occurred in 329/940–1, towards the end of the reign of Naṣr II ibn Aḥmad, *i.e.* long before the rebellion of Alptagín (see n. 2 on p. 15 *supra*). See Defrémery's *Samanides*, pp. 248 and 263–264. See Notes IV and V at the end.

[3] Better known as *Qúmis*, the arabicised form of the name. See B. de Meynard's *Dict. Géogr., Histor., et Litt. de la Perse*, pp. 454–455. For the three other towns mentioned, see the same work, pp. 213, 317 and 318.

march against him with seven thousand horsemen, suppress this rebellion, and put an end to this formidable insurrection in whatever way he deemed most expedient.

Now Tásh was mighty sagacious and clear in judgement, rashly involving himself in and skilfully extricating himself from the straitest passes; ever victorious in warfare, and never turning back disappointed from any enterprize, nor defeated from any campaign. While he lived, the dominion of the House of Sámán enjoyed the greatest brilliancy, and their affairs the utmost prosperity.

On this occasion, then, the Amír, being mightily preoccupied and distressed in mind, sent a messenger to summon Iskáfí, and held a private interview with him. "I am greatly troubled," said he, "by this business; for Mákán is a brave man, endowed with courage and manhood, and hath both ability and generosity, so that there have been few like him amongst the Daylamís. You must co-operate with Tásh, and whatever is lacking to him in military strength at this crisis, you must make good by your counsels. And I will establish myself at Níshápúr, so that the army may be supported from the base, and the foeman discouraged. Every day a swift messenger with a concise despatch[1] from you must come to me and in this you must set forth the pith of what may have happened, so that my anxieties may be assuaged." Iskáfí bowed and said, "I will obey."

So next day Tásh unfurled his standard, sounded his drums, and set out for the front from Bukhárá, crossing the Oxus with seven thousand horsemen; while the Amír followed him with the remainder of the army to Níshápúr. There he invested Tásh and the army with robes of honour; and Tásh marched out and entered Bayhaq, and went forth into Kúmish setting his face (١٦) towards Ray with fixed purpose and firm resolve.

Meanwhile Mákán, with ten thousand mailed warriors, was encamped at the gates of Ray, which he had made his base. Tásh arrived, passed by the city, and encamped over against him. Then messengers began to pass to and fro between them, but no settlement was effected, for Mákán was puffed up with pride on account of that high-hearted army which he had gathered together from every quarter. It was therefore decided that they should join battle.

Now Tásh was an old wolf who for forty years had held the position of Commander-in-chief, and had witnessed many such engagements; and he so arranged it that when the two armies confronted one another, and the doughty warriors and champions

[1] Mírzá Muḥammad (p. ١٠٦ of the Persian notes) has investigated the precise meaning of the word *mulaṭṭafa*, here translated "concise despatch," and shews by quotations that it is used for a minutely and concisely written note capable of being easily concealed and secretly carried.

of the army of Transoxiana and Khurásán moved forward from the centre, only half of Mákán's army was engaged, while the rest were not fighting. Mákán was slain, and Tásh, when he had ceased from taking and binding and slaying, turned to Iskáfí and said, "A carrier-pigeon must be sent in advance, to be followed later by a courier; but all the main features of the battle must be summed up in one sentence, which shall indicate all the circumstances, yet shall not exceed what a pigeon can carry, and shall adequately express our meaning."

Then Iskáfí took so much paper as two fingers would cover and wrote:—"*As for Mákán, he hath become as his name*[1]" [*Má kán* = "He hath not been" in Arabic]. By this "*má*" he intended the negative, and by "*kán*" the preterite of the verb, so that the Persian of it would be, "Mákán hath become like his name," that is to say, hath become nothing.

When the carrier-pigeon reached the Amír Núḥ, he was not more delighted at this victory than at this despatch, and he ordered Iskáfí's salary to be increased, saying, "Such a person must maintain a heart free from care in order to attain to such delicacies of expression[2]."

ANECDOTE IV.

One who pursues any craft which depends on reflection ought to be free from care and anxiety, for if it be otherwise the arrows of his thought will fly wide and will not be concentrated on the target of achievement, since only by a tranquil mind can one arrive at such diction.

It is related that a certain secretary of the 'Abbásid Caliphs was writing a letter to the governor of Egypt; and, his mind being tranquil and himself submerged in the ocean of reflection, was forming sentences precious as pearls of great price and fluent as running water. Suddenly his maid-servant entered, saying, "There is no flour left." The scribe was so put out and disturbed in mind (١٧) that he lost the thread of his theme, and was so affected that he wrote in the letter "There is no flour left." When he had finished it, he sent it to the Caliph, having no knowledge of these words which he had written.

When the letter reached the Caliph, and he read it, and arrived at this sentence, he was greatly astonished, being unable to account for so strange an occurrence. So he sent a messenger to summon the scribe, and enquired of him concerning this. The scribe was covered with shame, and gave the true explanation of the matter. The Caliph was mightily astonished and said, "The

[1] امّا مَاكَانَ فَصَارَ كَاَسْمِه

[2] The substance of this anecdote is given in the *Táríkh-i-Guzída*, and is cited by Defrémery at pp. 247–248 of his *Histoire des Samanides* (Paris, 1845).

beginning of this letter surpasses and excels the latter part by as much as the *súra* '*Say, He is God, the One*[1]' excels the *súra* '*The hands of Abú Lahab shall perish*[2],' and it is a pity to surrender the minds of eloquent men like you into the hands of the struggle for the necessaries of life." Then he ordered him to be given means sufficiently ample to prevent such an announcement as this ever entering his ears again. Naturally it then happened that he could compress into two sentences the ideas of two worlds.

ANECDOTE V.

The Ṣáḥib Isma'íl ibn 'Abbád[3], entitled *al-Káfí* ("the Competent") of Ray was minister to the Sháhansháh[4]. He was most perfect in his accomplishments, of which fact his correspondence and his poetry are two sufficient witnesses and unimpeachable arbiters.

Now the Ṣáḥib was a Mu'tazilite[5], and such are wont to be extremely pious and scrupulous in their religious duties, holding it right that a true believer should abide eternally in hell by reason of a grain of unrighteousness; and his servants, retainers and agents for the most part held the same opinion that he did.

Now there was at Qum a judge appointed by the Ṣáḥib in whose devoutness and piety he had a firm belief, though one after another men asserted the contrary. All this, however, left the Ṣáḥib unconvinced, until two trustworthy persons of Qum, whose statements commanded credence, declared that in a certain suit between So-and-so and Such-an-one this judge had accepted a bribe of five hundred *dínárs*. This was mightily displeasing to the Ṣáḥib for two reasons, first on account of the greatness of the bribe, and secondly on account of the shameless unscrupulousness of the judge. He at once took up his pen and wrote:

"*In the Name of God the Merciful the Clement. O Judge of Qum! We dismiss you,* (١٨) *so Come*[6]*!*"

Scholars and rhetoricians will notice and appreciate the high merit of this sentence in respect to its concision and clearness, and naturally from that time forth rhetoricians and stylists have inscribed this epigram on their hearts, and impressed it on their minds.

[1] *Qur'án*, cxii.

[2] *Qur'án*, cxi.

[3] For an account of this great minister and generous patron of literature, see de Slane's translation of *Ibn Khallikán*, vol. i, pp. 212–217, and Note VI at end.

[4] This old Persian title "King of kings" was borne by several of the House of Buwayh. Here either Mu'ayyidu'd-Dawla or his brother Fakhru'd-Dawla is intended.

[5] This, as Mírzá Muḥammad points out on p. ١٠٩ of the Persian notes, is the meaning of '*adlí madhhab*. The followers of this doctrine, called by their adversaries *al-Mu'tazila*, "the Seceders," called themselves "Partisans of the Divine Justice and Unity." See my *Lit. Hist. of Persia*, vol. i, p. 281.

[6] 'بسم الله الرّحمن الرّحيم، أيّها القاضي بقم قد عزلناك فقم'. I have endeavoured to preserve, feebly enough, the word-play in the original.

ANECDOTE VI.

Lamghán[1] is a city in the district of Sind, one of the dependencies of Ghazna; and at this present time one lofty mountain separates its inhabitants from the heathen, so that they live in constant dread of the attacks and raids of the unbelievers. Yet the men of Lamghán are of good courage, hardy and thrifty, and combining with their hardiness no small truculence, to such a degree that they think nothing of lodging a complaint against a tax-gatherer on account of a maund of chaff or a single egg; while for even less than this they are ready to come to Ghazna to complain of exactions, and to remain there one or two months, and not to return without having accomplished their object. In short they have a strong hand in obstinacy, and much back-bone in importunity.

Now in the reign of Sulṭán Maḥmúd *Yamínu'd-Dawla* (may God illuminate his proof!), the heathen one night attacked them, and damage of every sort befel them. But these were men who could roll in the dust[2] without soil; and when this event happened several of their chiefs and men of note rose up and came to the court of Ghazna, and, with their garments rent, their heads uncovered, and uttering loud lamentations, entered the bazaar of Ghazna, went to the King's Palace wailing and grieving, and so described their misfortune that even a stone would have been moved to tears. As their truculence, impudence, dissimulation and cunning had not yet become apparent, that great minister, Aḥmad-i-Ḥasan of Maymand[3], took pity upon them, and forgave them that year's taxes, exempting them from all exactions, and bidding them return home, strive more strenuously, and spend less, so that by the beginning of next year they might recover their former position.

So the deputation of Lamghánís returned with great contentment and huge satisfaction, and continued during that year in the easiest of circumstances, giving nothing to any one[4]. When the year came to an end, the same deputation returned to present another petition to the minister, simply setting forth that in the past year their lord the great minister had brightened their country by his grace and clemency and had preserved them by

[1] Or Lámaghán. See B. de Meynard's *Dict. Géogr. de la Perse*, p. 503; Pavet de Courteille's *Mém. de Baber*, ii, pp. 120–121.

[2] See the Editor's note on مراغه on p. ۱۰۹ of the text. This expression appears to denote extreme cunning and resourcefulness, as though one should say "to wash without water." An attractive if bold emendation would be—بی باك مراوغه كردندی "shamelessly evaded their obligations."

[3] See n. 8 on p. 14 *supra*.

[4] This is Mírzá Muḥammad's explanation of the expression آب بکس ندادند

his care and protection, (١٩) so that through that bounty and beneficence the people of Lamghán had reached their proper position and were able to dwell on that border; but that, since their prosperity was still somewhat shaken, they feared that, should he demand the contribution on their possessions that year, some of them would be utterly ruined, and that, as a consequence of this, loss might accrue to the royal coffers.

The minister, Aḥmad-i-Ḥasan, therefore, extending his favour, excused them the taxes of yet another year. During these two years the people of Lamghán grew rich, but this did not suffice them, for in the third year their greed reasserted itself, and, hoping again to be excused, the same deputation again appeared at Court and made a similar representation. Then it became apparent to all the world that the people of Lamghán were in the wrong. So the Prime Minister turned the petition over and wrote on the back of it:—"*Al-kharáju khurájun, adá'uhu dawá'uhu*"—that is to say, "*The tax is a running sore*[1]*: its cure is its discharge.*" And from the time of this great statesman this saying has become proverbial, and has proved useful in many cases. May the earth rest lightly on this great man!

ANECDOTE VII.

There arose great statesmen under the 'Abbásid dynasty, and indeed the history of the Barmecides is well known and famous, and to what extent and degree were their gifts and rewards. Ḥasan [ibn] Sahl, called *Dhu'r-Riyásatayn*[2] ("the lord of two commands"), and his brother Faḍl were exalted above the very heavens, so much so that Ma'mún espoused Faḍl's daughter and asked her in marriage. Now she was a damsel peerless in beauty and unrivalled in attainments; and it was agreed that Ma'mún should go to the bride's house and remain there for a month, and after the lapse of this period should return home with his bride. On the day fixed for their departure he desired, as is customary, to array himself in better clothes. Now Ma'mún always wore black; and people supposed that he wore it because black was the distinctive colour of the 'Abbásids; till one day Yaḥyá ibn Aktham[3] enquired of him, "Why is it that the Prince of Believers prefers black garments?" Ma'mún replied to the judge, "Black garments are for men and for the living; for no woman is married in black, nor is any dead man (٢٠) buried in black." Yaḥyá was

[1] Literally "a wound of a thousand fountains," probably a carbuncle.

[2] There appears to be a confusion here between the two brothers. Ḥasan ibn Sahl was the father of Púrán, al-Ma'mún's bride, while Faḍl bore the title of *Dhu'r-Riyásatayn*. See de Slane's *Ibn Khallikán*, vol. i, pp. 268–272, and 408–409; vol. ii, pp. 472–476. Also the *Laṭá'ifu'l-Ma'árif* of Ath-Tha'álibí (ed. de Jong), pp. 73–74, where a full account is given of this marriage.

[3] See de Slane's *Ibn Khallikán*, iv, pp. 33–51.

greatly surprised by this answer. Then on this day Ma'mún desired to inspect the wardrobe; but of a thousand coats of satin, *ma'diní, malikí, tamím*, hand-woven, cloth of gold, *miqrádí*, and fine black silk[1], he approved none, but clad himself in his [customary] black, and mounted, and turned his face towards the bride's house. Now on that day Faḍl had decked out his palace in such wise that the nobles were filled with wonder thereat, for he had collected so many rare things that words would fail to describe or enumerate them. So when Ma'mún reached the gate of this palace he saw a curtain suspended, fairer than a Chinese temple[2] yet withal more precious than the standards of the true Faith, whereof the design charmed the heart and the colour mingled with the soul. He turned to his courtiers and said, "Whichever of those thousand coats I had chosen, I should have been shamed here. Praise be to God and thanks that I restricted myself to this black raiment."

Now of all the elaborate preparations made by Faḍl on that day, one was that he had a dish filled with [pieces of] wax in the form of pearls, each in circumference like a hazel-nut, and in each one a piece of paper on which was inscribed the name of a village. These he poured out at Ma'mún's feet, and whosoever of Ma'mún's attendants obtained one of these pieces of wax, to him he sent the title-deeds of that village.

So when Ma'mún entered the bride's house, he saw a mansion plastered and painted, with a dado of china tiles[3], fairer than the East at the time of sunrise, and sweeter than a garden at the season of the rose; and therein spread out a full-sized mat of gold thread[4] embroidered with pearls, rubies and turquoises; and six cushions of like design placed thereon; and seated there, in the place of honour, a beauteous damsel sweeter than existence and life, and pleasanter than health and youth; in stature such that the cypress of Ghátafar[5] would have subscribed itself her servant; with cheeks which the brightest sun would have acknowledged as suzerain; with hair which was the envy of musk and ambergris; and eyes which were the despair of the onyx and the narcissus. She, rising to her feet like a cypress, and walking gracefully, advanced towards Ma'mún, and, with a profound obeisance and earnest apologies, took his hand, brought him forward, seated him in the chief seat, and stood before him in service. Ma'mún bade her be seated, whereupon she seated

[1] The exact nature of most of these fabrics I have been unable to ascertain. See Note VII at the end.

[2] This, not "spring," seems to be the meaning of *bahár* in this passage.

[3] *Izár* or *izára* appears to denote a kind of lower half-wall or dado against which one can lean while sitting.

[4] *Khánawár* seems to mean "large enough for [covering the floor of] a house," and *Shúsha-i-sar-kashída* "spun" or "thread-drawn gold."

[5] A quarter of Samarqand mentioned in the first story in Book i of the *Mathnawí*.

herself on her knees[1] hanging her head, and looking down at the carpet. Thereupon Ma'mún was overcome with love: (٢١) he had already lost his heart, and now he would have added thereunto his very soul. He stretched out his hand and drew forth from the opening of his coat eighteen pearls, each one as large as a sparrow's egg, brighter than the stars of heaven, more lustrous than the teeth of the fair, rounder, nay more luminous, than Saturn or Jupiter, and poured them out on the surface of the carpet, where, by reason of its smoothness and their roundness, they continued in motion, there being no cause for their quiescence. But the girl paid no heed to the pearls, nor so much as raised her head. Thereat was Ma'mún's passion further increased, and he extended his hand to open the door of amorous dalliance and to take her in his embraces. But the emotion of shame overwhelmed her, and the delicate damsel was so affected that she was overtaken by that state peculiar to women. Thereat the marks of shame and abashed modesty appeared in her cheeks and countenance, and she immediately exclaimed:—"*O Prince of Believers! The command of God cometh, seek not then to hasten it!*[2]"

Thereat Ma'mún withdrew his hand, and was near swooning on account of the extreme appositeness of this verse, and her graceful application of it on this occasion. Yet still he could not take his eyes off her, and for eighteen days he came not forth from this house and concerned himself with naught but her. And the affairs of Faḍl prospered, and he attained to that high position which was his.

ANECDOTE VIII.

Again in our own time one of the 'Abbásid Caliphs, al-Mustarshid bi'lláh[3], the son of al-Mustaẓhir bi'lláh, the Prince of Believers (may God render his dust fragrant and exalt his rank in Paradise!), came forth from the city of Baghdád with a well-equipped army in full panoply, treasure beyond compute, and many muniments of war, marching against Khurásán, seeking to establish his supremacy over the King of the World Sanjar[4].

Now this quarrel had been contrived by interested persons, and was due to the machinations and misrepresentations of wicked men, who had brought matters to this pass. When the Caliph reached Kirmánsháh, he there delivered on a Friday a homily which in eloquence transcended the highest zenith of the sun, and attained the height of the Heavenly Throne

[1] *I.e.* in the Persian fashion, on the heels, with the knees together in front.

[2] *Qur'án*, xvi, 1. Cf. de Slane's *Ibn Khallikán*, vol. i, p. 270.

[3] The 29th 'Abbásid Caliph, reigned A.H. 512–529 (A.D. 1118–1135).

[4] This happened in 529/1134–5. See Houtsma's *Recueil de Textes relatifs à l'Histoire des Seldjoucides*, vol. ii (1889), pp. 174–178. Sanjar is, however, a mistake for Mas'úd ibn Muḥammad ibn Malikshâh. See Note VIII at end.

and the Supreme Paradise. In the course of this harangue, in his great distress and extreme despair, he complained of the House of Saljúq, in such wise that the orators of Arabia and the rhetoricians of Persia are fain to confess that after the Companions of the Prophet (God's blessing rest on all of them), who were the disciples of the Point of the Prophetic Function (۲۲) and the expounders of his pithy aphorisms, no one had composed a discourse so weighty and eloquent. Said al-Mustarshid:—"*We entrusted our affairs to the House of Saljúq, but they rebelled against us:—'and the time lengthened over them, and their hearts were hardened, and most of them are sinners*[1],'" that is to say, withdrew their necks from our commands in [matters appertaining to] Religion and Islám.

ANECDOTE IX.

The Gúr-Khán of Khitá fought a battle with the King of the World Sanjar, the son of MalikSháh, at the gates of Samarqand, wherein such disaster befel the army of Islám as one cannot describe, and Transoxiana passed into his power[2]. After putting to death the Imám of the East Ḥusámu'd-Dín[3] (may God make bright his example, and extend over him His Peace!), the Gúr Khán bestowed Bukhárá on Atmatigín[4], the son of the Amír Bayábání[5] and nephew of Atsiz Khwárazmsháh, and, when he retired, entrusted him to the Imám *Táju'l-Islám* Aḥmad ibn 'Abdu'l-'Azíz, who was the Imám of Bukhárá and the son of Burhán[6], so that whatever he did he might do by his advice, and that he should do nothing without his orders, nor take any step without his knowledge. Then the Gúr-Khán turned back and retired to Barskhán[7].

Now his justice had no bounds, nor was there any limit to the effectiveness of his commands; and, indeed, in these two

[1] *Qur'án*, lvii, 15. The meaning of the Arabic is repeated in Persian in the text.

[2] See Mírkhwánd's *History of the Saljúqs*, ed. Vullers, pp. 176–180. Sir E. Denison Ross has pointed out to me that Gúr-Khán is a generic title. (See *History of the Moghuls of Central Asia* by Elias and Ross, pp. 287 *et seqq.*, and also Schefer's *Chrestomathie Persane*, vol. i, pp. 34 *et seqq.*) See also Mírzá Muḥammad's note on p. ۱۱۲ of the text, and Note IX at the end.

[3] Ḥusámu'd-Dín 'Umar ibn Burhánu'd-Dín 'Abdu'l-'Azíz ibn Máza. See Note XI at the end.

[4] The correct form of this name is uncertain, but *Alptigín*, the reading of the lithographed edition and of Schefer, *op. cit.*, p. ۱۹, is certainly wrong. See note on p. ۱۱۴ of the text, and Note X at the end.

[5] This name also is uncertain, and there are almost as many variants as there are texts. See Note X at the end.

[6] *I.e.* Burhánu'd-Dín 'Abdu'l-'Azíz mentioned in the last footnote but two. See Note XI at the end.

[7] The name of a city in Eastern Turkistán near Khutan. See G. le Strange's *Lands of the Eastern Caliphate*, p. 489, and Barthold in vol. i, part 4, p. 89, of the *Zapiski*, or *Mém. de l'Acad. Imp. des Sciences de St Pétersbourg, viii*[e] *Série. Classe hist.-philol.*, 1893–4.

things is comprised the essence of kingship. But when Atmatigín saw a clear field, he turned his hand to oppression, and began to levy contributions on Bukhárá. So several of the people of Bukhárá went as a deputation to Barskhán to seek redress. The Gúr-Khán, when he heard this, wrote a letter to Atmatigín [beginning] in the Muslim fashion:

"*In the Name of God the Merciful the Clement.* Let Atmatigín know that although far distance separates us, our approval and displeasure are near at hand. Let Atmatigín do that which [*Táju'l-Islám*] Aḥmad commands, and Aḥmad that which [the Prophet] Muḥammad commands. Farewell."

Again and again we have considered this and reflected on it. A thousand volumes or even more might be written to enlarge on this letter, yet its purport is extremely plain and clear, needing no explanation. Seldom have (٢٢) I seen anything like it.

ANECDOTE X.

|The extreme eloquence of the Qur'án lies in its concision of words and inimitable presentation of ideas; and such citations as those above given which have occurred to orators and eloquent writers are of a kind to inspire awe, so that the wise and eloquent man is moved from his [former] mental attitude. And this is a clear proof and trenchant argument to establish the fact that this Word did not proceed from the mouth of any created being, nor originate from any [human] lips or tongue, but that the stamp of Eternity is impressed on its prescriptions and sentences.|

It is related that one of the Muslims was reciting before Walíd ibnu 'l-Mughíra this verse:—"*And it was said, 'O Earth, gulp down thy waters, and O Heaven, draw them up': and the water abated. Thus was the matter effected. And it* [*i.e. the Ark*] *rested upon Mount Júdí*[1]." "By God," said Walíd ibnu 'l-Mughíra, "verily it hath beauty and sweetness; its highest part is fruitful, and its lowest part is luxuriant; nor is it the word of man!" When even enemies reached on the plane of equity such a level of enthusiasm concerning the eloquence of the Qur'án and its miraculous quality, see to what degree friends will attain.

ANECDOTE XI.

| It was formerly customary with the kings of old time and the autocrats of past ages, such as the Píshdádí, Kayání and Sásánian monarchs and the Caliphs, to vaunt themselves and compete with one another both in justice and erudition, and with every ambassador whom they despatched they used to send wise sayings,

riddles, and enigmatical questions. So the king, under these circumstances, stood in need of persons of intelligence and discrimination, and men of judgement and statesmanship; and several councils would be held and adjourned, until they were unanimous as to their answers, and these problems and enigmas were plain and apparent, when they would despatch the ambassador.

This practice was maintained until the time of that just king Maḥmúd ibn Subuktigín *Yamínu'd-Dawla* (may God have mercy upon him!). But when (٢٤) the Saljúqs succeeded him, they being nomads, ignorant of the conduct of affairs and the high achievements of kings, most of these royal customs became obsolete in their time, and many essentials of dominion fell into disuse. One of these was the Ministry of Posts, from which one can judge of the remainder. It is related that one day Sulṭán Maḥmúd *Yamínu'd-Dawla* despatched an ambassador to Bughrá Khán in Transoxiana, and in the letter which had been drafted occurred this passage:—"*God Almighty saith, 'Verily the most honourable of you in God's sight is he who is most pious of you*[1].' Investigators and critics are agreed that here he [*i.e.* the Prophet] guards himself from ignorance; for the souls of men are subject to no more grievous defect than this of ignorance, nor is there aught lower than the blemish of folly. To the truth of this proposition and the soundness of this assertion [God's] uncreated word also bears witness:—'[*God will raise up those of you who believe*] *and those to whom hath been given knowledge to* [*superior*] *degrees*[2].' Therefore we desire that the Imáms of the land of Transoxiana and the doctors of the East and scholars of the Kháqán's Court should impart [to us] this much information as to matters essential [to Salvation]. What is the Prophetic Office, what Saintship, what Religion, what Islám, what Faith, what Well-doing, what Godliness, what the Approbation of Right, what the Prohibition of Wrong, what the Path, what the Balance, what Mercy, what Pity, what Justice, and what Excellence?"

When this letter reached the Court of Bughrá Khán, and he had acquainted himself with its purport and contents, he summoned the Imáms of Transoxiana from the different towns and districts, and took counsel with them on this matter. Several of the greatest and most eminent of these Imáms agreed that they should severally compose a treatise on this subject, and in the course of their dissertation introduce into the text a reply to these interrogations. They craved a delay of four months for this purpose; which respite was fraught with all sorts of detriments, the worst of which were the disbursements from the treasury for the expenses of the ambassadors and king's messengers, and

[1] *Qur'án*, xlix, 13. [2] *Qur'án*, lviii, 12.

the maintenance of the Imáms, until at length Muḥammad ibn 'Abduh[1] the scribe, who was Bughrá Khán's secretary, and was deeply versed in learning and highly distinguished in scholarship, besides being profoundly skilled in verse and prose, and one of the eloquent and distinguished stylists of the Muslims, said, "I will reply to these questions in two words, in such wise that when the scholars of Islám and the most conspicuous men of the East shall see my answer, it shall command their approval and admiration." So he took up his pen and wrote (٢٠) under the questions, after the fashion of a legal decision (*fatwá*):— "*Saith God's Apostle (upon whom be the Blessing of God, and His Peace) 'Reverence for God's Command and loving-kindness towards God's people.'*" All the Imáms of Transoxiana bit their fingers [in amazement] and expressed their admiration, saying, "Here indeed is an answer which is perfect and an utterance which is comprehensive!" And the Kháqán was mightily pleased because the difficulty had been overcome by a scribe and there was no further need for the divines. And when the answer reached Ghazna, all applauded it.

It therefore results from these premises that an intelligent and accomplished secretary is the greatest ornament to a king's magnificence and the best means to his exaltation. And with this anecdote we conclude this Discourse, and so farewell.

(٢٦) SECOND DISCOURSE.

On the essence of the Poetic Art and the aptitude of the Poet.

Poetry is that art whereby the poet arranges imaginary propositions and blends fruitful analogies, in such wise that he can make a little thing appear great and a great thing small, or cause good to appear in the garb of evil and evil in the form of good. By acting on the imagination, he excites the faculties of anger and concupiscence in such a way that by his suggestion men's temperaments become affected with depression or exaltation; whereby he conduces to the accomplishment of great things in the order of the world.

ANECDOTE XII.

Thus they relate that Aḥmad ibn 'Abdu'lláh al-Khujistání[2] was asked, "How didst thou, who wert originally an ass-herd,

[1] See p. 14 *supra*, Note III at the end, and p. ٩٩ of the Persian notes.
[2] "Khujistán.—In the mountains near Herát. From this country issued Aḥmad ibn

become Amír of Khurásán?" He replied, "One day I was reading the Díwán of Ḥanẓala of Bádghís[1], in Bádghís of Khujistán, when I chanced on these two couplets:—

مهتری گر بکامِ شیر درست ، شو خطر کن ز کامِ شیر بجوی ،

یا بزرگی و ناز و نعمت و جاه ، یا چو مردانت مرگِ رویاروی ،

'If lordship lies within the lion's jaws,
Go, risk it, and from those dread portals seize
Such straight-confronting death as men desire,
Or riches, greatness, rank and lasting ease.'

An impulse stirred within me such that I could in no wise remain content with that condition wherein I was. I therefore sold my asses, bought a horse, and, quitting my country, entered the service of 'Alí ibn Layth, the brother of Ya'qúb and 'Amr. (۲۷) At that time the falcon of fortune of the Ṣaffárids[2] still hovered at the highest zenith of its prosperity. Of the three brothers, 'Alí was the youngest, and Ya'qúb and 'Amr had complete precedence over him. When Ya'qúb came from Khurásán to Ghazna over the mountains, 'Alí ibn Layth sent me back from *Ribáṭ-i-Sangín*[3] ('the Stone Rest-house') to act as agent to his feudal estates in Khurásán. I had a hundred horsemen of that army on the road, and had with me besides some twenty horsemen of my own. Now of the estates held in fief by 'Alí ibn Layth one was Karúkh[4] of Herát, a second Khwáf[5] of Níshápúr. When I reached Karúkh, I produced my warrant, and what was paid to me I divided amongst the army and gave to the soldiers. My horsemen now numbered three hundred. When I reached Khwáf[5], and again produced my warrant, the burghers of Khwáf contested it, saying, 'We want a prefect with [a body-guard of only] ten men.' I therefore decided to renounce my allegiance to the Ṣaffárís, looted Khwáf, proceeded to the village of Busht[6],

'Abdu'lláh al-Khujistání, who revolted at Níshápúr and died in 264/877–8." (Barbier de Meynard's *Dict. Géogr., Hist., et Litt. de la Perse*, p. 197.) The editor points out (Persian notes, p. ۱۲۳, and Note XIII at the end) that, according to Ibnu'l-Athír, Aḥmad was assassinated in Shawwál, 268/882, after having reigned at Níshápúr six six years. See the *Journal Asiatique* for 1845, pp. 345 *et seqq.* of the second half.

[1] See Ethé's *Rúdagí's Vorläufer und Zeitgenossen*, pp. 38–40, where these verses and others by the same poet are cited.

[2] The short-lived Ṣaffárid dynasty was founded by Ya'qúb ibn Layth in 254/867. On his death in 265/878 he was succeeded by his brother 'Amr, who was overthrown by Isma'íl the Sámánid in 287/900 and was subsequently put to death.

[3] This place, evidently situated between Ghazna and Khurásán, has not been identified, unless, as Muḥammad Iqbál suggests, it be identical with the *Ribáṭ-i-Sangbast* twice mentioned by Dawlatsháh (pp. ۱۷٦ and ۲۰٦ of my edition).

[4] A town situated at ten parasangs from Herát. See Barbier de Meynard's *Dict. Géogr., Hist., et Litt. de la Perse*, p. 487, and p. 33 *infra*.

[5] *Ibid.*, pp. 213–214.

[6] Busht or Pusht is also in the district of Níshápúr.

and came to Bayhaq[1], where two thousand horsemen joined me. I advanced and took Níshápúr, and my affairs prospered and continued to improve until I had subdued all Khurásán to myself. Of all this, these two verses of poetry were the original cause."

Sallámí[2] relates in his history that the affairs of Aḥmad ibn 'Abdu'lláh prospered so greatly that in one night in Níshápúr he distributed in largesse 300,000 *dínárs*, 500 head of horses, and 1000 suits of clothes, and to-day he stands in history as one of the victorious monarchs, all of which was brought about by these two verses of poetry. Many similar instances are to be found amongst both the Arabs and the Persians, but we have restricted ourselves to the mention of this one. So a king cannot dispense with a good poet, who shall provide for the immortality of his name, and shall record his fame in *díwáns* and books. For when the king receives that command which none can escape[3], no traces will remain of his army, his treasure, and his store; but his name will endure for ever by reason of the poet's verse, as Sharíf-i-Mujallidí of Gurgán says[4]:—

از آن چندان نعیم این جهانی، که ماند از آل ساسان و آل سامان،
ثنای رودکی ماندست و مدحش، نوای باربد ماندست و دستان،

"*From all the treasures hoarded by the Houses*
Of Sásán and of Sámán, in our days
Nothing survives except the song of Bárbad[5],
Nothing is left save Rúdakí's sweet lays."

The names of the monarchs of each age and the princes of all time are immortalized by the admirable verse and widely-diffused poetry of this company[6]; (٢٨) as, for example, the names of the House of Sámán through Master Abú 'Abdi'lláh Ja'far ibn Muḥammad ar-Rúdakí, Abu'l-'Abbás ar-Ribanjaní, Abu'l-Mathal al-Bukhárí, Abú Isḥáq-i-Júybárí, Abu'l-Ḥasan Ághají, Ṭaḥáwí,

[1] Bayhaq, also near Níshápúr, was according to Yáqút (who gives an unsatisfactory etymology) the ancient Khusrawjird and the later Sabzawár.

[2] *I.e.* Abú 'Alí as-Sallámí al-Bayhaqí, who died in 300/912–3. See p. ١٤٠ of the Persian notes, and Note XIV at the end.

[3] *I.e.* the summons of the Angel of Death.

[4] 'Awfí, who mentions this poet (*Lubáb*, i, pp. 13–14), calls him Abú Sharíf Aḥmad ibn 'Alí.

[5] Concerning Bárbad, the celebrated minstrel of Khusraw Parwíz, see my *Lit. Hist. of Persia*, vol. i, pp. 14–18 and foot-notes. and Noldeke's new edition of his *Persische Nationalepos*, p. 43, n. 2 *ad calc*.

[6] Of the poets included in this long list some account will be found in Note XIV at the end of this volume (derived in almost all cases from Mírzá Muḥammad's notes to the Persian text) save in the case of a few who are too well known to need further mention (such as 'Unṣurí, 'Asjadí, Farrukhí and Minúchihrí) and a rather larger number concerning whom no information is obtainable from the sources at present available, such as Lu'lu'í, Gulábí, 'Alí Sipihrí, Sughdí, Pisar-i-Tísha, Kafá'í, Kúsa-i-Fálí, Púr-i-Kalah, Abu'l-Qásim Rafí'í, Abú Bakr Jawharí and 'Alí Ṣúfí. Concerning Ja'far of Hamadán, see vol. ii of my *Lit. Hist. of Persia*, p. 260.

Khabbází of Níshápúr, and Abu'l-Ḥasan al-Kisá'í; the names of the kings of the House of Náṣiru'd-Dín[1] through such men as 'Unṣurí, 'Asjadí, Farrukhí, Bahrámí, Zínatí, Buzurjmihr of Qá'in, Muẓaffarí, Manshúrí, Minúchihrí, Mas'údí, Qaṣárámí, Abú Ḥanífa-i-Iskáf, Ráshidí, Abu'l-Faraj of Rúna, Mas'úd-i-Sa'd-i-Salmán, Muḥammad ibn Náṣir, Sháh Abú Rijá, Aḥmad-i-Khalaf, 'Uthmán Mukhtárí, and Majdúd as-Saná'í; the names of the House of Kháqán through Lú'lú'í, Gulábí, Najíbí of Farghána, 'Am'aq of Bukhárá, Rashídí of Samarqand, Najjár ("the Carpenter") of Ságharj, 'Alí Pánídhí, Pisar-i-Darghúsh, 'Alí Sipihrí, Jawharí, Sughdí, Pisar-i-Tísha, and 'Alí Shaṭranjí ("the Chess-player"); the names of the House of Buwayh by Master Manṭiqí, Kiyá Ghaḍá'irí, and Bundár; the names of the House of Saljúq by Farrukhí of Gurgán, Lámi'í of Dihistán, Ja'far of Hamadán, Dur-Fíruz-i-Fakhrí, Burhání, Amír Mu'izzí, Abu'l-Ma'álí of Ray, 'Amíd-i-Kamálí and Shihábí; the names of the kings of Ṭabaristán through Qamarí of Gurgán, Ráfí'í of Níshápúr, Kafá'í of Ganja, Kúsa-i-Fálí, and Púr-i-Kalah; and the names of the kings of Ghúr or House of Shansab (may God cause their kingdom to endure!) through Abu'l-Qásim Rafí'í, Abú Bakr Jawharí, this least of mankind Niẓámí-i-'Arúḍí, and 'Alí Ṣúfí. The *díwáns* of these poets are eloquent as to the perfection, splendour, equipment, military strength, justice, bounty, nobility, excellence, judgement, statecraft, heaven-sent success and influence of these former kings and bygone rulers (may God illuminate their tombs and enlarge unto them their resting-places!). How many princes there were who enjoyed the favours of kings, and made great gifts which they bestowed on these eminent poets, of whom to-day no trace remains, nor of their hosts and retinues any survivor, though many were the painted palaces and charming gardens which they created and embellished, but which to-day are levelled with the ground and indistinguishable from the deserts and ravines! Says the author:—

بسا کاخا که محمودش بنا کرد،
که از رفعت همی با مه مِرا کرد،

(۲۹) نه بینی زآن همه یك خشت بر پای،
مدیح عنصری ماندست بر جای،

"*How many a palace did great Maḥmúd raise,*
At whose tall towers the Moon did stand at gaze,
Whereof one brick remaineth not in place,
Though still re-echo 'Unṣurí's sweet lays."

The Monarch of the World, Sulṭán *'Alá'u'd-dunyá wa'd-Dín* Abú 'Alí al-Ḥusayn ibnu'l-Ḥusayn, the Choice of the Prince of

[1] *I.e.* the House of Ghazna.

Believers (may his life be long, and the umbrella of his dynasty victorious!), marched on Ghazna to avenge those two kings, the Prince-martyr and the Laudable Monarch[1], and Sulṭán Bahrámsháh fled before him. In vengeance for those two royal victims, whom they had treated with such indignity, and of whom they had spoken so lightly, he sacked the city of Ghazna, and destroyed the buildings raised by Maḥmúd, Mas'úd and Ibráhím, but he bought with gold the poems written in their praise, and placed them in his library. Alike in the army and in the city none dared call them king, yet the Conqueror himself would read from the *Sháhnáma* what Abu'l-Qásim Firdawsí says:—

چو کودک لب از شیرِ مادر بشست، ز گهواره محمود گوید نخست،

بتن زنده پیل و بجان جبرئیل، بکف ابرِ بهمن بدل رودِ نیل،

جهاندار محمود شاهِ بزرگ، بآبشخور آرد همی میش و گرگ،

"*Of the child in its cot, ere its lips yet are dry*
From the milk of its mother, 'Maḥmúd!' is the cry!
A mammoth in strength and an angel in style,
With a bounty like Spring and a heart like the Nile,
Maḥmúd, the Great King, who such order doth keep
That in peace from one pool drink the wolf and the sheep!"

All wise men know that herein was no reverence for Maḥmúd, but only admiration of Firdawsí and his verse. Had Sulṭán Maḥmúd understood this, he would presumably not have left that noble man disappointed and despairing.

EXCURSUS. *On the quality of the Poet and his verse.*

Now the poet must be of tender temperament, profound in thought, sound in genius, a powerful thinker, subtle of insight. He must be well versed in many divers sciences, and eclectic amidst divergent customs; for as poetry is of advantage in every science, so is every science of advantage in poetry. And the poet must be of pleasing conversation in social gatherings, of cheerful countenance on festive occasions; and his verse must have attained to such a level as to be written on the page of Time (۳۰) and celebrated on the tongues of the noble, and be such that they transcribe it in books and recite it in cities. For the richest portion and most excellent part of poetry is immortal fame, and until it be thus recorded and recited this idea will not be realized. And if poetry does not rise to this level, its influence is ineffectual, for it will die before its author. So, being impotent for the im-

[1] Quṭbu'd-Dín Muḥammad and Sayfu'd-Dín Súrí, both killed by Bahrámsháh the Ghaznawí towards the middle of the sixth century of the Flight. From his devastation of Ghazna (550/1155–6) their brother 'Alá'u'd-Dín Ḥusayn the Ghúrí received the title of *Jahán-súz* ("the World-consumer"). See Note XV at the end.

mortalizing of its own name, how can it confer immortality on the name of another?

But to this rank a poet cannot attain unless in the prime of his life and the season of his youth he commits to memory 20,000 couplets of the poetry of the Ancients, keeps in view [as models] 10,000 verses of the works of the Moderns, and continually reads and remembers the *díwáns* of the masters of his art, observing how they have acquitted themselves in the strait passes and delicate places of song, in order that thus the different styles and varieties of verse may become ingrained in his nature, and the defects and beauties of poetry may be inscribed on the tablet of his understanding. In this way his style will improve and his genius will develop. Then, when his genius has thus been firmly established in the power of poetical expression, and his verse has become even in quality, let him address himself seriously to the poetic art, study the science of Prosody, and familiarize himself with the works of Master Abu'l-Ḥasan Bahrámí of Sarakhs, such as the "Goal of Prosodists" (*Gháyatu'l-'Arúḍiyyín*)[1] and the "Treasure of Rhyme" (*Kanzu'l-Qáfiya*). Then let him make a critical study of poetic ideas and phraseology, plagiarisms, biographies, and all the sciences of this class, with such a Master as knows these matters, so that he in turn may merit the title of Master, and his name may appear on the page of Time like the names of those other Masters whom we have mentioned, that he may thus be able to discharge his debt to his patron and lord for what he obtains from him by immortalizing his name.

Now it behoves the King to patronize such a poet, so that he may enlist in his service and celebrate his praise. But if he fall below this level, no money should be wasted on him and no heed paid to his poetry, especially if he be old; for I have investigated this matter, and in the whole world have found nothing worse than an old poet, nor any money more ill spent than what is given to such. For one so ignoble as not to have discovered in fifty years that what he writes is bad, when will he discover it? But if he be young and has the right talent, even though his verse be not good, there is some hope that it may improve, (٣١) and according to the Code of Nobility it is proper to patronize him, a duty to take care of him, and an obligation to look after him.

Now in the service of kings naught is better than improvisation, for thereby the king's mood is cheered, his receptions are made brilliant, and the poet himself attains his object. Such favours as Rúdagí obtained from the House of Sámán by his improvisations and readiness in verse, none other hath experienced.

[1] Or perhaps *'Arúḍayn*, "the two Prosodies," *viz.* Arabic and Persian. See the Editor's note on p. ١٠٩.

ANECDOTE XIII.

They relate thus, that Naṣr ibn Aḥmad, who was the most brilliant jewel of the Sámánid galaxy, whereof the fortunes reached their zenith during the days of his rule, was most plenteously equipped with every means of enjoyment and material of splendour—well-filled treasuries, a far-flung army and loyal servants. In winter he used to reside at his capital, Bukhárá, while in summer he used to go to Samarqand or some other of the cities of Khurásán. Now one year it was the turn of Herát. He spent the spring season at Bádghís, where are the most charming pasture-grounds of Khurásán and 'Iráq, for there are nearly a thousand water-courses abounding in water and pasture, any one of which would suffice for an army.

When the beasts had well enjoyed their spring feed, and had regained their strength and condition, and were fit for warfare or to take the field, Naṣr ibn Aḥmad turned his face towards Herát, but halted outside the city at Margh-i-Sapíd and there pitched his camp. It was the season of spring; cool breezes from the north were stirring, and the fruit was ripening in the districts of Málin and Karúkh[1]—such fruit as can be obtained in but few places, and nowhere so cheaply. There the army rested. The climate was charming, the breeze cool, food plentiful, fruit abundant, and the air filled with fragrant scents, so that the soldiers enjoyed their life to the full during the spring and summer.

When Mihrgán[2] arrived, and the juice of the grape came into season, and the basil[3], rocket[4] and fever-few[5] were in bloom, they did full justice to the delights of youth, and took tribute of their juvenile prime. Mihrgán was protracted, for the cold did not wax severe, and the grapes ripened with exceptional sweetness. For in the district of Herát one hundred and twenty different varieties of the grape occur, each sweeter and more delicious than the other; and amongst them are in particular two kinds which are not to be found in any other region of the inhabited world, (٣٢) one called *Parniyán*[6] and the other *Kalanjarí*[7], thin-skinned,

[1] See Barbier de Meynard's *Dict. de la Perse*, pp. 487, 511–512, according to which the former village is distant from Herát two parasangs, the latter ten.

[2] The festival of the autumnal equinox, which fell in the old Persian month of Mihr.

[3] *Sháhisfaram* (Arabic *Rayḥán*) = Ocymum basilicum. See Schlimmer's *Terminologie*, p. 404; Achundow, pp. 226, 381.

[4] *Hamdḥim*, said to be equivalent to the Persian *Bustán-afrúz*.

[5] *Uqḥuwán* (Persian *Bábúna-i-Gaw-chashm*), Matricaria or Pyrethrum. See Schlimmer, p. 364.

[6] The Ṭihrán lithograph has *Tarniyán*, of which the usual meaning appears to be a sieve or basket made of osiers. See Horn's *Asadí*, p. 99, l. 1; Salemann's *Shams i Fachrīi Lexicon*, p. 96, l. 13 and note *ad calc*.

[7] This word, in the form *Kalanjar*, is given in the *Burhán-i-Qáṭi'*. The description seems to be based on this passage.

small-stoned, and luscious, so that you would say they contained no earthly elements. A cluster of Kalanjarí grapes sometimes attains a weight of five maunds, and each individual grape five dirhams' weight, they are black as pitch and sweet as sugar, and one can eat many by reason of the lusciousness that is in them. And besides these there were all sorts of other delicious fruits.

So the Amír Naṣr ibn Aḥmad saw Mihrgán and its fruits, and was mightily pleased therewith. Then the narcissus began to bloom, and the raisins were plucked and stoned[1] in Málin, and hung up on lines, and packed in store-rooms; and the Amír with his army moved into the two groups of hamlets called Ghúra and Darwáz. There he saw mansions of which each one was like highest paradise, having before it a garden or pleasure ground with a northern aspect. There they wintered, while the Mandarin oranges began to arrive from Sístán and the sweet oranges from Mázandarán; and so they passed the winter in the most agreeable manner.

When [the second] spring came, the Amír sent the horses to Bádghís and moved his camp to Málin [to a spot] between two streams. And when summer came and the fruits again ripened, Amír Naṣr ibn Aḥmad said, "Where shall we go for the summer? For there is no pleasanter place of residence than this. Let us wait till Mihrgán." And when Mihrgán came, he said, "Let us enjoy Mihrgán at Herát and then go"; and so from season to season he continued to procrastinate, until four years had passed in this way. For it was then the heyday of the Sámánian prosperity, and the land was flourishing, the kingdom unmenaced by foes, the army loyal, fortune favourable, and heaven auspicious; yet withal the Amír's attendants grew weary, and desire for home arose within them, while they beheld the king quiescent, the air of Herát in his head and the love of Herát in his heart; and in the course of conversation he would compare, nay, prefer Herát to the Garden of Eden, and would exalt its charms above those of a Chinese temple[2].

So they perceived that he intended to remain there for that summer also. Then the captains of the army and nobles of the kingdom went to Master Abú 'Abdi'lláh Rúdagí[3], than whom there was none more honoured of the king's intimates, and none whose words found so ready an acceptance. And they said to him, "We will present thee with five thousand *dínárs* if thou wilt contrive some artifice whereby the king may be induced to depart

[1] For this meaning of *munaqqa* the editor refers to the article *Zabíb* in the *Tuḥfatu'l-Mú'minín* of Muḥammad Mú'min al-Ḥusayní. For an account of this work, which was completed in A.D. 1669, see Fonahn's *Zur Quellenkunde der Persischen Medizin*, pp. 89–91.

[2] Or "Chinese Spring." See n. 2 on p. 22 *supra*.

[3] See Ethé's excellent monograph and his article in the *Encyclopaedia Britannica*; p. 62 of the *J.R.A.S.* for January, 1899; and Note XIV at the end, second paragraph.

hence, for our hearts are craving for our wives and children, and our souls (٣٣) are like to leave us for longing after Bukhárá." Rúdagí agreed; and, since he had felt the Amír's pulse and understood his temperament, he perceived that prose would not affect him, and so had recourse to verse. He therefore composed a *qaṣída*; and, when the Amír had taken his morning cup, came in and sat down in his place; and, when the musicians ceased, he took up the harp, and, playing the "Lover's air," began this elegy[1]:—

بوی جوی مولیان آید همی ، بوی یارِ مهربان آید همی

"The Jú-yi-Múliyán[2] we call to mind,
We long for those dear friends long left behind."

Then he strikes a lower key, and sings:—

ریگِ آموی و درشتی راه او ، زیرِ پایم پرنیان آید همی ،
آبِ جیحون از نشاطِ روی دوست ، خنگِ مارا تا میان آید همی ،
ای بخارا شاد باش و دیر زی ، میر زی تو شادمان آید همی ،
میر ماهست و بخارا آسمان ، ماه سوی آسمان آید همی ،
میر سَروست و بخارا بوستان ، سَرو سوی بوستان آید همی ،

"The sands of Oxus, toilsome though they be,
Beneath my feet were soft as silk to me.
Glad at the friends' return, the Oxus deep
Up to our girths in laughing waves shall leap.
Long live Bukhárá! Be thou of good cheer!
Joyous towards thee hasteth our Amír!
The Moon's the Prince, Bukhárá is the sky;
O Sky, the Moon shall light thee by and by!
Bukhárá is the mead, the Cypress he;
Receive at last, O Mead, thy Cypress-tree!"

When Rúdagí reached this verse, the Amír was so much affected that he descended from his throne, all unbooted bestrode the horse which was on sentry-duty[3], and set off for Bukhárá so precipitately that they carried his leggings and riding-boots

[1] This poem is very well known, being cited in almost all notices of Rúdagí's life (*e.g.* by Dawlatsháh), in Forbes' *Persian Grammar*, pp. ١٠, 161–163, and in Blochmann's *Prosody of the Persians*, pp. 2–3. See Note XVI at the end.

[2] The original name of this stream and the farms on its banks was, according to Narshakhí's *History of Bukhárá*, *Jú-yi-Mawáliyán*, "the Clients' Stream." See Note XVI at the end of this volume.

[3] *Khing-i-nawbatí.* To provide against any sudden emergency a horse, ready saddled and bridled, was kept always at the gate of the king's palace, and it is this "sentry-horse" to which reference is here made. See my *Lit. Hist. of Persia*, vol. i, p. 317, and n. 1 *ad calc.*

after him for two parasangs, as far as Burúna[1], and only then did he put them on; nor did he draw rein anywhere till he reached Bukhárá, and Rúdagí received from the army the double of that five thousand *dínárs*.

At Samarqand, in the year A.H. 504 (= A.D. 1110–1111), I heard from the Dihqán Abú Rijá Aḥmad ibn 'Abdu's-Ṣamad al-'Ábidí as follows: "My grandfather Abú Rijá related that on this occasion when Rúdagí reached Samarqand, he had four hundred camels laden with his baggage." And indeed that illustrious man was worthy of this splendid equipment, for no one has yet produced a successful imitation of that elegy, nor found means to surmount triumphantly the difficulties [which the subject presents]. Thus the Poet-laureate Mu'izzí was one of the sweetest singers and most graceful wits in Persia, for his poetry reaches the highest level in beauty and freshness, and excels in fluency and charm. Zaynu'l-Mulk Abú Sa'd [ibn] Hindú ibn Muḥammad ibn Hindú of Isfahán[2] requested him to compose an imitation of this *qaṣída*. Mu'izzí declared his inability to do so, but, being pressed, produced a few verses of which this is one:—

(۳۱) رستم از مازندران آید همی ، زینِ ملك از اصفهان آید همی ،

(۳۱) "*Now advanceth Rustam from Mázandarán,*
Now advanceth Zayn-i-Mulk from Isfahán."

All wise men will perceive how great is the difference between this poetry and that; for who can sing with such sweetness as does Rúdagí when he says:—

آفرین و مدح سود آید همی ، گر بگنج اندر زیان آید همی

"*Surely are renown and praise a lasting gain,*
Even though the royal coffers loss sustain!"

For in this couplet are seven admirable touches of art; first, the verse is apposite; secondly, antithetical; thirdly, it has a refrain; fourthly, it embodies an enunciation of equivalence; fifthly, it has sweetness; sixthly, style; seventhly, energy[3]. Every master of the craft who has deeply considered the poetic art will admit, after a little reflection, that I am right.

[1] L. has بها بروند, and in a marginal note explains *burúna* as meaning turban or handkerchief; but A. has به بروند, and I suspect that it is really a place-name. Cf. Sachau's remarks on the derivation of al-Bírúní's name at p. 7 of his translation of the *Chronology of Ancient Nations*.

[2] See Houtsma's ed. of al-Bundárí's *History of the Saljúqs*, pp. 93, 101, 105; and Ibnu'l-Athír under the year 506/1112–13, in which Zaynu'l-Mulk was put to death by his master Sulṭán Muḥammad ibn Malikshàh the Saljúq.

[3] Mírzá Muḥammad points out in his note on this passage (p. ۱۷۱) that the first three artifices are denoted by adjectives and the last four by substantives, and that the first and second (*muṭábiq* and *mutaḍádd*) are identical. Finally he justly observes that "style" or "elegance" (*faṣáḥat*) is not a rhetorical artifice but an indispensable attribute of all good writing, whether prose or verse.

ANECDOTE XIV.

The love borne by Sulṭán *Yamínu'd-Dawla* Maḥmúd to Ayáz the Turk is well-known and famous. It is related that Ayáz was not remarkably handsome, but was of sweet expression and olive complexion, symmetrically formed, graceful in his movements, sensible and deliberate in action, and mightily endowed with all the arts of pleasing, in which respect, indeed, he had few rivals in his time. Now all these are qualities which excite love and give permanence to friendship.

Now Sulṭán *Yamínu'd-Dawla* Maḥmúd was a pious and God-fearing man, and he wrestled much with his love for Ayáz so that he should not diverge by so much as a single step from the Path of the Law and the Way of Honour. One night, however, at a carousal, when the wine had begun to affect him and love to stir within him, he looked at the curls of Ayáz, and saw, as it were, ambergris rolling over the face of the moon, hyacinths twisted about the visage of the sun, ringlet upon ringlet like a coat of mail; link upon link like a chain; in every ringlet a thousand hearts and under every lock a hundred thousand souls. Thereupon love plucked the reins of self-restraint from the hands of his endurance, and lover-like he drew him to himself. But the watchman of "*Hath not God forbidden you to transgress against Him*[1]*?*" thrust forth his head from the collar of the Law, stood before Sulṭán [Maḥmúd] *Yamínu'd-Dawla*, and said, "O Maḥmúd, mingle not sin with love, nor mix the false with the true, for such a slip will raise the Realm of Love in revolt against thee, and like (٣٠) thy first father thou wilt fall from Love's Paradise, and remain afflicted in the world of Sin." The ear of his fortunate nature being quick to hear, he hearkened to this announcement, and the tongue of his faith cried from his innermost soul, "*We believe and we affirm.*" But he feared lest the army of his self-control might be unable to withstand the hosts of Ayáz's locks, so, drawing a knife, he placed it in the hands of Ayáz, bidding him take it and cut off his curls. Ayáz took the knife from his hands with an obeisance, and, having enquired where he should sunder them, was bidden to cut them in the middle. He therefore doubled back his locks to get the measurement, executed the king's command, and laid the two tresses before Maḥmúd. It is said that this ready obedience became a fresh cause of love; and Maḥmúd called for gold and jewels and gave to Ayáz beyond his usual wont and custom, after which he fell into a drunken sleep.

[1] Here and in the next sentence I have preferred the alternative reading of the MSS. to the printed text, which has "*We believe and we affirm*" in this place, and omits these and the preceding eleven words below.

When the morning breeze blew upon him, and he arose from sleep to ascend the Royal Throne, he remembered what he had done. He summoned Ayáz and saw the clipped tresses. The army of remorse invaded his heart, and the peevish headache born of wine vanquished his brain. He kept rising up and sitting down [aimlessly], and none of the courtiers or men of rank dared to address to him any enquiry as to the cause, until at length Ḥájib 'Alí [ibn] Qaríb, who was his Chief Chamberlain, turned to 'Unṣurí and said, "Go in before the King and shew thyself to him, and seek some way whereby he may be restored to good temper." So 'Unṣurí fulfilled the Chamberlain's command, came in and did obeisance. Sulṭán Yamínu'd-Dawla raised his head and said, "O 'Unṣurí, I was just thinking of you. You see what has happened: say something appropriate for us on this subject." 'Unṣurí did obeisance and extemporized as follows:—

کی عیبِ سرِ زلفِ بت از کاستن است ،
چه جای بغم نشستن و خاستن است ،
جای طرب و نشاط و می خواستن است ،
کآراستنِ سرو ز پیراستن است ،

"Why deem it shame a fair one's curls to shear,
Why rise in wrath or sit in sorrow here?
Rather rejoice, make merry, call for wine;
When clipped the Cypress doth most trim appear."

Maḥmúd was highly pleased with this quatrain, and bade them bring precious stones wherewith he twice filled the poet's mouth. Then he summoned the minstrels before him, and all that day until nightfall drank wine to [the accompaniment of] those two verses, whereby his melancholy was dissipated and he became mighty good-tempered.

Now you must know that improvisation is the chief pillar of the Poetic Art; and it is incumbent on the poet to train his talents to such a point as (۳٦) to be able to improvise on any subject, for thus can money be extracted from the treasury, and thus can the statement of any matter be adapted to the king's mood. All this is necessary to please the heart of one's master and the humour of one's patron; and whatever poets have earned in the way of great rewards has been earned by improvisations adapted to the occasion.

ANECDOTE XV.

Farrukhí was a native of Sístán, and was the son of Júlúgh, the slave of Amír Khalaf-i-Bánú[1]. He possessed excellent talents, composed pleasing verses, and was a dexterous performer on the harp; and he was retained in the service of one of the *dihqáns* of Sístán, who gave him a yearly allowance of two hundred measures of corn, each containing five maunds, and a hundred *dirhams* in silver coinage of Núḥ, which amply sufficed for his needs. But he sought in marriage a woman of Khalaf's clientage, whereby his expenses were increased and multiplied in all directions[2], so that Farrukhí remained without sufficient provision, nor was there in Sístán anyone else save his[3] nobles. He therefore appealed to the *dihqán* saying, "My expenses have been increased; how would it be if the *dihqán*, having regard to his generosity, should make my allowance of corn three hundred measures, and make my salary one hundred and fifty *dirhams*, so that my means may perhaps be equal to my expenditure?" The *dihqán* wrote on the back of the appeal, "So much shall not be refused you, but there is no possibility of any further increase."

Farrukhí, on hearing this, was in despair, and made enquiries of such as arrived and passed by to hear of some patron in some region or part of the world who might look upon him with favour, so that he might chance on a success; until at length they informed him that the Amír Abu'l-Muẓaffar-i-Chagháni in Chaghániyán[4] was a munificent patron of this class, conferring on them splendid presents and rewards, and was at that period unrivalled in this respect amongst the kings of the age and nobles of the time. So Farrukhí set out thither, having composed the *qaṣída* beginning:—

با کاروانِ حلّه برفتم ز سیستان ، با حُلّهٔ تنیده ز دل بافته ز جان ،

"*With caravan for Ḥilla bound from Sístán did I start,*
With fabrics spun within my brain and woven by my heart."

In truth it is a fine rhapsody in which he has admirably described the Poetic Art, while as a panegyric it is incomparable.

So Farrukhí, having furnished himself with what was necessary for the journey, set out for Chaghániyán. And when he

[1] *I.e.* the Amír Abú Aḥmad Khalaf ibn Aḥmad ibn Muḥammad ibn Khalaf ibn Layth aṣ-Ṣaffárí, King of Sístán, whose mother, called *Bánú* ("the Lady"), was the daughter of 'Amr ibn Layth. He died in captivity in 399/1008–9.

[2] See the *Farhang-i-Anjuman-árá-yi-Náṣirí*, *s.v.* زنبیل, where دبه و زنبیل is said to mean دبور و قبل.

[3] *I.e.* Khalaf's.

[4] Or, in its Arabicized form, *Ṣaghánián*, a place in Transoxiana, near Tirmidh and Qubádhiyán. See de Goeje's *Bibl. Geogr. Arab.*, where it is mentioned repeatedly.

arrived at the Court of Chagháníyán, it was the season of Spring and the Amír was at the branding-ground. Abu'l-Muẓaffar, as I have heard, had 18,000 breeding mares[1], each one of which was followed by its colt. And every year the Amír used to go out to brand (٣٧) the colts, and [at this moment he happened to be at the place where the branding was done; while[2]] 'Amíd As'ad, who was his steward, was at the court preparing provisions to be conveyed to the Amír. To him Farrukhí went, and recited a *qaṣída*, and submitted to him the poem he had composed for the Amír.

Now 'Amíd As'ad was a man of parts and a patron of poets, and in Farrukhí's verse he recognized poetry at once fresh, sweet, pleasing and masterly, while seeing the man himself to be an ill-proportioned Sagzí, clothed in a torn *jubba* worn anyhow[3], with a huge turban on his head after the manner of the Sagzís, with the most unpleasing feet and shoes; and this poetry, withal, in the seventh heaven. He could not believe that it had been composed by this Sagzí, and, to prove him, said, "The Amír is at the branding-ground, whither I go to wait upon him: and thither I will take thee also, for it is a mighty pleasant spot—

جهانی در جهانی سبزه بینی

"*World within world of verdure wilt thou see*"—

full of tents and lamps like stars, and from each tent come the strains of the lute, and friends sit together, drinking wine and making merry, while before the Amír's pavilion a great fire is kindled, in size like unto several mountains, whereat they brand the colts. And the Amír, with the goblet in one hand and the lassoo in the other, drinks wine and gives away horses. Compose, now, a *qaṣída*, suitable to the occasion, describing the branding-ground, so that I may take thee before the Amír."

That night Farrukhí went and composed a very fine *qaṣída*, which next morning he brought before 'Amíd As'ad. This is the *qaṣída*[4]:—

چون پرندِ نیلگون بر روی پوشد مرغزار
پرنیانِ هفت رنگ اندر سر آرد کوهسار

[1] The variant راهی is explained in the margin of L. as meaning گردنده و دونده, which I originally translated "roadster." The verb زهیدن, from which زهی seems to be derived, appears to be a variant of زادن.

[2] These words are omitted in the printed edition.

[3] *Písh u pas*, "hind before."

[4] See pp. ١١٤—١١٧ of the lithographed edition of Farrukhí's works published at Ṭihrán for Mírzá Mahdí Khán *Badáyi'-nigár*, poetically surnamed Mukhliṣ, in A.H. 1301. Of the 52 bayts there given, only 22 are cited in the *Chahár Maqála*. The poem is also given by Dawlatsháh (pp. ٥٥—٥٧ of my edition). Only the more important variants are given here.

خاکرا چون نافِ آهو مشك زاید بیقیاس،
بیدرا چون پرِّ طوطی برگ روید بیشمار،
دوش وقتِ نیم شب[1] بوی بهار آورد باد،
حبّذا بادِ شمال و خرّما بوی بهار،
باد گوئی مشكِ سوده دارد اندر آستین،
باغ گوئی لعبتانِ جلوه دارد در کنار،
(۳۸)نسترن لؤلؤی بیضا دارد اندر مُرْسَله[2]،
ارغوان لعلِ بدخشی دارد اندر گوشوار،
تا بر آمد جامهای سرخ مُل بر شاخ گُل،
پنجهها چون[3] دستِ مردم سر فرو کرد از چنار،
باغ بو قلمون لباس و شاخ بو قلمون نمای،
آب مروارید گون و ابر مروارید بار،
راست پنداری که خلعتهای رنگین یافتند،
باغهای پر نگار از داغگاهِ شهریار،
داغگاهِ شهریار اکنون چنان خرّم شود،
کاندرو از خرّمی خیره بماند روزگار،
سبزه اندر سبزه بینی چون سپهر اندر سپهر،
خیمه اندر خیمه بینی چون[4] حصار اندر حصار،
هرکجا خیمه است خفته عاشقی با دوست مست،
هرکجا سبزه است شادان یاری از دیدارِ یار،
سبزهها پر بانگِ چنگ و[5] مطربان چرب دست،
خیمهها پر بانگِ نوش و ساقیان میگسار،
عاشقان بوس و کنار و نیکوان ناز و عتاب،
مطربان رود و سرود و خفتگان خواب و خمار،

[1] The printed text has صُبْحدم for نیم شب.

[2] A gloss in the lithographed Ṭihrán edition explains this word as meaning "necklace" (گردن بند), which meaning is also given in the *Ghiyáthu'l-Lughát*.

[3] Variant ...پنجههای دست.

[4] The printed text has چون سیمین حصار.

[5] The printed text has با for پر and om. و after چنگ.

بر درِ پرده سرای خسرو[1] پیروز بخت،
از پیِ داغ آتشی افروخته خورشیدوار،
بر کشیده آتشی چون مِطْرَدِ دیبای زرد،
گرم چون طبع جوان و زرد چون زرّ عیار،
داغها چون شاخهای بسّد یاقوت رنگ،
هر یکی چون نار دانه گشته اندر زیر نار،
(۳۹) بردگانِ[2] خواب نا دیده مصاف اندر مصاف،
مرکبانِ داغ نا کرده قطار اندر قطار،
خسروِ فرّخ سیر بر بارهٔ دریا گذر،
با کمند اندر میانِ دشت چون اسفندیار،
همچو زلفِ دلبرانِ خُرْد ساله[3] تاب خورد،
همچو عهدِ دوستانِ سالخورده استوار،
میرِ عادل[4] بو المظفّر شاه با پیوستگان،
شهریارِ شهرگیر و پادشاهِ شهر دار[5]،
[اژدها کردار پیچان در کف رادش کمند،
چون عصای موسوی در دست موسی گشته مار][6]،
هر کرا اندر کمندِ شصت یازی در فَگَند،
گشت نامش[7] بر سرین و شانه و رویش نگار،
هرچه زین سو داغ کرد از سوی دیگر هدیه داد[8]،
شاعران‌را با لگام و زایران‌را با فسار،

[1] The *Majma'u'l-Fuṣaḥá*, as pointed out by the Editor (p. ۱٦٦), arbitrarily substitutes طاهر for خسرو, in order to support the theory that the poem was composed in honour of No. 6 not No. 7 of the House of Chagháníyán. See Note XVIII at the end.

[2] The printed text has ریدگان explained as "slave-boys" (غلام بچگان). The Ṭihrán ed. has دیدگان, "eyes."

[3] The printed text has نیکوانِ مرو گیسو.

[4] The lithograph substitutes "*Fakhr-i-Dawlat.*"

[5] Both the printed and the lithographed editions have:—

شادمان و شادخوار و کامران و کامکار،

[6] This verse only occurs in the Ṭihrán lithographed edition (L.).

[7] The lithographed edition has دابش.

[8] A., B. and L. have میدهد.

"*Since the meadow hides its face in satin shot with greens and blues,*
And the mountains wrap their brows in silken veils of seven hues,
Earth is teeming like the musk-pod with aromas rich and rare,
Foliage bright as parrot's plumage doth the graceful willow wear.
Yestere'en the midnight breezes brought the tidings of the spring:
Welcome, O ye northern gales, for this glad promise which ye bring!
Up its sleeve the wind, meseemeth, pounded musk hath stored away,
While the garden fills its lap with shining dolls, as though for play.
On the branches of syringa necklaces of pearls we see,
Ruby ear-rings of Badakhshán sparkle on the Judas-tree.
Since the branches of the rose-bush carmine cups and beakers bore
Human-like five-fingered hands reach downwards from the sycamore.
Gardens all chameleon-coated, branches with chameleon whorls,
Pearly-lustrous pools around us, clouds above us raining pearls!
On the gleaming plain this coat of many colours doth appear
Like a robe of honour granted in the court of our Amír.
For our Prince's Camp of Branding stirreth in these joyful days
So that all this age of ours in joyful wonder stands agaze.
Green within the green you see, like skies within the firmament;
Like a fort within a fortress spreads the army tent on tent.
Every tent contains a lover resting in his sweetheart's arms,
Every patch of grass revealeth to a friend a favourite's charms.
Harps are sounding 'midst the verdure, minstrels sing their lays divine,
Tents resound with clink of glasses as the pages pour the wine.
Kisses, claspings from the lovers; coy reproaches from the fair;
Wine-born slumbers for the sleepers, while the minstrels wake the air.
Branding-fires, like suns ablaze, are kindled at the spacious gate
Leading to the state-pavilion of our Prince so fortunate.
Leap the flames like gleaming standards draped with yellow-hued brocade,
Hotter than a young man's temper, yellower than gold assayed.
Branding tools like coral branches ruby-tinted glow amain
In the fire, as in the ripe pomegranate glows the crimson grain.
Rank on rank of active boys, whose watchful eyes no slumber know;
Steeds which still await the branding, rank on rank and row on row.
On his horse, the river-forder, roams our genial Prince afar,
Ready to his hand the lassoo, like a young Isfandiyár.
Like the locks of pretty children see it how it curls and bends,
Yet be sure its hold is stronger than the covenant of friends.
Bu'l-Muẓaffar Sháh the Just, surrounded by a noble band,
King and conqueror of cities, brave defender of the land.
Serpent-coiled in skilful hands fresh forms his whirling noose doth take,
Like unto the rod of Moses metamorphosed to a snake.
Whosoever hath been captured by that noose and circling line,
On the face and flank and shoulder ever bears the Royal Sign.
But, though on one side he brands, he giveth also rich rewards,
Leads his poets with a bridle, binds his guests as though with cords."

When 'Amíd As'ad heard this rhapsody, he was overwhelmed with amazement, for never had the like of it reached his ears. He put aside all his business, mounted Farrukhí on a horse, and set out for the Amír, whose presence he entered about sun-down, saying, "O Sire, I bring thee a poet the like of whom no one hath seen since Daqíqí's face was veiled in the tomb." Then he related what had passed.

Then the Amír accorded Farrukhí an audience, and when he came in he did reverence, and the Amír gave him his hand and assigned him an honourable place, enquiring after his health, treating him with kindness, and inspiring him with hopes of favours to come. When the wine had gone round several times[1], Farrukhí arose, and, in a sweet and plaintive voice, recited his elegy beginning:—

با کاروانِ حِلّه برفتم ز سیستان، با حُلّه تنیده ز دل بافته ز جان،

"With caravan for Ḥilla bound from Sístán did I start,
With fabrics spun within my brain and woven by my heart."

When he had finished, the Amír, who appreciated poetry and was himself something of a poet, expressed his astonishment at this rhapsody. 'Amíd As'ad said, "O Sire, wait till you see something still better!" Farrukhí was silent and held his peace until the wine had produced its full effect on the Amír, then he arose and recited this rhapsody (٤٠) on the branding-ground. The Amír was amazed, and in his admiration turned to Farrukhí, saying, "They have brought in a thousand colts, all with white foreheads, fetlocks and feet, bred in Khatlán[2]. The way is [open] to thee! Thou art a cunning rascal, a Sagzí; catch as many as thou art able, that they may be thine." Farrukhí, on whom the wine had produced its full effect, came out, straightway took his turban from his head, hurled himself into the midst of the herd, and chased a drove of them before him across the plain; but, though he caused them to gallop right and left in every direction, he could not catch a single one. At length a ruined rest-house situated on the edge of the camping-ground came into view, and thither the colts fled. Farrukhí, being utterly tired out, placed his turban under his head in the porch of the rest-house, and at once went to sleep, by reason of his extreme weariness and the effects of the wine. When they counted the colts, they were forty-two in number. They went and told the Amír, who, greatly surprised, laughed heartily and said, "He is a lucky fellow, and will come to great things. Look after him and the colts as well, and when he awakes, waken me too." So they obeyed the King's orders.

Next day, at sunrise, Farrukhí arose. The Amír had already risen, and, when he had performed his prayers, he gave Farrukhí an audience, treated him with great consideration, and handed over the colts to his attendants. He also ordered Farrukhí to be given a horse and equipments suitable to a man of rank, as well as two tents, three mules, five slaves, wearing apparel and carpets. So Farrukhí prospered in his service, and enjoyed the greatest circumstance. Then he waited upon Sulṭán Yamínu'd-Dawla

[1] I prefer the reading دَوْرِی to دَرْ وَی, and Mírzá Muḥammad concurs.

[2] The Editor shews in a note (pp. ١٦٦–١٦٨ of the text) that *Khatlán* is the Persian and *Khuttal* the Arabic name of a place in Transoxiana celebrated for its fine horses, called *Khatlí*.

Maḥmúd, who, seeing him thus magnificently equipped, regarded him with the same regard, and his affairs reached such a pitch of prosperity that twenty servants girt with silver girdles rode behind him.

ANECDOTE XVI.

In the year A.H. 510 (A.D. 1116–1117) the King of Islám, Sanjar the son of Malikshâh the Saljúq (may God prolong his existence and continue his exaltation to the heights!), chanced to be encamped at the spring season within the marches of Ṭús, in the plain of Turúq[1], where he remained for two months. There I, in hopes of obtaining some favour, joined his Court from Herát, having then nothing in the way of equipment (٤١) or provision. I composed a *qaṣída* and went to Mu'izzí the Poet-laureate, to seek an opening through him. Having looked at my poem, he tested me in several ways, and I satisfied his expectations. He then behaved in the most generous manner, and deemed it his duty to act in the way befitting so great a man.

One day I expressed in his presence a hope that fortune would be more favourable to me, and complained of my luck. He encouraged me, saying, "Thou hast laboured hard to acquire this science, and hast fully mastered it: surely this will have its effect. My own case was precisely similar; and good poetry has never yet been wasted. Thou hast a goodly share in this art: thy verse is even and melodious, and is still improving. Wait and see the advantages which thou wilt reap from this science. For though Fortune should at first be grudging, matters will eventually turn out as thou wishest.

"My father Burhání, the Poet-laureate (may God be merciful to him!) passed away from this transitory to that eternal world in the town of Qazwín in the early part of the reign of Malikshâh, entrusting me to the King in this verse, since then become famous[2]:—

من رفتم و فرزندِ من آمد خلفِ صدق ‘ اورا بخدا و بخداوند سپردم

"*I am flitting, but I leave a son behind me,*
And commend him to my God and to my King."

[1] This place is not mentioned in the geographies, but the Editor (p. ١٦٨ of the notes) believes it to be identical with the modern *Ṭuruq*, a large village distant two parasangs from Mashhad on the road to Ṭihrán.

[2] This verse, to which are added several others, is commonly ascribed to the Niẓámu'l-Mulk, *e.g.* by Dawlatsháh (p. ٥٩ of my edition). Apart from the improbability that one who lay dying of a mortal wound would be in the mood to compose verses, we learn from this anecdote that the Niẓámu'l-Mulk "had no opinion of poets because he had no skill in their art." The verse which gives his age as 94 at the time of his death, when he was in reality some fifteen or twenty years younger (born 408/1017, assassinated 485/1092), is alone enough to discredit the legend, while the authority of the *Chahár Maqála*, of which the author derived his information directly from Mu'izzí, the son of Burhání, is far superior to any other source of the story. Compare my *Lit. Hist. of Persia*, vol. ii, pp. 188–193, and the Persian notes, pp. ١٦٨–١٦٩.

"So my father's salary and allowances[1] were transferred to me, and I became Malikshāh's court-poet, and spent a year in the King's service; yet during this time I was unable to see him save once from a distance, nor did I get one *dínár* of my salary or one maund of my allowances, while my expenditure was increased I became involved in debt, and my brain was perplexed by my affairs. For that great Minister the Niẓámu'l-Mulk (may God be merciful to him!), had no opinion of poetry, because he had no skill in it; nor did he pay any attention to any one except religious leaders and mystics.

"One day—it was the eve of the day on which [the new moon of] Ramaḍán was due [to appear], and I had not a farthing for all the expenses incidental to that month and the feast which follows it—I went thus sad at heart to the Amír 'Alí ibn Farámarz[2] 'Alá'u'd-Dawla, a man of royal parentage, a lover of poetry, and the intimate companion of the King, with whom he was connected by marriage and enjoyed the highest honour, and before whom he could speak boldly, for he held high rank under that administration. And he had already been my patron. I said, 'May my lord's life be long! Not all that the father could do (٤٢) can the son do, nor does that which accrued to the father accrue to the son. My father was a bold and energetic man, and was sustained by his art, and the martyred King Alp Arslán, the lord of the world, entertained the highest opinion of him. But what he could do that can I not, for modesty forbids me, and my retiring disposition supports it. I have served [this prince] for a year, and have contracted debts to the extent of a thousand *dínárs*, and have not received a farthing. Crave permission, then, for thy servant to go to Níshápúr, and discharge his debts, and live on that which is left over, and pray for this victorious Dynasty.'

"'Thou speakest truly,' replied Amír 'Alí: 'We have all been at fault, but this shall be so no longer. The King, at the time of Evening Prayer, will come out to look for the new moon. Thou must be present there, and we will see what chance Fortune will offer.' Thereupon he at once ordered me to receive a hundred *dínárs* to defray my Ramaḍán expenses, and a purse[3] containing

[1] According to the Editor's note (p. ١٦٩ of the text) *jámagí* is equivalent to the modern *mawájib* or *mustamirrí*, and means wages in cash, while *ijrá* (the modern *jíra*) means allowances, especially in kind.

[2] 'Alí ibn Farámarz the Kákwayhid is intended. See S. Lane-Poole's *Muhammadan Dynasties*, p. 145, and Mírzá Muḥammad's note on pp. ١٦٩–١٧٠ of the text. He is called *Dámád* ("son-in-law," but here in the wider sense of "sib") because in 469/1076–7 he married Malikshāh's paternal aunt, Arslán Khátún, widow of the Caliph al-Qá'im biamri'lláh. He ultimately fell in battle in 488/1095.

[3] *Muhr* ordinarily means a seal, but Mírzá Muḥammad (p. ١٧٠ of the Persian notes) quotes other passages shewing that it was also used in the sense of a sealed purse, containing a definite and certified sum of money.

this sum in Nísnapúr coinage was forthwith brought and placed before me. So I returned mightily well pleased, and made my preparations for Ramaḍán, and at the time of the Evening Prayer went to the entrance of the King's pavilion. It chanced that 'Alá'u'd-Dawla arrived at the very same moment, and I paid my respects to him. 'Thou hast done excellently well,' said he, 'and hast come punctually.' Then he dismounted and went in before the King.

"At sun-down the King came forth from his pavilion, with a cross-bow in his hand and 'Alá'u'd-Dawla on his right side. I ran forward to do obeisance. Amír 'Alí continued his kindnesses, and they then busied themselves in looking for the moon. The King, however, was the first to see it, whereat he was mightily pleased. Then 'Alá'u'd-Dawla said to me, 'O son of Burhání, say something original about this moon,' and I at once recited these two couplets:—

ای ماه چو ابروانِ یاری گوئی ، یا نی چو کمانِ شهریاری گوئی ،
نعلی زده از زرِّ عیاری گوئی ، در گوشِ سپهر گوشواری گوئی ،

"*Methinks, O Moon, thou art our Prince's bow,*
Or his curved eyebrow, which doth charm us so,
Or else a horse-shoe wrought of gold refined,
Or ring from Heaven's ear depending low."

"When I had submitted these verses, Amír 'Alí applauded much, and the King said, 'Go, loose from the stable whichever horse thou pleasest'; for at that moment we were standing close to the stable. Amír 'Alí designated a horse which was brought out and given to my attendants, and which proved to be worth three hundred *dínárs* of Níshápúr. The King then went to his oratory, and I performed the evening prayer with him, after which we sat down to meat. At the table Amír 'Alí said, 'O son of Burhání! Thou hast not yet said anything about this favour conferred on thee by the lord of the world. (۴۳) Compose a quatrain at once!' I thereupon sprang to my feet, did obeisance and immediately recited these two verses just as they came to me:—

چون آتشِ خاطرِ مرا شاه بدید ،
از خاك مرا بر زبرِ ماه کشید ،
چون آب یکی ترانه از من بشنید ،
چون باد یکی مرکبِ خاصم بخشید ،

"*The King beheld the* fire *which in me blazed:*
Me from low earth *above the moon he raised:*
From me a verse, like water *fluent, heard,*
And swift as wind *a noble steed conferred.*"

"When I recited these verses 'Alá'u'd-Dawla warmly applauded me, and by reason of his applause the King gave me a thousand *dínárs*. Then 'Alá'u'd-Dawla said, 'He hath not yet received his salary and allowances. To-morrow I will sit on the Minister's skirt until he writes a draft for his salary on Ispahán, and orders his allowances to be paid out of the treasury.' Said the King, 'Thou must do it, then, for no one else has sufficient assurance. And call this poet after my title.' Now the King's title was *Mu'izzu'd-Dunyá wa'd-Dín*, so Amír 'Alí called me 'Master Mu'izzí.' '*Amír* Mu'izzí,' said the King, [correcting him]. And this noble and nobly born lord so wrought for me that next day, by the time of the afternoon prayer, I had received a thousand *dínárs* as a gift, twelve hundred more as allowances, and likewise an order for a thousand maunds of corn. And when the month of Ramaḍán was past, he summoned me to court, and caused me to become the King's boon-companion. So my fortune began to improve, and thenceforth he made continuing provision for me, and to-day whatever I have I possess by the favour of that Prince. May God, blessed and exalted is He, rejoice his dust with the lights of His Mercy, by His Favour and His Grace!"

ANECDOTE XVII.

The House of Saljúq were all fond of poetry, but none more so than Ṭughánsháh ibn Alp Arslán[1], whose conversation and intercourse was entirely with poets, and whose favourite companions were almost all of this class—men such as Amír Abú 'Abdu'lláh Qurashí, Abú Bakr Azraqí[2], Abú Manṣúr the son of Abú Yúsuf[3], Shujá'í of Nasá, Aḥmad Badíhí[4], Ḥaqíqí and Nasímí, all of whom were ranked in his service, while many others kept coming and going, all departing with gifts and joyful countenances.

One day the King was playing backgammon with Aḥmad Badíhí. They were finishing a game for [a stake of] ten thousand [? *dirhams*], (٤٤) and the Amír had two pieces in the sixth house and

[1] His full names and titles were *Shamsu'd-Dawla Abu'l-Fawáris Ṭughánsháh ibn Alp Arslán Muḥammad ibn Chaghrí Beg ibn Míká'íl ibn Saljúq*. During the reign of Alp Arslán he governed Khurásán from Herát. By Riḍá-qulí Khán (*Majma'u'l-Fuṣaḥá*, i, 139) and other biographers he has been confused with Ṭughánsháh ibn Mu'ayyad Áy-ába. See the Editor's note on the text, pp. ١٧٠–١٧٣, where many passages from poems in his praise by Azraqí are cited.

[2] See Note XX at the end, and the Editor's long note on pp. ١٧٤–١٧٨ of the text; 'Awfí's *Lubáb*, ch. x, No. 3; Dawlatsháh (pp. 72–73 of my ed.), Ṭabaqa II, No. 1; and *Majma'u'l-Fuṣaḥá*, vol. i, pp. ١٣٩–١٥٢.

[3] Abú Manṣúr 'Abdu'r-Rashíd ibn Aḥmad ibn Abí Yúsuf al-Hirawí. See 'Awfí's *Lubáb*, vol. ii, p. ٦١. A few lines lower in this story the author mentions having met him at Herát in 509/1115–6.

[4] *Majma'u'l-Fuṣaḥá*, i, p. ١٦٩. His *laqab* was Majdu'd-Dín and his *nisba* Sajáwandí.

Aḥmad Badíhí two pieces in the first house[1]; and it was the Amír's throw. He threw with the most deliberate care, in order to cast two sixes, instead of which he threw two ones, whereat he was mightily vexed and lost his temper (for which, indeed, he had good cause), while his anger rose so high and reached such a pitch that each moment he was putting his hand to his sword, while his courtiers trembled like the leaves of a tree, seeing that he was a King, and withal a boy angered at such spite of Fortune.

Then Abú Bakr Azraqí arose, and, approaching the minstrels, recited this quatrain:—

گر شاه دو شش خواست دو یك زخم افتاد،
تا ظن نبری که کعبتَین داد نداد،
آن زخم که کرد رای شاهنشه یاد،
در خدمتِ شاه روی بر خاك نهاد،

"Reproach not Fortune with discourteous tricks,
If by the King, desiring double six,
Two ones were thrown; for whomsoe'er he calls
Face to the earth before him prostrate falls."

When I was at Herát in the year A.H. 509 (A.D. 1115–1116), Abú Manṣúr the son of Abú Yúsuf related to me that the Amír Ṭughánsháh was so charmed and delighted with these two verses that he kissed Azraqí on the eyes, called for gold, and successively placed five hundred *dínárs* in his mouth, continuing thus to reward him so long as one gold piece was left. Thus did he recover his good humour and such largesse did he bestow, and the cause of all this was one quatrain. May God Almighty have mercy on both of them, by His Favour and Grace!

ANECDOTE XVIII.

In the year A.H. 472 (A.D. 1079–1080)[2] a certain spiteful person laid a statement before Sulṭán Ibráhím to the effect that his son, Amír Maḥmúd Sayfu'd-Dawla, intended to go to 'Iráq to wait on Maliksháh. The King's jealousy was aroused, and it so worked on him that suddenly he had his son seized, bound, and interned

[1] For the explanation of this passage I am indebted to my friend Mírzá 'Abdu'l-Ghaffár of the Persian Legation. The six "houses" on each side of the backgammon board are named (proceeding from left to right) as follows: (1) *khál-khán* or *yak-gáh*, (2) *dú-khán*, (3) *si-khán*, (4) *chahár-khán*, (5) *báf-dar*, (6) *shish-khán* or *shish-dar-gáh*. The numbers contained in these names allude to the numbers which must be thrown with the dice to get the pieces which occupy them off the board.

[2] The MSS. and L. all have "572," an evident error, for (1) Sulṭán Ibráhím the Ghaznawí reigned A.H. 451–492 (A.D. 1059–1099); (2) Maliksháh reigned A.H. 465–485 (A.D. 1072–1092); (3) the poet in question died in A.H. 515 or 525 (A.D. 1121 or 1130); (4) the *Chahár Maqála*, as we have already seen, was written during the lifetime of Sulṭán 'Alá'u'd-Dín Ḥusayn *Jahán-súz*, i.e. before A.H. 556 (A.D. 1161).

in a fortress. His son's intimates (١٠) also he arrested and interned, amongst them Mas'úd-i-Sa'd-i-Salmán, whom he sent to Wajíristán[1], to the Castle of Náy[2]; whence he sent the following quatrain to the King:—

در بندِ تو ای شاه ملك شه باید، تا بندِ تو پای تاجداری ساید،
آن کس که ز پُشتِ سعدِ سلمان آید، کر زهر شود ملكِ ترا نگزاید،

"O King, 'tis Malik Shah should wear thy chain,
That royal limbs might fret with captive's pain,
But Sa'd-i-Salmán's offspring could not hurt,
Though venomous as poison, thy domain!"

Alí Kháṣṣ brought this quatrain to the King, but it produced no effect on him, though all wise and impartial critics will recognize what rank Mas'úd's "Songs of Prison" hold in lofty feeling, and what degree in eloquence. Sometimes, when I read his verses, the hair stands on end on my body, and the tears are like to trickle from my eyes. All these verses were read to the King, and he heard them, yet they affected him not at all, and not one particle of his being was warmed to enthusiasm, so that he departed from this world leaving that noble man in prison. Khwája Salmán says[3]:—

مقصور شد مصالحِ کارِ جهانیان،
بر حبس و بندِ این تنِ مهجور ناتوان،
بر حبس و بند نیز ندارندم استوار،
تا گرد من ندارد ده تن نگاهبان،
هر ده نشسته بر در و در بامِ سجنِ من،
با یکدکر دمادم گویند هر زمان،
هان بر جهید زود که حیلتگریست او،
کز آفتاب پل کند از سایه نردبان،
گیرم که ساخته شوم از بهرِ کارزار،
بیرون جهم ز گوشهٔ این سجن ناگهان،
با چند کس بر آیم در قلعه گرچه من،
شیری شوم معربد و پیلی شوم دمان

[1] Mírzá Muḥammad (Persian notes, p. ١٧٩) at first failed to identify Wajíristán, but now believes it to be identical with the modern Wazíristán.

[2] The only mention of Náy hitherto discovered in Persian geographical works occurs in the *Nuzhatu'l-Qulúb*, where it is briefly mentioned in the section dealing with Marw-i-Sháhján.

[3] These verses are inserted in the margin of A. (f. 20ᵃ) only. They are omitted in the printed text.

پس بی سلاح جنگ چگونه کنم مگر،
من سینه‌را سپر کنم و پشت‌را کمان،

"Naught served the ends of statesmen save that I,
A helpless exile, should in fetters lie,
Nor do they deem me safe within their cells,
Unless surrounded by ten sentinels;
Which ten sit ever by the gates and walls,
And ever one unto his comrade calls:
'Ho there! On guard! This cunning rogue is one
To fashion bridge and steps from shade and sun!'
Why, grant I stood arrayed for such a fight,
And suddenly sprang forth, attempting flight,
Could elephant or raging lion hope,
Thus cramped in prison-cage, with ten to cope?
Can I, bereft of weapons, take the field,
Or make of back and bosom bow and shield?"

So, by reason of his relation to Sayfu'd-Dawla, he remained imprisoned for twelve[1] years in the days of Sulṭán Ibráhím, and, on account of his like relation to Abú Naṣr of Párs[2], for eight years more in the reign of Sulṭán Mas'úd ibn Ibráhím, though none hath been heard of who hath produced so many splendid elegies and rare gems of verse as were born of his brilliant genius. After eight years Thiqatu'l-Mulk Ṭáhir ibn 'Alí ibn Mushkán[3] brought him forth from his bondage, so that, in short, during these two reigns this illustrious man spent all his life in captivity, and the ill repute of this deed remained on this noble House. I hesitate as to the motives which are to be assigned to this act, and whether it is to be ascribed to strength of purpose, recklessness, hardness of heart, or a malicious disposition. In any case it was not a laudable deed, and I have never met with any sensible man who was prepared to praise that administration for such inflexibility of purpose or excess of caution. And I heard it remarked by the King of the world Ghiyáthu'd-Dunyá wa'd-

[1] As Mírzá Muḥammad has pointed out (Persian notes, pp. ۱۷۹–۱۸۰) there is some confusion of facts here. Mas'úd suffered two separate periods of imprisonment, the first for ten years, of which seven were spent in Sú and Dahak (between Zaranj and Bust in Sístán), the second for seven or eight years in Maranj in India. Sulṭán Ibráhím's death took place in A.H. 492 (A.D. 1098–9), so that, if he was still suffering his first imprisonment at that time, it cannot have begun earlier than A.H. 482 (A.D. 1089–1090). We have Mas'úd's own authority for fixing the duration of his imprisonment at ten (not twelve) years. See his verses quoted at the top of p. ۱۸۰ of the Persian notes.

[2] Qiwámu'l-Mulk Niẓámu'd-Dín Abú Naṣr Hibatu'lláh al-Fársí, a leading statesman during these two reigns and a friend and patron of our poet, fell into disgrace in the reign of Sulṭán Mas'úd, together with his clients and protégés. He died about 510/1116.

[3] He was prime minister to Sulṭán Mas'úd ibn Ibráhím, and patron of many poets, including, besides Mas'úd-i-Sa'd-i-Salmán, Abu'l-Faraj-i-Rúní, Mukhtárí and Saná'í, all of whom have sung his praises. His uncle Abú Naṣr Manṣúr ibn Mushkán was secretary to Sulṭán Maḥmúd and Sulṭán Mas'úd, author of a volume of Memoirs and teacher of the historian Abu'l-Faḍl-i-Bayhaqí.

Dín Muḥammad[1], the son of Malikshah, at the gates of Hamadán, on the occasion of the rebellion of his son-in-law (may God make fragrant their dust, and exalt their station in Paradise!) Amír Shihábu'd-Dín Qutulmush Alp Ghází, "It is the sign of a malicious heart to keep a foe imprisoned; for one of two things, either he is loyal or seditious. Then, if the former, it is an injustice to keep him in prison; and if the latter, it is again an injustice to suffer an ill-doer to live." (٤٦) In short that misery of Mas'úd passed, while this ill repute will endure till the Resurrection.

ANECDOTE XIX.

In the time of Sulṭán Khiḍr ibn Ibráhím[2] the power of the Kháqánís[3] was at its most flourishing period, while the strength of their administration and the respect in which it was held were such as could not be surpassed.

Now he was a wise and just ruler and an ornament to the throne, and to him appertained the dominion of Transoxiana and Turkistán, while he enjoyed the most complete security on the side of Khurásán, wherewith he was allied by friendly relations, kinship, and firm treaties and covenants. And of the splendour maintained by him one detail was this, that when he rode out they carried before his horse, besides other arms, seven hundred maces of gold and silver. He was, moreover, a great patron of poets, and in his service were Amír 'Am'aq[4], Master Rashídí, Najjár-i-Ságharchí, 'Alí Pánídhí, the son of Darghúsh, the son of Isfaráyiní, 'Alí Sipihrí and Najíbí of Farghána, all of whom obtained rich rewards and vast honours. The Poet-Laureate was Amír 'Am'aq, who had profited abundantly by that dynasty and obtained the most ample circumstance, comprising Turkish slaves, fair damsels, well-paced horses, golden vessels, sumptuous apparel, and servants, biped and quadruped[5], innumerable. He was greatly honoured at the King's Court, so that of necessity the other poets

[1] The seventh Saljúq king, who reigned A.H. 498–511 (A.D. 1104–1117). There is, as pointed out by Mírzá Muḥammad (pp. ١٨٢–١٨٤ of the Persian notes) an extraordinary confusion of dates and persons in this story. See also Note XXI at the end.

[2] Sulṭán Khiḍr Khán ibn Tafgháj Khán Ibráhím ibn Naṣr Arslán (known as Ílak) ibn 'Alí ibn Músá ibn Sutuq succeeded his brother Shamsu'l-Mulk Naṣr ibn Ibráhím in A.H. 474 (A.D. 1081–2), but died shortly afterwards. See Ibnu'l-Athír *sub anno* A.H. 408, and the *Ta'ríkh-i-Jahán-árá* (Or. 141 of the British Museum, f. 133a).

[3] This Turkish Muslim dynasty, also known as Khániyya, Ílak Khans, and Ál-i-Afrásiyáb, reigned for about 230 lunar years (A.H. 380–609 = A.D. 990–1212) in Transoxiana, and was finally overthrown by the Khwárazmsháhs. See S. Lane-Poole's *Muhammadan Dynasties*, pp. 134–135; Note XXII at the end; and pp. ١٨٤–١٨٩ of the Persian notes.

[4] Mention has already been made of all these poets on p. ٢٨ of the text (= pp. 29–30 of this translation) with the exception of "the son of Isfaráyiní." See pp. ١٠١–١٠٢ of the Persian notes, and Note XIV at the end.

[5] Literally, "speaking and silent," or "articulate and dumb."

must needs do him reverence. Such homage as from the others he desired from Master Rashídí also, but herein he was disappointed, for Rashídí, though still young, was nevertheless learned in his art. The Lady Zaynab was the special object of his panegyrics, while all Khiḍr Khán's women were at his command, and he enjoyed the fullest favour of the King, who was continually praising him and asserting his merits, so that Rashídí's affairs prospered, the title of "Prince of poets[1]" was conferred on him, he continued to rise higher in the King's opinion, and from him received gifts of great value.

One day, in Rashídí's absence, the King asked 'Am'aq, "What thinkest thou of the verse of Rashídí, 'the Prince of poets'?" "His verse," replied he, "is extremely good and chaste and correct, but it wants a little spice."

After some while had elapsed, Rashídí (٤٧) came in and did obeisance, and was about to sit down when the King called him before himself, and said, teasing him as is the way of Kings, "I asked the Poet-Laureate just now, 'How is Rashídí's poetry?' He replied that it was good, but wanted spice. Now you must compose a couple of verses on this subject." Rashídí, with a bow, sat down in his place and improvised the following fragment:—

شعرهای مرا به بینمکی ' عیب کردی روا بود شاید '
شعرِ من همچو شکّر و شهدست ' و اندرین دو نمك نکو ناید '
شلغم و باقلاست گفتهٔ تو ' نمك ای قلتبان ترا باید '

"You stigmatise my verse as 'wanting spice,'
And possibly, my friend, you may be right.
My verse is honey-flavoured, sugar-sweet,
And spice with such could scarcely cause delight.
Spice is for you, you blackguard, not for me,
For beans and turnips is the stuff you write!"

When he submitted these verses the King was mightily pleased. And in Transoxiana it is the custom and practice to place in the audience-chambers of kings and others gold and silver in trays, which they call *sím-ṭáqá* or *juft*; and in this audience of Khiḍr Khán's there were set for largesse four trays of red gold, each containing two hundred and fifty *dínárs*; and these he used to dispense by the handful. On this day he ordered Rashídí to receive all four trays, so he obtained the highest honour, and became famous. For just as a patron becomes famous by the verse of a good poet, so do poets likewise achieve renown by receiving a great reward from the King, these two things being interdependent.

[1] Sayyidu'sh-Shu'ará.

ANECDOTE XX.

Master Abu'l-Qásim Firdawsí[1] was one of the Dihqáns (landowners) of Ṭús, from a village called Bázh[2] in the district of Ṭabarán[3], a large village capable of supplying a thousand men. There Firdawsí enjoyed an excellent position, so that he was rendered quite independent of his neighbours by the income which he derived from his lands, and he had but one child, a daughter. His one desire in putting the Book of Kings (*Sháhnáma*) into verse was, out of the reward which he might obtain for it, to supply her with an adequate dowry. He was engaged for twenty-five years on this work ere he (۱۸) finished the book, and to this end he left nothing undone, raising his verse as high as heaven, and causing it in sweet fluency to resemble running water. What genius, indeed, could raise verse to such a height as he does in the letter written by Zál to Sám the son of Narímán in Mázandarán when he desired to ally himself with Rúdába the daughter of the King of Kábul[4]:—

یکی نامه فرمود نزدیکِ سام، سراسر درود و نوید و سلام،[5]
نخست از جهان آفرین یاد کرد، که هم داد فرمود و هم داد کرد،
وزو باد بر سامِ نیرم درود، خداوندِ شمشیر و گوپال و خود،
چمانندهٔ چرمه هنگامِ گرد، چرانندهٔ کرگس اندر نبرد،
فزایندهٔ باد آوردگاه، فشانندهٔ خون ز ابرِ سیاه،
بمردی هنر در هنر ساخته، هنرش[6] از هنر گردن افراخته،

"*Then to Sám straightway sent he a letter,*
Filled with fair praises, prayers and good greeting.
First made he mention of the World-Maker,
Who doom dispenseth and doom fulfilleth.
'*On Nírám's son Sám,*' *wrote he*, '*the sword-lord,*
Mail-clad and mace-girt, may the Lord's peace rest!

[1] This anecdote is cited by Ibn Isfandiyár in his *History of Ṭabaristán* (A.H. 613, A.D. 1216. See Rieu's *Persian Catalogue*, pp. 202–204 and 533[b]), whence it was excerpted and published, with a German translation, by Ethé (*Z.D.M.G.*, vol. xlviii, pp. 89–94). It was also utilized by Nöldeke in 1896 in his *Iranische Nationalepos* (*Grundriss d. Iran. Philologie*, vol. ii, pp. 150 *et seqq.*). A revised edition of this valuable monograph has just appeared (Berlin and Leipzig, 1920). The references here given are, unless otherwise specified, to the original edition.

[2] The *Burhán-i-Qáṭi'* is the only Persian or Arabic book of reference which makes mention of this place as situated near Ṭús.

[3] See Nöldeke, *loc. cit.*, p. 151 (p. 25 of the new edition), and Yáqút, *s.v.* The city of Ṭús comprised the two districts of Ṭabarán (or Ṭábarán) and Núqán.

[4] These verses (with some variants) will be found on pp. 124–125 of vol. i of Turner Macan's edition of the *Sháhnáma* (Calcutta, 1829).

[5] The printed text has خرام for سلام.

[6] The text has سرش for هنرش.

Hurler of horse-troops in hot-contested fights,
Feeder of carrion-fowls with foemen's flesh-feast,
Raising the roar of strife on the red war-field,
From the grim war-clouds grinding the gore-shower.
Who, by his manly might merit on merit
Heaps, till his merit merit outmeasures[1].'"

In eloquence I know of no poetry in Persian which equals this, and but little even in Arabic.

When Firdawsí had completed the *Sháhnáma*, it was transcribed by 'Alí Daylam[2] and recited by Abú Dulaf[2], both of whom he mentions by name in tendering his thanks to Ḥuyayy-i-Qutayba[3], the governor of Ṭús, who had conferred on Firdawsí many favours:—

ازین نامه از نامدارانِ شهر، علی دیلم و بو دلف راست بهر،
نیامد جز اَحْسَنْتَشَان بهره‌ام، بکَفْت اندر اَحْسَنْتَشَان زهره‌ام،
حُیَیِّ قتیبه است از آزادگان، که از من نخواهد سخن رایگان،
نیَم آگه از اصل و فرع خراج، همی غلطم اندر میانِ دواج،

"*Of the men of renown of this city 'Alí Daylam and Abú Dulaf have participated in this book.*
From them my portion was naught save 'Well done!'
My gall-bladder was like to burst with their 'Well dones[4].'
Ḥuyayy the son of Qutayba is a nobleman who asks me not for unrewarded verse.
I know nothing either of the root nor the branches of the land-tax;
I lounge [at ease] in the midst of my quilt[5]."

Ḥuyayy the son of Qutayba was the revenue-collector of Ṭús, and deemed it his duty at least to abate the taxes payable by Firdawsí; hence naturally his name will endure till the Resurrection and Kings will read it.

So 'Alí Daylam transcribed the *Sháhnáma* in seven volumes, and Firdawsí, taking with him Abú Dulaf, set out for the Court of Ghazna. There, by the help of the great Minister Aḥmad ibn Ḥasan[6], the secretary, he presented it, and it was accepted, Sulṭán

[1] Poor as this rendering is, I am strongly of opinion that for an English rendering of the *Sháhnáma* (which always seems to me very analogous in aim, scope, and treatment to that little-read English Epic, the Brut of Layamon) the old English alliterative verse would be the most suitable form.

[2] See Nöldeke, *op. cit.*, p. 153 (p. 27 of the new edition), and n. 2 *ad calc.*

[3] So A. and L. B. has the more usual "Ḥusayn b. Qutayba." Cf. Nöldeke, *loc. cit.*

[4] *I.e.* I am sick of their barren and unprofitable plaudits. As these poor men rendered him material service in other ways, Firdawsí's remarks seem rather ungrateful.

[5] What follows is evidently an explanation of this couplet. Firdawsí means that being no longer vexed with the exactions of the tax-gatherer, he can now repose in peace.

[6] This celebrated minister had the title *Shamsu'l-Kufát* and the *nisba* of al-Maymandí. He died in 424/1033 after twenty years' service as Minister to Sulṭán Maḥmúd.

Maḥmúd expressing himself as greatly indebted to his Minister. But the Prime Minister had enemies who were continually casting the dust of misrepresentation into the cup of his rank, and Maḥmúd (٥٩) consulted with them as to what he should give Firdawsí. They replied, "Fifty thousand *dirhams*, and even that is too much, seeing that he is in belief a Ráfiḍí and a Mu'tazilite. Of his Mu'tazilite views this verse is a proof:—

به بینندگان آفریننده‌را ، نبینی مرنجان دو بیننده‌را ،

'Thy gaze the Creator can never descry;
Then wherefore, by gazing, dost weary thine eye?'

" while to his Ráfiḍí proclivities these verses of his witness:—

خردمند گیتی چو دریا نهاد ، بر انگیخته موج از آن تند باد ،
چو هفتاد کشتی دران ساخته ، همه بادبانها ، بر افراخته ،
میانه یکی خوب کشتی عروس ، بر آراسته همچو چشمِ خروس ،
پیمبر بدو اندرون با علی ، همه اهلِ بیتِ نبیّ و ولی ،
اگر خلد خواهی بدیگر سرای ، بنزدِ نبیّ و وصی گیر جای ،
گرت زین بد آید گناهِ منست ، چنین دان و این راه راهِ منست ،
برین زادم و هم برین بگذرم ، یقین دان که خاكِ پیِ حیدرم ،

'The wise man conceives the world as a sea, wherefrom the fierce wind has stirred up waves.
Thereon are seventy ships[1] afloat, all with sails set,
And amongst them one vessel, fair as a bride, decked with colour like the eye of the cock,
Wherein are the Prophet and 'Alí, with all the Family of the Prophet and his Vicar.
If thou desirest Paradise in the other World, take thy place by the Prophet and his Trustee.
If ill accrues to thee thereby, it is my fault: know this, that this way is my way.
In this I was born, and in this I will pass away: know for a surety that I am as dust at feet of 'Alí.'"

Now Sulṭán Maḥmúd was a zealot, and he listened to these imputations and caught hold of them, and in all only twenty thousand *dirhams* were paid to Ḥakím Firdawsí. He was bitterly disappointed, went to the bath, and, on coming out, bought a draft of sherbet[2], and divided the money between the bath-man and the sherbet-seller. Knowing, however, Maḥmúd's

[1] That is the seventy (or seventy-two) sects of Islám "all of which are doomed to Hell-fire save one which shall be saved."

[2] *Fuqá'*, described as a kind of beer. See Schlimmer's *Terminologie Pharmaceutique* (lith. Ṭihrán, 1874), p. 75, and Abdul-Chalig Akhundow's German translation, with notes, of the Pharmacology of Abú Manṣúr Muwaffaq ibn 'Alí al-Hirawí, pp. 241 and 388–389.

severity, he fled from Ghazna by night, and alighted in Herát at the shop of Azraqí's father, Isma'íl the bookseller (*Warráq*), where he remained in hiding for six months, until Maḥmúd's messengers had reached Ṭús and had turned back thence, when Firdawsí, feeling secure, set out from Herát for Ṭús, taking the *Sháhnáma* with him. Thence he came to Ṭabaristán to the Sipahbad Shahriyár[1] of the House of Báwand, who was King there; and this is a noble house which traces its descent from Yazdigird[2] the son of Shahriyár.

Then Firdawsí wrote a satire of a hundred couplets on Sulṭán Maḥmúd in the Preface, and read it to Shahriyár[3], saying, "I will dedicate this book to you instead of to Sulṭán Maḥmúd, for this book deals wholly with the legends and deeds of thy forebears." Shahriyár treated him with honour and shewed him many kindnesses, and said, "O Master, Maḥmúd was induced to act thus by others, who did not submit your book to him under proper conditions, (..) and misrepresented you. Moreover you are a Shí'ite, and whosoever loves the Family of the Prophet his worldly affairs will prosper no more than theirs. Maḥmúd is my liege-lord: let the *Sháhnáma* stand in his name, and give me the satire which you have written on him, that I may expunge it and give you some little recompense; and Maḥmúd will surely summon thee and seek to satisfy thee fully, for the labour spent on such a book must not be wasted." And next day he sent Firdawsí 100,000 *dirhams*, saying, "I buy each couplet at a thousand *dirhams*, give me those hundred couplets, and be reconciled to Maḥmúd." So Firdawsí sent him these verses, and he ordered them to be expunged; and Firdawsí also destroyed his rough copy of them, so that this satire was done away with and only these six verses of it remained[4]:—

مرا غمز کردند کآن پر سخن، بمهرِ نبیّ و علی شد کهن،
اگر مهرشان من حکایت کنم، چو محمودرا صد حمایت کنم،
پرستار زاده نیاید بکار، و گرچند باشد پدر شهریار،
ازین در سخن چند رانم همی، چو دریا کرانه ندانم همی،
به نیکی نبد شاه‌را دستگاه، و گرنه مرا بر نشاندی بگاه،
چو اندر تبارش بزرگی نبود، ندانست نامِ بزرگان شنود،

[1] The MSS. have Shahrzád and the lithographed edition Shírzád, both of which readings are erroneous. The correct reading Shahriyár is given by Ibn Isfandiyár in his citation of this passage. His full genealogy, with references to the histories in which mention is made of him, is given on p. ۱۹۰ of the Persian notes.

[2] The last Sásánian king.

[3] Cf. Nöldeke, *loc. cit.*, p. 155, and n. 4 *ad calc.*

[4] This is a remarkable statement, and, if true, would involve the assumption that the well-known satire, as we have it, is spurious. Cf. Nöldeke (*op. cit.*), pp. 155–156, and n. 1 on the latter, and pp. 30-31 of his new edition of *Das Iran. Nationalepos.*

'They cast imputations on me, saying, 'That man of many words
Hath grown old in the love of the Prophet and 'Alí.'
If I speak of my love for these
I can protect a hundred such as Maḥmúd.
No good can come of the son of a slave,
Even though his father hath ruled as King.
How long shall I speak on this subject?
Like the sea I know no shore.
The King had no aptitude for good,
Else would he have seated me on a throne.
Since in his family there was no nobility
He could not bear to hear the names of the noble."

In truth good service was rendered to Maḥmúd by Shahriyár, and Maḥmúd was greatly indebted to him.

When I was at Níshápúr in the year A.H. 514 (A.D. 1120–1121), I heard Amír Mu'izzí say that he had heard Amír 'Abdu'r-Razzáq at Ṭús relate as follows: "Maḥmúd was once in India, and was returning thence towards Ghazna. On the way, as it chanced, there was a rebellious chief possessed of a strong fortress, and next day Maḥmúd encamped at the gates of it, and sent an ambassador to him, bidding him come before him on the morrow, do homage, pay his respects at the Court, receive a robe of honour and return to his place. Next day Maḥmúd rode out with the Prime Minister[1] on his right hand, for the ambassador had turned back and was coming to meet the King. 'I wonder,' said the latter to the Minister, 'what answer he will have given?' Thereupon the Minister recited this verse of Firdawsí's:—

'اگر جز بکامِ من آید جواب' من و گرز و میدان وافراسیاب'

Should the answer come contrary to my wish,
Then for me the mace, and the field [of battle], and Afrásiyáb." (۵۱)

Whose verse,' enquired Maḥmúd, 'is that, for it is one to inspire courage?' 'Poor Abu'l-Qásim Firdawsí composed it,' answered the Minister; 'he who laboured for five and twenty years to complete such a work, and reaped from it no advantage.' 'You have done well,' said Maḥmúd, 'to remind me of this, for I deeply regret that this noble man was disappointed by me. Remind me at Ghazna to send him something.'

"So when the Minister returned to Ghazna, he reminded Maḥmúd, who ordered Firdawsí to be given sixty thousand *dínárs'* worth of indigo, and that this indigo should be carried to Ṭús on the King's own camels, and that apologies should be made to Firdawsí. For years the Minister had been working for this, and at length he had achieved his work; so now he despatched the camels, and the indigo arrived safely at Ṭabarán[2].

[1] *Khwája-i-Buzurg.* This was the title commonly given to *Shamsu'l-Kufát* Aḥmad ibn Ḥasan al-Maymandí. See n. 6 at the foot of p. 55 *supra*.

[2] Ṭabarán is the name of a portion of the city of Ṭús. See B. de Meynard's *Dict. de la Perse*, pp. 374–375, and p. 54 *supra*, n. 3 *ad calc.*

But as the camels were entering through the Rúdbár Gate, the corpse of Firdawsí was being borne forth from the Gate of Razán[1]. Now at this time there was in Ṭabarán a preacher whose fanaticism was such that he declared that he would not suffer Firdawsí's body to be buried in the Musulmán Cemetery, because he was a Ráfiḍí (Shí'a); and nothing that men could say served to move this doctor. Now within the Gate there was a garden belonging to Firdawsí, and there they buried him, and there he lies to this day." And in the year A.H. 510 (A.D. 1116–1117) I visited his tomb[2].

They say that Firdawsí left a daughter, of very lofty spirit, to whom they would have given the King's gift; but she would not accept it, saying, "I need it not." The Post-master wrote to the Court and represented this to the King, who ordered that doctor to be expelled from Ṭabarán as a punishment for his officiousness, and to be exiled from his home, and the money to be given to the Imám Abú Bakr ibn Isḥáq-i-Kirámí[3] for the repair of the rest-house of Cháha, which stands on the road between Merv and Níshápúr on the boundaries of Ṭús. When this order reached Ṭús it was faithfully carried out; and the restoration of the rest-house of Cháha was effected by this money.

ANECDOTE XXI.

At the period when I was in the service of my Lord the King of the Mountains[4] (may God illuminate (٥٣) his tomb and exalt his station in Paradise!), that august personage had a high opinion of me, and shewed himself a most generous patron towards me. Now on the Festival of the Breaking of the Fast one of the nobles of the city of Balkh (may God maintain its prosperity!), Amír 'Amíd Ṣafiyyu'd-Dín Abú Bakr Muḥammad ibn al-Ḥusayn Rawánsháhí, came to the Court. He was a young man, accomplished and highly esteemed, an expert writer, a qualified secretary of state, well endowed with culture and its fruits, popular with all, whose praises were on all tongues. And at this time I was not in attendance.

[1] See Nöldeke's new edition of his *Pers. Nationalepos*, p. 32, n. 2 *ad calc.* There are several places called *Rúdbár*, of which one situated near Ṭabarán is probably meant. See B. de Meynard's *Dict. de la Perse*, p. 266. A *Razán* in Sístán is mentioned by al-Baládhurí (pp. ٣٩٦–٣٩٧), and another (رزان) in the district of Nasá in Khurásán (*Dict. de la Perse*, p. 259).

[2] I am not sure at what point the inverted commas should be inserted, but the last sentence of this paragraph is certainly Niẓámí's.

[3] This divine, Abú Bakr Muḥammad ibn Isḥáq ibn Maḥmashád, was the head of the Kirámí sect at Níshápúr, and his biography is given in the *Ta'ríkhu'l-Yamíní* (ed. Cairo, pp. ٣٠٩–٣٣٠). The Kirámí sect inclined to anthropomorphism. A full account of their doctrines will be found in Shahristání's *Kitábu'l-Milal wa'n-Niḥal.*

[4] This, as already stated, was the title assumed by the kings of Ghúr generally, and by the first of them, Quṭbu'd-Dín Muḥammad ibn 'Izzu'd-Dín Ḥusayn, especially. He it was whose death was avenged by his brother Sulṭán 'Alá'u'd-Dín *Jahán-súz* in the sack of Ghazna, and who was our author's patron. See Note XV at the end.

Now at a reception the King chanced to say, "Call Niẓámí." Said the Amír 'Amíd Ṣafiyyu'd-Dín, "Is Niẓámí here?" They answered "Yes." But he supposed that it was Niẓámí-Munírí[1]. "Ah," said he, "a fine poet and a man of wide fame!" When the messenger arrived to summon me, I put on my shoes, and, as I entered, did obeisance, and sat down in my place. When the wine had gone round several times, Amír 'Amíd said, "Niẓámí has not come." "He is come," replied the King; "see, he is seated over there." "I am not speaking of this Niẓámí," answered Amír 'Amíd, "that Niẓámí of whom I speak is another one, and as for this one, I do not even know him." Thereupon I saw that the King was vexed; he at once turned to me and said, "Is there somewhere else another Niẓámí besides thee?" "Yes, Sire," I answered, "there are two other Niẓámís, one of Samarqand, whom they call Niẓámí-i-Munírí, and one of Níshápúr, whom they call Niẓámí-i-Athírí; while me they call Niẓámí-i-'Arúḍí." "Art thou better, or they?" demanded he. Then Amír 'Amíd perceived that he had made an unfortunate remark and that the King was annoyed. "Sire," said he, "those two Niẓámís are quarrelsome fellows, apt to break up and spoil social gatherings by their quarrelsomeness." "Wait," said the King jestingly, "till you see this one drain five bumpers of strong wine[2] and break up the meeting: but of these three Niẓámís which is the best poet?" "Of those two," said the Amír 'Amíd, "I have personal knowledge, having seen them, while this one I have not previously seen, nor have I heard his poetry. If he will compose a couple of verses on this subject which we have been discussing, so that I may see his talents and hear his verse, I will tell you which of these three is best."

Then the King turned to me, saying, "Now, O Niẓámí, do not shame us, (٥٣) and when thou speakest say what 'Amíd desires."

Now at that time, when I was in the service of this sovereign, I possessed a prolific talent and a brilliant genius, and the favours and gifts of the King had stimulated me to such a point that my improvisations came fluent as running water; so I took up a pen, and, ere the wine-cup had gone twice round, composed these five couplets:—

در جهان سه نظامییم ای شاه، که جهانی ز ما بافغانند،
من بورساد پیشِ تختِ شهم، وآن دو در مَرْو پیشِ سلطانند،
بحقیقت که در سخن امروز، هر یکی مفخرِ خراسانند،

[1] The reading of this *nisba* is very doubtful in all three texts, both here and lower. In some it appears to read *Minbarí*.

[2] The correct reading, *si-yakí*, is that given in the text, not *sangí*, which most of the MSS. have. It is wine reduced by evaporation to one-third of its original bulk; in Arabic it is similarly called *muthallath*. See the *Anjuman-áráyi-Náṣirí*, *s.v.*

گرچه همچون روان سخن گویند، ورچه همچون خرد سخن دانند،
من شرابم که شان چو در یابم، هر دو از کارِ خود فرو مانند،

"*We are three Nizámís in the world, O King, on account of whom a whole world is filled with outcry.*
I am at Warsád[1] *before the King's throne, while those two others are in Merv before the Sulṭán.*
To-day, in truth, in verse each one is the Pride of Khurásán.
Although they utter verse subtle as spirit, and although they understand the Art of Speech like Wisdom,
I am the Wine, for, when I get hold of them, both desist from their work."

When I submitted these verses, the Amír 'Amíd Ṣafiyyu'd-Dín bowed and said, "O King, let alone the Niẓámís, I know of no poet in all Transoxiana, 'Iráq, or Khurásán capable of improvising five such verses, more especially in respect of strength, energy, and sweetness, conjoined with such grace of diction and filled with ideas so original. Be of good cheer, O Niẓámí, for thou hast no peer on the face of the earth. O Sire, he hath a graceful wit, a mind strong in apprehension, and a finished art. The good fortune of the King of the age and his generosity (may God exalt them!) hath increased them, and he will become a unique genius, and will become even more than this, for he is young, and hath many days before him."

Thereat the countenance of my King and Lord brightened mightily; a great cheerfulness appeared in his gracious temperament, and he applauded me, saying, "I give thee the lead-mine of Warsád from this Festival until the Festival of the Sheep-sacrifice[2]. Send an agent there." I did so, sending Isḥáq the Jew. It was the middle of summer and the time of active work, and they melted much of the ore, so that in seventy days twelve thousand maunds of lead appertaining to the tithe[3] accrued to me, while the King's opinion of me was increased a thousand-fold. May God (blessed and exalted is He) illuminate his august ashes with the light of His approval and rejoice his noble soul by the accumulation of wealth, by His Favour and Grace!

[1] Warsád or Warshád was the residence of this king, Quṭbu'd-Dín Muḥammad, in Ghúr, as mentioned in the *Ṭabaqát-i-Náṣirí* (Raverty's translation, p. 339).

[2] *I.e.* from the end of Ramaḍán until the 10th of Dhu'l-Ḥijja, a period of two months and ten days.

[3] The exact meaning of this sentence is not clear even to the learned editor Mírzá Muḥammad (p. ۱۹۲ of the Persian notes). He suggests that our author, Niẓámí, was a Sayyid, or descendant of the Prophet, and that the *khums*, or fifth part of the profits, to which Sayyids are entitled, was in this case made over wholly to him. If this be the meaning, we should probably read *dar isti khums* for *az ín-i-khums*. An alternative conjecture is to read *bi-dún-i-khums*, and to translate "not counting the *khums*," *i.e.* that the net profit, after deducting the *khums* or tithe, was 12,000 maunds of lead.

(١٠) THIRD DISCOURSE.

On the Lore of the Stars and the excellence of the Astronomer in that Science.

Abú Rayḥán al-Bírúní[1] says, in the first chapter of his "Explanation of the Science of Astronomy" (*Kitábu't-Tafhím fí ṣiná'ati't-Tanjím*)[2]:—"A man doth not merit the title of Astronomer until he hath attained proficiency in four sciences; *first*, Geometry; *secondly*, Arithmetic; *thirdly*, Cosmography; and *fourthly*, Judicial Astrology."

Now *Geometry* is that science whereby are known the dispositions of lines and the shapes of plane surfaces and solid bodies, the general relations existing between determinates and determinants, and the relation between them and what has position and form. Its principles are included in the book of Euclid the Geometrician[3] in the recension of Thábit ibn Qurra[4].

Arithmetic is that science whereby are known the nature of all sorts of numbers, especially each species thereof in itself; the nature of their relation to one another; their generation from each other; and the applications thereof, such as halving, doubling, multiplication, division, addition, subtraction, and Algebra. The principles thereof are contained in the book of the 'Αριθμητική, and the applications in the "Supplement" (*Takmila*) of Abú Manṣúr of Baghdád[5], and the "Hundred Chapters" (*Ṣad Báb*) of as-Sajzí[6].

Cosmography is that science whereby are known the nature of the Celestial and Terrestrial Bodies, their shapes and positions, their relations to one another, and the measurements and distances which are between them, together with the nature of the movements of the stars and heavens, and the co-ordination of the spheres and segments whereby these movements are fulfilled.

[1] The best account of this great scholar is that given by Dr Edward Sachau in the German Introduction to his edition of *al-Átháru'l-Báqiya* (Leipzig, 1876), and, in a shorter form, in his English translation of the same (London, 1879). The substance of this is given by Mírzá Muḥammad on pp. ١٩٣–١٩٧ of the Persian notes. See Note XXIII at the end.

[2] This book was composed simultaneously in Arabic and Persian in A.H. 420 (A.D. 1029). There is a fine old MS. of the Persian version dated A.H. 685 (A.D. 1286), and bearing the class-mark Add. 7697, in the British Museum. See Rieu's *Persian Catalogue*, pp. 451–452.

[3] *Najjár*, literally, "the Carpenter."

[4] I take this to be the sense of 'که ثابت بن قرّه دستی کرده است'. Concerning Thábit ibn Qurra, see Wüstenfeld's *Gesch. d. Arabischen Aerzte*, pp. 34–36; Brockelmann's *Gesch. d. Arab. Litteratur*, vol. i, pp. 217–218, etc. He was born in A.H. 221 (A.D. 836) and died in A.H. 288 (A.D. 901).

[5] Abú Manṣúr 'Abdu'l-Qáhir ibn Ṭáhir al-Baghdádí, d. A.H. 429 (A.D. 1037). See Ḥájjí Khalífa, No. 3253.

[6] Abú Sa'íd Aḥmad ibn Muḥammad ibn 'Abdu'l-Jalíl as-Sajzí (or Sijazí, *i.e.* of Sajistán or Sístán). See Brockelmann, *op. cit.*, vol. i, p. 219, and Note XXIII at the end.

This science is contained in [Ptolemy's] *Almagest*, whereof the best commentaries (..) and elucidations are the Commentary of Nayrízí[1] and the *Almagest* in the *Shifá*[2]. And amongst the applications of this science is the science of Astronomical Tables and Almanacs.

Judicial Astrology is a branch of Natural Science, and its special use is prognostication, by which is meant the deducing by analogy from the configurations of the stars in relation to one another, and from an estimation of their degrees in the zodiacal signs, the fulfilment of those events which are brought about by their movements, such as the conditions of the world-cycles, empires, kingdoms, cities, nativities, changes, transitions, decisions, and other questions. It is contained, as above defined by us, in the writings of Abú Ma'shar of Balkh[3], Aḥmad [ibn Muḥammad] ibn 'Abdu'l-Jalíl-i-Sajzí[4], Abú Rayḥán Bírúní[5], and Kúshyár-i-Jílí[6].

So the astrologer must be a man of acute mind, approved character, and great natural intelligence, though apparently [some degree of] folly, madness and a gift for soothsaying are amongst the conditions and essentials of this branch [of the subject]. And the Astrologer who would pronounce prognostications must have the Part of the Unseen[7] in his own Ascendant, or in a position which stands well in relation to the Ascendant, while the Lord of the Mansion of the Part of the Unseen must be fortunate and in a favourable position, in order that such pronouncements as he gives may be near the truth. And one of the conditions of being a good astrologer is that he should know by heart the whole of the "Compendium of Principles" (*Mujmalu'l-Uṣúl*) of Kúshyár[6], and should continually study the "Opus Major[8]," and should look frequently into the *Qánún-i-Mas'údí*[9] and the *Jámi'-i-Sháhí*[10], so that his knowledge and concepts may be refreshed.

[1] Abu'l-'Abbás al-Faḍl ibn Ḥátam of Nayríz (near Dárábjird in Fárs). He flourished in the latter half of the third century of the Flight (late ninth and early tenth of the Christian era).

[2] Presumably Avicenna's great philosophical work of this name is intended.

[3] See Brockelmann's *Gesch. d. Arab. Litt.*, vol. i, pp. 221–222, pp. ١٩٨–٩ of the Persian notes, and Note XXIII at the end.

[4] See n. 6 on p. 62 *supra*. [5] See n. 1 on p. 62 *supra*.

[6] See *Ibid.*, pp. 222–223. Kiyá Abu'l-Ḥasan Kúshyár ibn Labbán ibn Báshahrí al-Jílí (of Gílán) was a very notable astronomer who flourished in the second half of the fourth century of the Flight (tenth of the Christian era). A fine MS. of his *Mujmal* (Add. 7490) exists in the British Museum. See also p. ٢٠٢ of the Persian notes, and Note XXIII at the end.

[7] For this and other Astrological terms see Note XXIV at the end.

[8] *Kár-i-Mihtar* by Ḥasan ibnu'l-Khaṣíb, a notable astronomer of the second century of the Flight.

[9] Composed about A.D. 1031–6 for Sulṭán Mas'úd, to whom it is dedicated, by al-Bírúní. A fine MS. transcribed at Baghdád in 570/1174–5 is described in Rieu's *Arabic Supplement*, pp. 513–519.

[10] A collection of fifteen treatises by Aḥmad ibn Muḥammad ibn 'Abdu'l-Jalíl as-Sajzí, a notable astronomer who flourished in the latter half of the tenth century of the Christian era. See p. 62 *supra*, n. 6 *ad calc.*

ANECDOTE XXII.

Ya'qúb ibn Isḥáq al-Kindí[1], though he was a Jew, was the philosopher of his age and the wisest man of his time, and stood high in the service of al-Ma'mún. One day he came in before al-Ma'mún, and sat down above one of the prelates of Islám. Said this man, "Thou art of a subject race; why then dost thou sit above the prelates of Islám?" "Because," said Ya'qúb, "I know what thou knowest, while thou knowest not what I know."

Now this prelate knew of his skill in Astrology, but had no knowledge of his other attainments in science. "I will write down," said he, "something on a piece of paper, and if thou canst divine what I have written, I will admit thy claim." Then they laid a wager, on the part of the prelate a cloak, and on the part of Ya'qúb (٦٠) a mule and its trappings, worth a thousand *dínárs*, which was standing at the door. Then the former asked for an inkstand and paper, wrote something on a piece of paper, placed it under the Caliph's quilt, and cried, "Out with it!" Ya'qúb ibn Isḥáq asked for a tray of earth, rose up, took the altitude, ascertained the Ascendant, drew an astrological figure on the tray of earth, determined the positions of the stars and located them in the Signs of the Zodiac, and fulfilled all the conditions of divination and thought-reading[2]. Then he said, "O Commander of the Faithful, on that paper he has written something which was first a plant and then an animal." Al-Ma'mún put his hand under the quilt and drew forth the paper, on which was written "The Rod of Moses." Ma'mún was filled with wonder, and the prelate expressed his astonishment. Then Ya'qúb took the cloak of his adversary, and cut it in two before al-Ma'mún, saying, "I will make it into two putties."

This matter became generally known in Baghdád, whence it spread to 'Iráq and Khurásán, and became widely diffused. A certain doctor of Balkh[3], prompted by that fanatical zeal which characterises the learned, took a knife and placed it in the middle of a book on Astrology, intending to go to Baghdád, attend the lectures of Ya'qúb ibn Isḥáq al-Kindí, make a beginning in Astrology, and, when he should find a suitable opportunity, suddenly kill him. Stage by stage he advanced in this resolve, until he reached Baghdád, went in to the hot bath and came out, arrayed himself in clean clothes, and, placing the book in his sleeve, set out for Ya'qúb's house.

[1] See Wüstenfeld's *Gesch. d. Arab. Aerzte*, pp. 21–22. He died about A.H. 260 (A.D. 873). The author's assertion that the celebrated al-Kindí, called *par excellence* "the Philosopher of the Arabs," was a Jew, is, as the Editor has pointed out (Persian notes, pp. ٢٠٣–٢٠٦), so absurd as to go near to discrediting the whole story.

[2] *Khaby* means guessing the nature of a hidden object and *ḍamír* of a hidden thought, according to al-Bírúní's *Tafhím*. See Note XXIV at the end.

[3] *I.e.* Abú Ma'shar, as appears from the conclusion of the story.

When he reached the gate of the house, he saw standing there many handsomely-caparisoned horses belonging to descendants of the Prophet[1] and other eminent and notable persons of Baghdád. Having made enquiries, he went in, entered the circle in front of Ya'qúb, greeted him, and said, "I desire to study somewhat of the Science of the Stars with our Master." "Thou hast come from the East to slay me, not to study Astrology," replied Ya'qúb, "but thou wilt repent of thine intention, study the Stars, attain perfection in that science, and become one of the greatest Astrologers amongst the People of Muḥammad (on whom be God's Blessing and Peace)." All the great men there assembled were astonished at these words; and Abú Ma'shar[2] confessed and produced the knife from the middle of the book, broke it, and cast it away. Then he bent his knees and studied for fifteen years, until he attained in Astrology that eminence which was his. (٥٧)

ANECDOTE XXIII.

It is related that once when *Yamínu'd-Dawla* Sulṭán Maḥmúd ibn Náṣiru'd-Dín[3] was sitting on the roof of a four-doored summer-house in Ghazna, in the Garden of a Thousand Trees, he turned his face to Abú Rayḥán[4] and said, "By which of these four doors shall I go out?" (for all four were practicable). "Decide and write the decision on a piece of paper, and put it under my quilt." Abú Rayḥán called for an astrolabe, took the altitude, determined the Ascendant, reflected for a while, and then wrote down his decision on a piece of paper, and placed it under the quilt. "Hast thou decided?" asked Maḥmúd. He answered, "I have."

Then Maḥmúd bade them bring a navvy with pick-axe and spade, and in the wall which was on the eastern side they dug out a fifth door, through which he went out. Then he bade them bring the paper. So they brought it, and on it Abú Rayḥán had written, "He will go out through none of these four doors, but they will dig a fifth door in the eastern wall, by which door he will go forth." Maḥmúd, on reading this, was furious, and bade them cast Abú Rayḥán down in the midst of the palace, and so they did. Now there was stretched a net from the middle floor, and on it Abú Rayḥán fell. The net tore, and he subsided gently to the ground, so that he received no injury. "Bring him in," said Maḥmúd. So they brought him in, and Maḥmúd said, "O Abú Rayḥán, at all events thou didst not know about this event!"

[1] Literally, "of the Banú Háshim."
[2] See n. 3 on p. 63 *supra* and Note XXIII at the end.
[3] *I.e.* the great Sulṭán Maḥmúd of Ghazna (reigned A.H. 388–421, A.D. 998–1030).
[4] Al-Bírúní. See n. 1 on p. 62 *supra*, and Note XXIII at the end.

"I knew it, Sire," answered he. Said Maḥmúd, "Where is the proof?" So Abú Rayḥán called for his servant, took the Almanac from him, and produced the prognostications out of the Almanac; and amongst the predictions of that day was written:—"To-day they will cast me down from a high place, but I shall reach the earth in safety, and arise sound in body."

All this was not according to Maḥmúd's mind. He waxed still angrier, and ordered Abú Rayḥán to be detained in the citadel. So Abú Rayḥán was confined in the citadel of Ghazna, where he remained for six months.

ANECDOTE XXIV.

It is said that during that period of six months none dared speak to Maḥmúd about Abú Rayḥán; (۵۸) but one of his servants was deputed to wait upon him, and go out to get what he wanted, and return therewith. One day this servant was passing through the Park (*Marghzár*) of Ghazna when a fortune-teller called him and said, "I perceive several things worth mentioning in your fortune: give me a present, that I may reveal them to you." The servant gave him two *dirhams*, whereupon the Sooth-sayer said, "One dear to thee is in affliction, but ere three days are past he will be delivered from that affliction, will be invested with a robe of honour and mark of favour, and will again become distinguished and ennobled."

The servant proceeded to the citadel and told this incident to his master as a piece of good tidings. Abú Rayḥán laughed and said, "O foolish fellow, dost thou not know that one ought not to loiter in such places? Thou hast wasted two *dirhams*." It is said that the Prime Minister Aḥmad ibn Ḥasan of Maymand (may God be merciful to him!) was for six months seeking an opportunity to say a word on behalf of Abú Rayḥán. At length, when engaged in the chase, he found the King in a good humour, and, working from one topic to another, he brought the conversation round to Astrology. Then he said, "Poor Abú Rayḥán uttered two such good prognostications, and, instead of decorations and a robe of honour, earned only bonds and imprisonment." "Know, my lord," replied Maḥmúd, "for I have discovered it, and all men admit it, that this man has no equal in the world save Abú 'Alí [ibn] Síná (Avicenna). But both his prognostications were opposed to my will; and kings are like little children; in order to receive rewards from them, one should speak in accordance with their views. It would have been better for him on that day if one of those two prognostications had been wrong. But to-morrow order him to be brought forth, and to be given a horse caparisoned with gold, a royal robe, a satin turban, a thousand *dínárs*, a boy slave and a handmaiden."

So, on the very day specified by the sooth-sayer, they brought forth Abú Rayḥán, and the gift of honour detailed above was conferred upon him, and the King apologized to him, saying, "O Abú Rayḥán, if thou desirest to reap advantage from me, speak according to my desire, not according to the dictates of thy science." So thereafter Abú Rayḥán altered his practice; and this is one of the conditions of the king's service, that one must be with him in right or wrong, and speak according to his wish[1].

Now when Abú Rayḥán went to his house and the learned came to congratulate him, he related to them the incident of the sooth-sayer, whereat they were amazed, (٠٩) and sent to summon him. They found him quite illiterate, knowing nothing. Then Abú Rayḥán said, "Hast thou the horoscope of thy nativity?" "I have," he replied. Then he brought the horoscope and Abú Rayḥán examined it, and the Part of the Unseen fell directly on the degree of his Ascendant, so that whatever he said, though he spoke blindly, came near to the truth.

ANECDOTE XXV.

I had in my employment a woman-servant, who was born on the 28th of Ṣafar, A.H. 511[2] (July 1st, A.D. 1117), when the Moon was in conjunction with the Sun and there was no distance between them, so that in consequence of this the Part of Fortune and the Part of the Unseen both fell on the degree of the Ascendant. When she reached the age of fifteen years, I taught her Astrology, in which she became so skilful that she could answer difficult questions in this science, and her prognostications came mighty near the truth. Ladies used to come to her and question her, and the most part of what she said coincided with the pre-ordained decrees of Fate.

One day an old woman came to her and said, "It is now four years since a son of mine went on a journey and I have no news of him, neither of his life nor of his death. See whether he is of the living or the dead, and wherever he is acquaint me with his condition." So the woman-astrologer arose, took the altitude, worked out the degree of the Ascendant, drew out an astrological figure, and determined the positions of the stars; and the very first words she said were, "Thy son hath returned!"

The old woman was annoyed and said, "O child, I have no hopes of his coming: tell me this much, is he alive or dead?"

[1] Cf. *Gulistán*, ed. Platts, p. 40, last two lines.

[2] A. and B. have "512," and L. "510." Although the text has عجوزه, "an old woman," I have substituted "a woman-servant" as more appropriate, for since she was born in A.H. 511 and the *Chahár Maqála* was composed about A.H. 551 or 552, she can only have been at most about forty years of age, even if the incident described took place shortly before it was here recorded.

"I tell you," said the other, "thy son hath come. Go, and if he hath not come, return that I may tell thee how he is."

So the old woman went to her house, and lo, her son had arrived and they were unloading his ass. She embraced him, took two veils, and brought them to the woman-astrologer, saying, "Thou didst speak truly; my son hath come," and gave her a blessing with her present. When I came home and heard tidings of this, I enquired of her, "By what indication didst thou speak, and from what house didst thou deduce this prognostication?" She answered, "I had not reached so far as this. When I had finished the figure of the Ascendant, (٦٠) a fly came and settled on the number of the degree of the Ascendant, wherefore it so seemed in my mind that this young man had returned. When I had thus spoken, and the mother had gone to find out, it became as certain to me that he had come as though I actually saw him unloading his ass."

Then I perceived that it was the Part of the Unseen which had effected all this on the degree of the Ascendant, and that this [success of hers] arose from nothing else but this.

ANECDOTE XXVI.

Maḥmúd Dá'údí, the son of Abu'l-Qásim Dá'údí, was a great fool, nay, almost a madman, and had no great amount of knowledge of the stars; though of astrological operations he could cast a nativity, and in his note-book were figures, declaring "it is" or "it is not." He was in the service of Amír-Dád Abú Bakr ibn Mas'úd at Panj-dih; and his prognostications mostly came nearly right.

Now his madness was such that when my master the King of the Mountains[1] sent Amír-Dád a pair of Ghúrí dogs, very large and formidable, he fought with them of his own free will, and escaped from them in safety. Years afterwards we were sitting with a number of persons of learning in the Druggists' Bázár at Herát, in the shop of Muqrí the surgeon-barber, and discussing all manner of subjects. One of these learned men happening to remark, "What a great man was Avicenna (Ibn Síná)!" I saw Dá'údí fly into such a passion that the veins of his neck became hard and prominent, and all the symptoms of anger appeared in him, and he cried, "O So-and-so, who was Abú 'Alí ibn Síná? I am worth a thousand Abú 'Alís, for he never even fought with a cat, whilst I fought before Amír-Dád with two Ghúrí dogs." So on that day I knew him to be mad; yet for all his madness, I witnessed the following occurrence.

[1] *I.e.* Quṭbu'd-Dín Muḥammad ibn 'Izzu'd-Dín Ḥusayn, the first king of the Ghúrí dynasty, poisoned by Bahrám Sháh. See Note I at the end.

In the year A.H. 508 (A.D. 1114–1115), when Sulṭán Sanjar encamped in the Plain of Khúzán[1], on his way to Transoxiana to fight with Muḥammad Khán[2], Amír-Dád made a mighty great entertainment for the King at Panj-dih. On the third day he came to the river-brink, and entered a boat to amuse himself (٦١) with fishing. In the boat he summoned Dá'údí before him to talk in that mad way of his, while he laughed, for Dá'údí would openly abuse Amír-Dád.

Presently the King said to Dá'údí, "Prognosticate how many maunds the fish which I shall catch this time will weigh." Dá'údí said, "Draw up your hook." So the King drew it up; and he took the altitude, paused for a while, and then said, "Now cast it." The King cast, and he said, "I prognosticate that this fish which you will draw out will weigh five maunds." "O knave," said Amír-Dád, "whence should fish of five maunds' weight come into this stream?" "Be silent," said Dá'údí; "what do you know about it?" So Amír-Dád was silent, fearing that, should he insist further, he would only get abuse.

After a while there was a pull on the line, indicating that a fish had been taken captive. The King drew in the line with a very large fish on it, which, when weighed, scaled six[3] maunds. All were amazed, and the King of the World expressed his astonishment, for which, indeed, there was good occasion. "Dá'údí," said the King, "what dost thou wish for?" "O King of the face of the Earth," said he with an obeisance, "I desire but a coat of mail, a shield and a spear, that I may do battle with Báwardí." And this Báwardí was an officer attached to Amír-Dád's Court, and Dá'údí entertained towards him a fanatical hatred, because the title of *Shujá'u'l-Mulk* ("the Champion of the Kingdom") hac been conferred on him, while Dá'údí himself bore the title of *Shujá'u'l-Ḥukamá* ("the Champion of the Philosophers"), and grudged that the other should also be entitled *Shujá'*. And Amír-Dád, well knowing this, used continually to embroil Dá'údí with him, and this good Musulmán was at his wit's end by reason of him.

In short, as to Maḥmúd Dá'údí's madness there was no doubt, and I have mentioned this matter in order that the King may know that as regards astrological predictions folly and insanity are amongst the conditions of this craft.

[1] See Barbier de Meynard's *Dict. de la Perse*, pp. 215–216.

[2] The person meant is Muḥammad Khán (known as Arslán Khán) ibn Sulaymán ibn Dá'úd ibn Bughrá Khán of the Khániyya dynasty. The event alluded to in the text took place in A.H. 507 (A.D. 1113–1114).

[3] L. has "five," which corresponds better with the prognostication, but the MS. authority is in favour of the reading here adopted.

ANECDOTE XXVII.

Ḥakím-i-Mawṣilí was one of the order of Astrologers in Níshápúr, and was in the service of that Great Minister Niẓámu'l-Mulk of Ṭús, who used to consult with him on matters of importance, and seek his advice (٦٤) and opinion. Now when Mawṣilí's years were drawing to a close, and failure of his faculties began to manifest itself, and feebleness of body began to appear, so that he was no longer able to perform these long journeys, he asked the Minister's permission to go and reside at Níshápúr, and to send thence, annually, an almanac and forecast for the year.

Now the Minister Niẓámu'l-Mulk was also in the decline of life and near the term of existence; and he said, "Calculate the march of events and see when the dissolution of my elemental nature will occur, and at what date that inevitable doom and unavoidable sentence will befall."

Ḥakím-i-Mawṣilí answered, "Six months after my death." So the Minister bestowed on him in increased measure all things needful for his comfort, and Mawṣilí went to Níshápúr, and there abode in ease, sending each year the forecast and calendar. And whenever anyone came to the Minister from Níshápúr, he used first to enquire, "How is Mawṣilí?" and so soon as he had ascertained that he was alive and well, he would become joyous and cheerful.

At length in the year A.H. 485 (A.D. 1092–3) one arrived from Níshápúr, and the Minister enquired of him concerning Mawṣilí. The man replied, with an obeisance, "May he who holdeth the chief seat in Islám be the heir of many life-times! Mawṣilí hath quitted this mortal body." "When?" enquired the Minister. "In the middle of Rabí' the First" (April 11—May 11, A.D. 1092), answered the man, "he yielded up his life for him who sitteth in the chief seat of Islám."

The Minister thereat was mightily put about; yet, being thus warned, he looked into all his affairs, confirmed all his pious endowments, gave effect to his bequests, wrote his last testament, set free such of his slaves as had earned his approval, discharged the debts which he owed, and, so far as lay in his power, made all men content with him, and sought forgiveness from his adversaries, and so sat awaiting his fate until the month of Ramaḍán (A.H. 485 = Oct. 5—Nov. 4, A.D. 1092), when he fell a martyr at Baghdád[1] at the hands of that Sect (*i.e.* the Assassins); may God make illustrious his Proof, and accord him an ample approval!

[1] This is an error of the author's, for the evidence that Niẓámu'l-Mulk was assassinated at Nihávand is overwhelming.

Since the observed Ascendant of the nativity, the Lord of the House, and the dominant influence (*hayláj*) were rightly determined, and the Astrologer was expert and accomplished, naturally the prognostication came true[1]. *And He* [*God*] *knoweth best.*

ANECDOTE XXVIII.

In the year A.H. 506 (A.D. 1112–1113) Khwája Imám 'Umar-i-Khayyámi[2] and Khwája Imám Muẓaffar-i-Isfizárí[3] had alighted in the city of Balkh, in the Street of the Slave-sellers, in the house of Amír (٦٣) Abú Sa'd Jarrah, and I had joined that assembly. In the midst of our convivial gathering I heard that Argument of Truth (*Ḥujjatu'l-Ḥaqq*) 'Umar say, "My grave will be in a spot where the trees will shed their blossoms on me twice a year[4]." This thing seemed to me impossible, though I knew that one such as he would not speak idle words.

When I arrived at Níshápúr in the year A.H. 530 (A.D. 1135–6), it being then four[5] years since that great man had veiled his countenance in the dust, and this nether world had been bereaved of him, I went to visit his grave on the eve of a Friday (seeing that he had the claim of a master on me), taking with me one to point out to me his tomb. So he brought me out to the Ḥíra[6] Cemetery; I turned to the left, and found his tomb situated at the foot of a garden-wall, over which pear-trees and peach-trees thrust their heads, and on his grave had fallen so many flower-leaves that his dust was hidden beneath the flowers. Then I remembered that saying which I had heard from him in the city of Balkh, and I fell to weeping, because on the face of the earth, and in all the regions of the habitable globe, I nowhere saw one like unto him. May God (blessed and exalted is He!) have mercy

[1] I confess that these astrological terms are beyond me. Several of them (*e.g. hayláj* and *kadkhudá*) are explained in the section of the *Mafátíḥu'l-'ulúm* which treats of Astrology (ed. van Vloten, pp. 225–232). See, however, Note XXIV at the end.

[2] The MSS. have *Khayyámí*, the form usually found in Arabic books. See Note XXV at the end.

[3] A notable astronomer who collaborated with 'Umar-i-Khayyám and others in A.H. 467 (A.D. 1074–1075) in the computation of the Jalálí era by command of Malikshdh. Ibnu'l-Athír mentions him under the above year by the name of Abu'l-Muẓaffar al-Isfizárí.

[4] The editor of the text has adopted the reading of the Constantinople MS., "every spring-tide the north wind will scatter blossoms on me," but the reading here adopted seems to me preferable, for there would be nothing remarkable in the grave being covered with fallen blossoms *once* a year; what was remarkable was that it should happen *twice*.

[5] The Constantinople MS., which is the oldest and most reliable, alone has this reading, the others having "some years." If "four" be correct, it follows that 'Umar-i-Khayyám died in A.H. 526 (A.D. 1132) and not, as stated by most authorities, in A.H. 515 (A.D. 1121–1122) or 517 (A.D. 1123–1124).

[6] Ḥíra, according to as-Sam'ání and Yáqút, was a large and well-known quarter lying outside Níshápúr on the road to Merv.

upon him[1], by His Grace and His Favour![2] Yet although I witnessed this prognostication on the part of that Proof of the Truth 'Umar, I did not observe that he had any great belief in astrological predictions; nor have I seen or heard of any of the great [scientists] who had such belief.

ANECDOTE XXIX.

In the winter of the year A.H. 508 (A.D. 1114–1115) the King sent a messenger to Merv to the Prime Minister Ṣadru'd-Dín [Abú Ja'far] Muḥammad ibn al-Muẓaffar[3] (on whom be God's Mercy) bidding him tell Khwája Imám 'Umar to select a favourable time for him to go hunting, such that therein should be no snowy or rainy days. For Khwája Imám 'Umar was in the Minister's company, and used to lodge at his house.

The Minister, therefore, sent a messenger to summon him, and told him what had happened. So he went and looked into the matter for two days, and made a careful choice; and he himself went and superintended the mounting of the King at the auspicious moment. When the King was mounted and had gone but a short distance[4], the sky became over-cast with clouds, a wind arose, (٦٤) and snow and mist supervened. All present fell to laughing, and the King desired to turn back; but Khwája Imám ['Umar] said, "Let the King be of good cheer, for this very hour the clouds will clear away, and during these five days there will not be a drop of moisture." So the King rode on, and the clouds opened, and during those five days there was no moisture, and no one saw a cloud.

But prognostication by the stars, though a recognized art, is not to be relied on, nor should the astronomer have any far-reaching faith therein; and whatever the astrologer predicts he must leave to Fate.

ANECDOTE XXX.

It is incumbent on the King, wherever he goes, to prove such companions and servants as he has with him; and if one is a believer in the Holy Law, and scrupulously observes the rites and duties thereof, he should make him an intimate, and treat

[1] A. and C. have—"cause him to dwell in Paradise."

[2] In the printed text "Anecdote XXIX" begins here with the following sentence, which is omitted in the Ṭihrán lithographed edition.

[3] He was the grandson of the great Niẓámu'l-Mulk. His father, Fakhru'l-Mulk Abu'l-Fatḥ al-Muẓaffar, was put to death by Sulṭán Sanjar, whose Minister he was, in A.H. 500 (A.D. 1106–1107). Ṣadru'd-Dín himself was murdered by one of Sanjar's servants in A.H. 511 (A.D. 1117–1118).

[4] I suppose this to be the meaning of the words:—و یك بانگ زمین برفت, which is the reading of all the texts. It perhaps means the distance which the human voice will carry when raised to its highest pitch.

him with honour and confide in him; but if otherwise, he should drive him away, and guard even the outskirts of his environment from his very shadow. Whoever does not believe in the religion of God (great and glorious is He!) and the law of Muḥammad the Chosen One, in him can no man trust, and he is unlucky, both to himself and to his master.

In the beginning of the reign of the King Sulṭán *Ghiyáthu'd-Dunyá wa'd-Dín* Muḥammad ibn Maliksháh, styled *Qasímu Amíri'l-Múminín* (may God illuminate his tomb!)[1], the King of the Arabs Ṣadaqa[2] revolted and withdrew his neck from the yoke of allegiance, and with fifty thousand Arabs marched on Baghdád from Ḥilla[3]. The Prince of Believers al-Mustaẓhir bi'lláh had sent off letter after letter and courier after courier to Iṣfahán, summoning the Sulṭán, who sought from the astrologers the determination of the auspicious moment. But no such determination could be made which would suit the Lord of the King's Ascendant, which was retrograde. So they said, "O Sire, we find no auspicious moment." "Seek it, then," said he; and he was very urgent in the matter, and much vexed in mind. And so the astrologers fled.

Now there was a man of Ghazna who had a shop in the Street of the Dome and who used to practise sooth-saying, and women used to visit him, and he used to write them love-charms, but he had no profound knowledge. By means of an acquaintance with one of the King's servants he brought himself to the King's notice, and said, "I will find an auspicious moment; depart in that, and if (١٠) thou dost not return victorious, then cut off my head."

So the King was pleased, and mounted his horse at the moment declared auspicious by him, and gave him two hundred *dínárs* of Níshápúr, and went forth, fought with Ṣadaqa, defeated his army, took him captive, and put him to death. And when he returned triumphant and victorious to Iṣfahán, he heaped favours on the sooth-sayer, conferred on him great honours, and made him one of his intimates. Then he summoned the astrologers and said, "You did not find an auspicious moment, it was this Ghaznawí who found it; and I went, and God justified his forecast. Wherefore did ye act thus? Probably Ṣadaqa had sent you a bribe so that you should not name the auspicious time." Then they all fell to the earth, lamenting and exclaiming, "No astrologer was satisfied with that choice. If you wish, write a message

[1] Reigned A.H. 498–511 (A.D. 1104–1117).

[2] For an account of this event and the doings of Ṣadaqa ibn Mazyad, the "King of the Arabs" here mentioned, see Ibnu'l-Athír's Chronicle *sub anno* A.H. 501 (A.D. 1107–1108).

[3] This is an error, for Ṣadaqa never attacked Baghdád nor quarrelled with the Caliph al-Mustaẓhir bi'lláh, his quarrel being with Muḥammad ibn Malikshsháh.

and send it to Khurásán, and see what Khwája Imám 'Umar-i-Khayyámí says."

The King saw that the poor wretches did not speak amiss. He therefore summoned one of his accomplished courtiers and said, "Hold a wine-party at your house to-morrow. Invite this astrologer of Ghazna, give him wine, and, when he is overcome with wine, enquire of him, saying, 'That moment determined by thee was not good, and the astrologers find fault with it. Tell me the secret of this.'"

Then the courtier did so, and, when his guest was drunk, made this enquiry of him. The Ghaznawí answered, "I knew that one of two things must happen; either that army would be defeated, or this one. If the former, then I should be loaded with honours; and if the latter, who would concern himself about me?"

Next day the courtier reported this conversation to the King, who ordered the Ghaznawí sooth-sayer to be expelled, saying, "Such a man holding such views about good Musulmáns is unlucky." Then[1] he summoned his own astrologers and restored his confidence to them, saying, "I myself held this sooth-sayer to be an enemy, because he never said his prayers, and one who agrees not with our Holy Law, agrees not with us."

ANECDOTE XXXI.

In the year A.H. 547 (A.D. 1152–3)[2] a battle was fought between the King of the World Sanjar ibn (١١) Malikshāh and my lord the King 'Alá'u'd-Dunyá wa'd-Dín at the Gates of Awba[3]; and the army of Ghúr was defeated, and my lord the King of the East (may God perpetuate his reign!) was taken prisoner, and my lord's son the Just King *Shamsu'd-Dawla wa'd-Dín* Muhammad ibn Mas'úd[4] was taken captive at the hands of the Commander-in-Chief (*Amír-i-sipahsálár*) Yaranqush Haríwa. The ransom was fixed at fifty thousand *dínárs*, and a messenger from him was to go to the court at Bámiyán to press for this sum; and when it reached Herát the Prince was to be released, being already accorded his liberty by the Lord of the World (Sanjar)[5], who, moreover, at the time of his departure from Herát, granted him a robe of honour. It was under these circumstances that I arrived to wait upon him.

[1] A. adds:—"they killed him, and...."

[2] This is the correct date, but the *Ta'ríkh-i-Guzída* gives A.H. 544 (A.D. 1149–1150).

[3] A village near Herát.

[4] The second of the Kings of Shansab or Ghúr who ruled over Bámiyán, and the son of Fakhru'd-Dín Mas'úd. See p. ٩٢ of the Persian notes and Note I at the end.

[5] The meaning appears to be that a ransom was demanded by the Amír Yaranqush, the Prince's actual captor, but not by his over-lord Sanjar.

One day, being extremely sad at heart, he signed to me, and enquired when this deliverance would finally be accomplished, and when this consignment would arrive. So I took an observation that day with a view to making this prognostication, and worked out the Ascendant, exerting myself to the utmost, and [ascertained that] there was an indication of a satisfactory solution to the question on the third day. So next day I came and said, "To-morrow at the time of the afternoon prayer the messenger will arrive." All that day the Prince was thinking about this matter. Next day I hastened to wait on him. "To-day," said he, "is the time fixed." "Yes," I replied; and continued in attendance on him till the afternoon prayer. When the call to prayer was sounded, he remarked reproachfully, "The afternoon prayer has arrived, but still no news!" Even while he was thus speaking, a courier arrived bringing the good tidings that the consignment had come, consisting of fifty thousand *dínárs*, sheep, and other things, and that 'Izzu'd-Dín Maḥmúd Ḥájji, the steward of Prince Ḥusámu'd-Dawla wa'd-Dín, was in charge of the convoy. Next day my lord Shamsu'd-Dawla wa'd-Dín was invested with the King's dress of honour, and released. Shortly afterwards he regained his beloved home, and from that time onwards his affairs have prospered more and more every day (may they continue so to do!). And it was during these nights that he used to treat me with the utmost kindness and say, "Niẓámí, do you remember making such a prognostication in Herát, and how it came true? I wanted to fill thy mouth with gold, but there I had no gold, though here I have." Then he called for gold, and twice filled my mouth therewith. Then he said, "It will not hold enough; hold out thy sleeve." (٦٧) So I held it out, and he filled it also with gold. May God (blessed and exalted is He!) maintain this dynasty in daily-increasing prosperity, and long spare these two Princes to my august and royal Master, by His Favour, Bounty and Grace!

(٦٨) FOURTH DISCOURSE.

On the Science of Medicine, and the right direction of the Physician.

Medicine is that art whereby health is maintained in the human body; whereby, when it wanes, it is restored; and whereby the body is embellished by long hair, a clear complexion, fragrance and vigour[1].

[1] The ordinary definition of Medicine ends at the word "restored," but the whole of Book VIII of the *Dhakhíra-i-Khwárazmsháhí* deals with the care of the hair, nails, complexion, etc.

[*Excursus.*]

The physician should be of tender disposition and wise nature, excelling in acumen, this being a nimbleness of mind in forming correct views, that is to say a rapid transition to the unknown from the known. And no physician can be of tender disposition if he fails to recognize the nobility of the human soul; nor of wise nature unless he is acquainted with Logic, nor can he excel in acumen unless he be strengthened by God's aid; and he who is not acute in conjecture will not arrive at a correct understanding of any ailment, for he must derive his indications from the pulse, which has a systole, a diastole, and a pause intervening between these two movements[1].

Now here there is a difference of opinion amongst physicians, one school maintaining that it is impossible by palpation to gauge the movement of contraction; but that most accomplished of the moderns, that Proof of the Truth Abú 'Alí al-Ḥusayn ibn 'Abdu'lláh ibn Síná (Avicenna)[2], says in his book the *Qánún*[3] that the movement of contraction also can be gauged, though with difficulty, in thin subjects. Moreover the pulse is of ten sorts, each of which is divided into three subordinate varieties, namely its two extremes and its mean; but, unless the Divine guidance assist the physician in his search for the truth, his thought will not hit the mark. So also in the inspection of the urine, the observing of its colours and sediments, and the deducing of some special condition from each colour (٦٩) are no easy matters; for all these indications depend on Divine help and Royal patronage. This quality [of discernment] is that which we have indicated under the name of acumen. And unless the physician knows Logic, and understands the meaning of genus and species, he cannot discriminate between that which appertains to the category, that which is peculiar to the individual, and that which is accidental, and so will not recognize the cause [of the disease]. And, failing to recognize the cause, he cannot succeed in his treatment. But let us now give an illustration, so that it may be known that it is as we say. Disease is the genus; fever, headache, cold, delirium, measles and jaundice are the species, each of which is distinguished from the others by a diagnostic sign, and in turn itself constitutes a genus. For example, "Fever" is the genus, wherein quotidian, tertian, double tertian and quartan are the

[1] Some notes on the varieties of pulse recognized by the Arabian physicians will be found in Note XXVI at the end.

[2] See de Slane's translation of *Ibn Khallikán*, vol. i, pp. 440–446; von Kremer's *Culturgeschichte d. Orients*, vol. ii, pp. 455–456; Wüstenfeld's *Gesch. d. Arab. Aerzte*, pp. 64–75; and Note XXVII, No. 10, at the end.

[3] The *Qánún* was printed at Rome, A.D. 1593, and the Latin translation at Venice in A.D. 1544. According to Steinschneider, Gerard of Cremona's Latin translation was printed more than thirty times, and fifteen times before A.D. 1500.

species, each of which is distinguished from the other by a special diagnostic sign. Thus, for instance, quotidian is distinguished from other fevers by the fact that the longest period thereof is a day and a night, and that in it there is no languor[1], heaviness, lassitude, nor pain. Again inflammatory fever[2] is distinguished from other fevers by the fact that when it attacks it does not abate for several days; while tertian is distinguished by the fact that it comes one day and not the next; and double tertian by this, that one day it comes with a higher temperature and a shorter interval, and another day in a milder form with a longer interval; while lastly quartan is distinguished by the fact that it attacks one day, does not recur on the second and third days, but comes again on the fourth. Each of these in turn becomes a genus comprising several species; and if the physician be versed in Logic and possessed of acumen and knows which fever it is, what the *materies morbi*[3] is, and whether it is simple or compound, he can then at once proceed to treat it. But if he fail to recognize the disease, then let him turn to God and seek help from Him; and so likewise, if he fail in his treatment, let him have recourse to God and seek help from Him, seeing that all issues are in His hands.

ANECDOTE XXXII.

In the year A.H. 512 (A.D. 1118–19), in the Druggist's Bazaar of Níshápúr, at the shop of Muhammad (٧٠) ibn Muhammad the Astrologer-Physician[4], I heard Khwája Imám Abú Bakr Daqqáq saying, "In the year A.H. 502 (A.D. 1108–9) a certain notable man of Níshápúr was seized with the colic and called me in. I examined him, and proceeded to treat him, trying every remedy suggested in this malady; but no improvement in his health took place. Three days elapsed. At the time of evening prayer I returned in despair, convinced that the patient would pass away at midnight. In this distress I fell asleep. In the morning I awoke, not doubting that he had passed away. I went up on to the roof, and turned my face in that direction to listen, but heard no sound [of lamentation] which might indicate his decease. I repeated the *Fátiha*, breathing it in that direction and adding, 'O my God, my Master and my Lord, Thou Thyself hast said in the Sure Book and Indubitable Scripture, "*And we will send*

[1] Perhaps "languor" is hardly strong enough. The original is *takassur*, literally "contrition," "being broken to pieces."

[2] تب مطبقة. See Schlimmer's *Terminologie Médico-Pharmaceutique* (lithographed at Ṭihrán, A.D. 1874), pp. 192–197 and 285. Perhaps, however, it should here be translated "remittent" or even "continuous." See Note XXVI at the end.

[3] *I.e.*, whether it be primary or secondary, from which of the four humours it arises, etc.

[4] The readings vary, A. has—محمّد ضمهر; B. محمّد صمیور; L. ضمهور only. The reading adopted in the text is no doubt correct.

down in the Qur'án what shall be a Healing and a Mercy to true believers[1].'" For I was filled with regret, seeing that he was a young man, and wealthy, and in easy circumstances, and had all things needful for a pleasant life. Then I performed the minor ablution, went to the oratory and acquitted myself of the customary prayer[2]. One knocked at the door of the house. I looked and saw that it was one of his people, who gave good tidings, saying, 'Open!' I enquired what had happened, and he replied, 'This very hour he obtained relief.' Then I knew that this was through the blessing of the *Fátiḥa* of the Scripture, and that this draught had been issued from the Divine Dispensary. For I have put this to the proof, administering this draught in many cases, in all of which it proved beneficial, and resulted in restoration to health." Therefore the physician should be of good faith, and should venerate the commands and prohibitions of the Holy Law.

On the Science of Medicine the student should procure and read the "Aphorisms" (*Fuṣúl*) of Hippocrates, the "Questions" (*Masá'il*) of Ḥunayn ibn Isḥáq[3], the "Guide" (*Murshid*) of Muḥammad ibn Zakariyyá of Ray (ar-Rází)[4], and the Commentary of Nílí[5], who has made abstracts of these. After he has carefully read [these works] with a kind and congenial master, he should diligently study with a sympathetic teacher the following intermediate works, to wit, the "Thesaurus" (*Dhakhíra*) of Thábit ibn Qurra[6], the [*Kitábu'ṭ-Ṭibbi'l-*] *Manṣúrí* of Muḥammad ibn Zakariyyá of Ray[7]; the "Direction" (*Hidáya*) of Abú Bakr Ajwíní, or the "Sufficiency" (*Kifáya*) of Aḥmad [ibn] Faraj and the "Aims" (*Aghráḍ*) of Sayyid Isma'íl Jurjání[8]. Then he

[1] *Qur'án*, xvii, 84.

[2] Each prayer consists of three parts, what is obligatory (*farḍ*), what is customary after the Prophet's example (*sunnat*), and what is supererogatory (*náfila*). The *sunnat* portion comes first, so that in the story the narrator was interrupted before he had performed the obligatory prostrations.

[3] See Wüstenfeld's *Geschichte d. Arab. Aerzte*, No. 69, pp. 26–29. He was born A.H. 194 (A.D. 809) and died A.H. 260 (A.D. 873). A fuller account of all these writers and their works will be found in Note XXVII at the end.

[4] *Ibid.*, No. 98, pp. 40–49. He is known in Europe as Rasis or Rhazes. The *Murshid* here mentioned is identified by the Editor with the work properly entitled *al-Fuṣúl fi'ṭ-Ṭibb*, or "Aphorisms in Medicine." See p. ۲۳۰ of the Persian notes, and Note XXVII at the end.

[5] See p. ۲۳۱ of the Persian notes. His full name was Abú Sahl Sa'íd ibn 'Abdu'l-'Azíz, and he was a native of Níshápúr. The *nisba* "Nílí" is explained in Sam'ání's *Ansáb* (Vol. XX of the Gibb Series, f. 574b) as referring to a place called Níl between Baghdád and Kúfa, or to connection with the trade in indigo (*níl*). Here the latter sense is evidently required. Mention is made of the brother of our physician, a poet and man of letters named Abú 'Abdi'r-Raḥmán ibn 'Abdu'l-'Azíz, who died about 440/1048–9.

[6] Al-Qiftí in his *Ta'ríkhu'l-Ḥukamá* (ed. Lippert, p. 120) mentions this work, but expresses a doubt as to its authorship.

[7] See Wüstenfeld, *op. cit.*, p. 43, No. 2. This celebrated work was composed for Manṣúr ibn Isḥáq, Governor of Ray, A.D. 903–9.

[8] See Wüstenfeld, *op. cit.*, No. 165, p. 95.

should take up one of the more detailed treatises, such as the "Sixteen (Treatises," *Sitta 'ashar*) of Galen, or the "Continens" (*Ḥáwí*)[1] of Muhammad ibn Zakariyyá, or the "Complete Practitioner" (*Kámilu'ṣ-Ṣiná'at*)[2], or the "Hundred Chapters" (*Ṣad Báb*) of Abú Sahl Masíḥí[3], or the *Qánún* of Abú 'Alí ibn Síná (Avicenna)[4], or the *Dhakhíra-i-Khwárazm-sháhí*[5], and read it in his leisure moments; or, if he desires to be independent of other works, he may content himself with the *Qánún*.

The Lord (٧١) of the two worlds and the Guide of the two Grosser Races says: "Every kind of game is in the belly of the wild ass[6]": all this of which I have spoken is to be found in the *Qánún*, with much in addition thereto; and whoever has mastered the first volume of the *Qánún*, to him nothing will be hidden of the general and fundamental principles of Medicine, for could Hippocrates and Galen return to life, it were meet that they should do reverence to this book. Yet have I heard a wonderful thing, to wit that one hath taken exception to Abú 'Alí [ibn Síná] in respect of this work, and hath embodied his objections in a book, which he hath named "the Rectification of the *Qánún*[7]"; and it is as though I looked at both, and perceived what a fool the author was, and how detestable is the book which he has composed! For what right has anyone to find fault with so great a man when the very first question which he meets with in a book of his which he comes across is difficult to his comprehension? For four thousand years the wise men of antiquity travailed in spirit and melted their very souls in order to reduce the Science of Philosophy to some fixed order, yet could not effect this, until, after the lapse of this period, that incomparable philosopher and most powerful thinker Aristotle weighed this coin in the balance of Logic, assayed it with the touchstone of definitions, and measured it by the scale of analogy, so that all doubt and ambiguity departed from it, and it became established

[1] This, known to mediaeval Europe as the "Continens," is the most detailed and most important of ar-Rází's works. The original Arabic exists only in manuscript, and that partially. The Latin translation was printed at Brescia in A.D. 1486, and in 1500, 1506, 1509 and 1542 at Venice. See Note XXVII at the end, No. 4.

[2] This notable work, also known as *al-Kitábu'l-Malikí* ("Liber Regius") was composed by 'Alí ibnu'l-'Abbás al-Majúsí ("Haly Abbas" of the mediaeval physicians of Europe), who died in A.H. 384 (A.D. 994). The Arabic text has been lithographed at Lahore in A.H. 1283 (A.D. 1866) and printed at Bulàq in A.H. 1294 (A.D. 1877). There are two editions of the Latin translation (Venice, A.D. 1492, and Lyons, A.D. 1523).

[3] Avicenna's master, d. A.H. 390 (A.D. 1000). See Wüstenfeld, *loc. cit.*, pp. 59–60, No. 118; p. ٢٢٠ of the Persian notes; and Note XXVII, No. 9, at the end.

[4] See Note XXVII, No. 10, at the end.

[5] See Rieu's *Persian Catalogue*, pp. 466–467.

[6] Meaning that every kind of game is inferior to the wild ass. It is said proverbially of any one who excels his fellows. See Lane's *Arabic Lexicon*, p. 2357, *s.v.* فرأ.

[7] اصلاح قانون.

on a sure and critical basis. And during these fifteen centuries which have elapsed since his time, no philosopher hath won to the inmost essence of his doctrine, nor travelled the high road of his method, save that most excellent of the moderns, the Philosopher of the East, the Proof of God unto His creatures, Abú 'Alí al-Ḥusayn ibn 'Abdu'lláh ibn Síná (Avicenna). He who finds fault with these two great men will have cut himself off from the company of the wise, placed himself in the category of madmen, and exhibited himself in the ranks of the feeble-minded. May God (blessed and exalted is He!) keep us from such stumblings and vain desires, by His Favour and His Grace!

So, if the physician hath mastered the first volume of the *Qánún*, and hath attained to forty years of age, he will be worthy of confidence; yet even if he hath attained to this degree, he should keep ever with him some of the smaller treatises composed by proved masters, such as the "Gift of Kings" (*Tuḥfatu'l-Mulúk*)[1] of Muḥammad ibn Zakariyyá [ar-Rází], or the *Kifáya* of Ibn Mandúya of Iṣfahán[2], or the "Provision against all sorts of errors in Medical Treatment" (*Tadáruku anwá'i'l-khaṭá fi 't-tadbíri't-ṭibbí*)[3] of which Abú 'Alí (Avicenna) is the author; or the *Khuffiyy-i-'Alá'í*[4], or the "Memoranda" (*Yádigár*)[5] of Sayyid Isma'íl Jurjání. For no reliance can be placed on the Memory, which is located in the most posterior (٧٤) part of the brain[6], and when it is slow in its operation these books may prove helpful.

Therefore every King who would choose a physician must see that these conditions which have been enumerated are found in him; for it is no light matter to commit one's life and soul into the hands of any ignorant quack, or to entrust the care of one's health to any reckless charlatan.

[1] No mention of such a work is made in any of the biographies of ar-Rází.

[2] Abú 'Alí Aḥmad ibn 'Abdu'r-Raḥmán ibn Mandúya of Iṣfahán was a notable physician of the fourth century of the *hijra* (tenth of the Christian era). He was one of the four and twenty physicians appointed by 'Aḍudu'd-Dawla to the hospital which he founded at Baghdád. The proper title of the work to which our author here refers appears to be *al-Káfí*, not *al-Kifáya*.

[3] This book was printed in 1305/1887–8 at Buláq in the margins of the *Manáfi'u'l-Aghdhiya wa Maḍárru-há* ("Beneficial and injurious properties of Foods") of ar-Rází.

[4] A small manual of Medicine in Persian by the author of the *Dhakhíra-i-Khwárazm-sháhí*, written by command of Átsiz Khwárazm-sháh (succeeded to the throne in 521/1127) and called after him, his title being 'Alá'u'd-Dawla.

[5] Another small manual by the same author as the last. See Adolf Fonahn's *Zur Quellenkunde der Persischen Medizin* (Leipzig, 1910), p. 105, No. 280, and p. 129.

[6] Concerning the Five Internal Senses and their supposed location in the brain, see p. 8 *supra*, and also my *Year amongst the Persians*, pp. 144–145.

ANECDOTE XXXIII.

Bukht-Yishú'[1], a Christian of Baghdád, was a skilful physician and a true and tender man; and he was attached to the service of al-Ma'mún [the Caliph]. Now one of the House of Háshim, a kinsman of al-Ma'mún, was attacked with dysentery, and al-Ma'mún, being greatly attached to him, sent Bukht-Yishú' to treat him. So he, for al-Ma'mún's sake, rose up, girt himself with his soul[2], and treated him in various ways, but to no purpose, and tried such recondite remedies as he knew, but to no advantage, for the case had passed beyond his powers. So Bukht-Yishú' was ashamed before al-Ma'mún, who, divining this, said to him, "O Bukht-Yishú', be not abashed, for thou didst fulfil thine utmost endeavour, and rendered good service, but God Almighty doth not desire [that thou shouldst succeed]. Acquiesce in Fate, even as we have acquiesced." Bukht-Yishú', seeing al-Ma'mún thus hopeless, replied, "One other remedy remains, and it is a perilous one; but, trusting to the fortune of the Prince of Believers, I will attempt it, and perchance God Most High may cause it to succeed."

Now the patient was going to stool fifty or sixty times a day. So Bukht-Yishú' prepared a purgative and administered it to him; and on the day whereon he took the purgative, his diarrhœa was still further increased; but next day it stopped. So the physicians asked him, "What hazardous treatment was this which thou didst adopt?" He answered, "The *materies morbi* of this diarrhœa was from the brain, and until it was dislodged from the brain the flux would not cease. I feared that, if I administered a purgative, the patient's strength might not be equal to the increased diarrhœa; but, when all despaired, I said to myself, 'After all, there is hope in giving the purgative, but none in withholding it.' So I gave it, relying on God, for He is All Powerful; and God Most High vouchsafed a cure and the patient recovered; and my opinion was justified, namely that if the purgative were withheld, only the death of the patient was to be expected, (٧٢) but that if it were administered, there was a possibility of either life or death. So I deemed it best to administer it."

[1] See Wüstenfeld, *op. cit.*, p. 17, No. 30, and Note XXVII, No. 1, at the end. Concerning this and similar names, see Noldeke's *Geschichte d. Artakhshír-i-Pápakán*, p. 49, n. 4.

[2] *I.e.* "Put his whole heart into his task."

ANECDOTE XXXIV.

The great Shaykh and Proof of the Truth Abú 'Alí ibn Síná (Avicenna) relates as follows in the "Book of the Origin and the Return" (*Kitábu'l-Mabda' wa 'l-Ma'ád*)[1], at the end of the section on "the possibility of the production of exceptional psychical phenomena":—He says "A curious anecdote hath reached me which I have heard related. A certain physician was attached to the court of one of the House of Sámán, and there attained so high a position of trust that he used to enter the women's apartments and feel the pulses of its carefully-guarded and closely-veiled inmates. One day he was sitting with the King in the women's apartments in a place where it was impossible for any [other] male creature to penetrate. The King demanded food, and it was brought by the hand-maidens. One of these who was laying the table took the tray off her head, bent down, and placed it on the ground. When she desired to stand upright again, she was unable to do so, but remained as she was, by reason of a rheumatic swelling of the joints[2]. The King turned to the physician and said, "You must cure her at once in whatever way you can." Here was no opportunity for any physical method of treatment, for which no appliances were available, no drugs being at hand. So the physician bethought himself of psychical treatment, and bade them remove the veil from her head and expose her hair, so that she might be ashamed and make some movement, this condition being displeasing to her, to wit that all her head and face should be thus exposed. As, however, she underwent no change, he proceeded to something still more shameful, and ordered her trousers to be removed. She was overcome with shame, and a warmth was produced within her such that it dissolved that thick rheum and she stood up straight and sound, and regained her normal condition[3].

Had this physician not been wise and capable, he would never have thought of this treatment and would have been unable to effect this cure; while had he failed he would have forfeited the King's regard. Hence a knowledge of natural phenomena and an apprehension of the facts of Nature form part of this subject. And God knoweth best!

[1] The original passage is cited by Mírzá Muḥammad (on p. ۲۴۰ of the Persian notes) from Add. 16,659 of the British Museum, f. 488.

[2] Literally, "by reason of a thick rheum which was produced in her joints."

[3] This anecdote is told by al-Qifṭí (p. ۱۳۴) and Ibn Abí Uṣaybi'a (Vol. i, p. ۱۲۷) of the physician Bukht-Yishú' and the Caliph Hárúnu'r-Rashíd. A versified rendering of it is given in Jámí's "Chain of Gold" (*Silsilatu'dh-Dhahab*), composed in A.D. 1485. The text of this version is given in Note XXVIII at the end.

(v1) ANECDOTE XXXV.

Another of the House of Sámán, Amír Manṣúr ibn Núḥ ibn Naṣr[1], became afflicted with an ailment which grew chronic, and remained established, and the physicians were unable to cure it. So the Amír Manṣúr sent messengers to summon Muḥammad ibn Zakariyyá ar-Rází to treat him. Muḥammad ibn Zakariyyá came as far as the Oxus, but, when he reached its shores and saw it, he said, "I will not embark in the boat, for God Most High saith—'*Do not cast yourselves into peril with your own hands*[2]'; and again it is surely a thing remote from wisdom voluntarily to place one's self in so hazardous a position." Ere the Amír's messenger had gone to Bukhárá and returned, he had composed the *Kitáb-i-Manṣúrí*, which he sent by the hand of that person, saying, "I am this book, and by this book thou canst attain thine object, so that there is no need of me."

When the book reached the Amír he was grievously afflicted, wherefore he sent a thousand *dínárs* and one of his own private horses fully caparisoned, saying, "Show him every kindness, but, if this proves fruitless, bind his hands and feet, place him in the boat, and fetch him across." They did so, but their entreaties moved him not at all. Then they bound his hands and feet, placed him in the boat, and, when they had ferried him across the river, released his limbs. Then they brought the led-horse, fully caparisoned, before him, and he mounted in the best of humours, and set out for Bukhárá. So they enquired of him, saying, "We feared lest, when we should cross the water and set thee free, thou wouldst cherish enmity against us, but thou didst not so, nor do we see thee annoyed or vexed in heart." He replied, "I know that every year twenty thousand persons cross the Oxus without being drowned, and that I too should probably not be drowned; still, it was possible that I might perish, and if this had happened they would have continued till the Resurrection to say, 'A foolish fellow was Muḥammad ibn Zakariyyá, in that, of his own free will he embarked in a boat and so was drowned.' So should I be one of those who deserve blame, not of those who are held excused."

[1] That is Manṣúr I, who reigned A.H. 350–366 (A.D. 961–976). This anecdote is given in the *Akhláq-i-Jalálí* (ed. Lucknow, A.H. 1283), pp. 168–170. It is, however, a tissue of errors, for this Manṣúr came to the throne at least thirty years after the death of the great physician ar-Rází, who died either in A.H. 311 or 320 (A.D. 923–4 or 932). The Manṣúr to whom his *Kitábu'l-Manṣúrí* was dedicated was an entirely different person. See Note XXVII, No. 4, at the end, *s.v. Al-Kitábu'l-Manṣúrí*. This anecdote, as Mírzá Muḥammad has pointed out to me, appears to be based, so far as the refusal to cross the Oxus is concerned, on an incident in the life of the geographer Abú Zayd al-Balkhí. See al-Maqdisí's *Aḥsanu't-Taqásím fí ma'rifati'l-Aqálím*, p. 4.

[2] *Qur'án*, ii, 191.

When he reached Bukhárá, the Amír came in and they saw one another and he began to treat him, exerting his powers to the utmost, but without relief to the patient. One day he came in before the Amír and said, "To-morrow (٧٠) I am going to try another method of treatment, but for the carrying out of it you will have to sacrifice such-and-such a horse and such-and-such a mule," the two being both animals noted for their speed, so that in one night they would go forty parasangs.

So next day he took the Amír to the hot bath of Jú-yi-Múliyán[1], outside the palace, leaving that horse and mule ready equipped and tightly girt in the charge of his own servant at the door of the bath; while of the King's retinue and attendants he suffered not one to enter the bath. Then he brought the King into the middle chamber of the hot bath, and poured over him tepid water, after which he prepared a draught, tasted it, and gave it to him to drink. And he kept him there till such time as the humours in his joints had undergone coction.

Then he himself went out and put on his clothes, and, [taking a knife in his hand][2], came in, and stood for a while reviling the King, saying, "O such-and-such, thou didst order thy people to bind and cast me into the boat and to threaten my life. If I do not destroy thee as a punishment for this, I am no true son of [my father] Zakariyyá!"

The Amír was furious and rose from his place to his knees. Muḥammad ibn Zakariyyá drew a knife and threatened him yet more, until the Amír, partly from anger, partly from fear, completely rose to his feet. When Muḥammad ibn Zakariyyá saw the Amír on his feet, he turned round and went out from the bath, and both he and his servant mounted, the one the horse, the other the mule, and turned their faces towards the Oxus. At the time of the afternoon prayer they crossed the river, and halted nowhere till they reached Merv. When Muḥammad ibn Zakariyyá alighted at Merv, he wrote a letter to the Amír, saying, "May the life of the King be prolonged in health of body and effective command! I your servant undertook the treatment and did all that was possible. There was, however, an extreme failure in the natural caloric, and the treatment of the disease by ordinary means would have been a protracted affair. I therefore abandoned it in favour of psychical treatment, carried you to the hot bath, administered a draught, and left you so long as to bring about a coction of the humours. Then I angered the King, so as to aid the natural caloric, and it gained strength until those humours, already softened, were dissolved. But henceforth it is not expedient that a meeting should take place between myself and the King."

[1] See n. 2 on p. 35 *supra*, and Note XVI at the end.

[2] This sentence, though omitted in the printed text, seems on the whole to be an improvement.

Now after the Amír had risen to his feet and Muḥammad ibn Zakariyyá had gone out and ridden off, the Amír at once fainted. When he came to himself he went forth from the bath and (٧٦) called to his servants, saying, "Where has the physician gone?" They answered, "He came out from the bath, and mounted the horse, while his attendant mounted the mule, and went off."

Then the Amír knew what object he had had in view. So he came forth on his own feet from the hot bath; and tidings of this ran through the city. Then he gave audience, and his servants and retainers and people rejoiced greatly, and gave alms, and offered sacrifices, and held high festival. But they could not find the physician, seek him as they might. And on the seventh day Muḥammad ibn Zakariyyá's servant arrived, riding the mule and leading the horse, and presented the letter. The Amír read it, and was astonished, and excused him, and sent him an honorarium consisting of a horse fully caparisoned, a cloak, turban and arms, and a slave-boy and a handmaiden; and further commanded that there should be assigned to him in Ray from the estates of al-Ma'mún[1] a yearly allowance of two thousand *dínárs* in gold and two hundred ass-loads of corn. This honorarium and pension-warrant he forwarded to him at Merv by the hand of a man of note. So the Amír completely regained his health, and Muḥammad ibn Zakariyyá attained his object.

ANECDOTE XXXVI.

Abu'l-'Abbás Ma'mún Khwárazmsháh[2] had a Minister named Abu'l-Ḥusayn Aḥmad ibn Muḥammad as-Suhaylí[3]. He was a man of philosophical disposition, magnanimous nature and scholarly tastes, while Khwárazmsháh likewise was a philosopher and friend of scholars. In consequence of this many philosophers and men of erudition, such as Abú 'Alí ibn Síná, Abú Sahl-i-Masíḥí, Abu'l-Khayr ibnu'l-Khammár, Abú Naṣr-i-'Arráq and Abú Rayḥán al-Bírúní[4], gathered about his court.

Now Abú Naṣr-i-'Arráq was the nephew of Khwárazmsháh,

[1] The precise meaning of these words has not yet been determined.

[2] See p. viii of the Preface to Sachau's translation of al-Bírúní's *Chronology of the Ancient Nations*, and the same scholar's article *Zur Geschichte und Chronologie von Chwarezm* in the *Sitzungsberichte d. Wiener Akademie* for 1863. See also Note XXIX at the end, and pp. ٢٤١–٤ of the Persian notes. Ma'mún II, to whom this anecdote refers, was the third ruler of this House, and was killed in 407/1016–17.

[3] Or "as-Sahlí," but Mírzá Muḥammad considers "Suhaylí" to be the correct form. He died at Surra man ra'a in 418/1027–8.

[4] The first, second, and last of these learned men have been already mentioned. The third is Abu'l-Khayr al-Ḥasan ibnu'l-Khammár (Wüstenfeld's *Geschichte d. Arab. Aerzte*, No. 115, pp. 58–59) who died A.H. 381 (A.D. 991). See also Note XXVII at the end, Nos. 5, 6, 9 and 10.

and in all branches of Mathematics he was second only to Ptolemy; and Abu'l-Khayr ibnu'l-Khammár was the third after Hippocrates and Galen in the science of Medicine; and Abú Rayḥán [al-Bírúní] in Astronomy held the position of Abú Ma'shar and Aḥmad ibn 'Abdu'l-Jalíl; while Abú 'Alí [ibn Síná] and Abú Sahl Masíḥí were the successors of Aristotle in the Science of Philosophy, which includes all sciences. And all these were, in this their service, independent of worldly cares, and maintained with one another familiar intercourse and pleasant correspondence.

But Fortune disapproved of this and Heaven disallowed it; their pleasure was spoiled and their happy life was marred. (٧٧) A notable arrived from Sulṭán Maḥmúd Yamínu'd-Dawla with a letter, whereof the purport was as follows. "I have heard that there are in attendance on Khwárazmsháh several men of learning who are beyond compare, such as so-and-so and so-and-so. Thou must send them to my court, so that they may attain the honour of attendance thereat, while we may profit by their knowledge and skill. So shall we be much beholden to Khwárazmsháh."

Now the bearer of this message was Khwája Ḥusayn ibn 'Alí ibn Míká'íl, who was one of the most accomplished and remarkable men of his age, and the wonder of his time amongst his contemporaries, while the affairs of Sulṭán Maḥmúd Yamínu'd-Dawla were at the zenith of prosperity, his Kingdom enjoyed the utmost splendour, and his Empire the greatest elevation, so that the Kings of the time used to treat him with every respect and at night lay down in fear of him. So Khwárazmsháh assigned to Ḥusayn [ibn 'Alí] ibn Míká'íl the best of lodgings, and ordered him the most ample entertainment; but, before according him an audience, he summoned the philosophers and laid before them the King's letter, saying: "Maḥmúd hath a strong hand and a large army: he hath annexed Khurásán and India and covets 'Iráq, and I cannot refuse to obey his order or execute his mandate. What say ye on this matter?"

Abú 'Alí ibn Síná and Abú Sahl answered, "We will not go"; but Abú Naṣr, Abu'l-Khayr and Abú Rayḥán were eager to go, having heard accounts of the King's munificent gifts and presents. Then said Khwárazmsháh, "Do you two, who have no wish to go, take your own way before I give audience to this man." Then he equipped Abú 'Alí [ibn Síná] and Abú Sahl, and sent with them a guide, and they set off by the way of the wolves[1] towards Gurgán.

[1] I imagine that a word-play is here intended between Gurgán (the old Hyrcania, of which the present capital is Astarábád) and *az ráh-i-gurgán* ("by the Wolves' Way"), *i.e.* "across the desert." This is the reading of C.; the other texts have 'across the desert to Mázandarán."

Next day Khwárazmsháh accorded Ḥusayn ibn 'Alí ibn Míká'íl an audience, and heaped on him all sorts of favours. "I have read the letter," said he, "and have acquainted myself with its contents and with the King's command. Abú 'Alí and Abú Sahl are gone, but Abú Naṣr, Abú Rayḥán and Abu'l-Khayr are making their preparations to appear at [Maḥmúd's] court." So in a little while he provided their outfit, and despatched them in the company of Khwája Ḥusayn ibn 'Alí ibn Míká'íl. And in due course they came into the presence of Sulṭán Yamínu'd-Dawla Maḥmúd at Balkh, and there joined his court.

Now it was Abú 'Alí [ibn Síná] whom the King chiefly desired. He commanded Abú Naṣr-i-'Arráq, who was a painter, to draw his portrait on paper, (٧٨) and then ordered other artists to make forty copies of the portrait, and these he despatched with proclamations in all directions, and made demand of the neighbouring rulers, saying, "There is a man after this likeness, whom they call Abú 'Alí ibn Síná. Seek him out and send him to me."

Now when Abú 'Alí and Abú Sahl departed from Khwárazmsháh with Abu'l-Ḥusayn as-Suhaylí's man, they so wrought that ere morning they had travelled fifteen parasangs. When it was morning they alighted at a place where there were wells, and Abú 'Alí took up an astrological table to see under what Ascendant they had started on their journey. When he had examined it he turned to Abú Sahl and said, "Judging by this Ascendant under which we started, we shall lose our way and experience grievous hardships." Said Abú Sahl, "We acquiesce in God's decree. Indeed I know that I shall not come safely through this journey, for during these two days the passage of the degree of my Ascendant[1] falls in Capricorn, which is the sector, so that no hope remains to me. Henceforth only the intercourse of souls will exist between us." So they rode on.

Abú 'Alí relates that on the fourth day a wind arose and stirred up the dust, so that the world was darkened. They lost their way, for the wind had obliterated the tracks. When the wind lulled, their guide was more astray than themselves; and, in the heat of the desert of Khwárazm, Abú Sahl-i-Masíḥí, through lack of water and thirst, passed away to the World of Eternity, while the guide and Abú 'Alí, after experiencing a thousand hardships, reached Báward. There the guide turned back, while Abú 'Alí went to Ṭús, and finally arrived at Níshápúr.

There he found a number of persons who were seeking for Abú 'Alí. Filled with anxiety, he alighted in a quiet spot, where he abode several days, and thence he turned his face towards

[1] The term *tasyír* is explained at p. ٢٣٠ of Van Vloten's ed. of the *Mafátíḥu'l-'ulúm*.

Gurgán, for Qábús[1], who was King of that province, was a great and philosophically-minded man, and a friend of scholars. Abú 'Alí knew that there no harm would befall him. When he reached Gurgán, he alighted at a caravanseray. Now it happened that one fell sick in his neighbourhood, and Abú 'Alí treated him, and he got better. Then he treated another patient, who also got better, and so people began to bring him their water in the morning for him to look at, and he began to earn an income, which continued to increase day by day. Some time elapsed thus, until an illness befell one of the relatives of Qábús ibn Washmgír, who was the King of Gurgán. The physicians set themselves to treat him, (٧٩) striving and exerting themselves to the utmost, but the disease was not cured. Now Qábús was greatly concerned about this, till one of his servants said to him, "Into such-and-such a caravanseray a young man hath entered who is a great physician, and whose efforts are singularly blessed, so that several persons have been cured at his hands." So Qábús bade them seek him out and bring him to the patient, that he might treat him, seeing that the effort of one may be more blessed than that of another.

So they sought out Abú 'Alí and brought him to the patient, whom he beheld to be a youth of comely countenance, whereon the hair had scarcely begun to shew itself, and of symmetrical proportions, but now laid low. He sat down, felt his pulse, asked to see his urine, inspected it, and said, "I want a man who knows all the houses and districts of Gurgán." So they brought one, saying, "Here you are"; and Abú 'Alí placed his hand on the patient's pulse, and bade the other mention the names of the different districts of Gurgán. So the man began, and continued to name the districts until he reached one at the mention of which the patient's pulse gave a strange flutter. Then Abú 'Alí said, "Now give the streets in this quarter." The man gave them, until he arrived at the name of a street whereat that strange flutter recurred. Then Abú 'Alí said, "We need someone who knows all the houses in this street." They brought such an one, who proceeded to give out the houses till he reached a house at the mention of which the patient's pulse gave the same flutter. "Now," said Abú 'Alí, "I want someone who knows the names of all the household and can repeat them." They brought such an one, and he began to repeat them until he reached a name at the mention of which that same flutter was apparent.

Then said Abú 'Alí, "It is finished." Thereupon he turned to the confidential advisers of Qábús, and said, "This lad is in

[1] *Shamsu'l-Ma'álí* Qábús ibn Washmgír reigned A.H. 366–371 (A.D. 976–981) and again A.H. 388–403 (A.D. 998–1012). To him al-Bírúní dedicated his *Chronology of Ancient Nations*. See Sachau's English translation of that work, Preface, p. viii.

love with such-and-such a girl, so-and-so by name, in such-and-such a house, in such-and-such a street, in such-and-such a quarter: union with that girl is his remedy, and the sight of her his cure." The patient, who was listening, and heard all that Abú 'Alí said, hid his face in shame beneath the bed-clothes. When they made enquiries, it was even as Abú 'Alí had said[1]. Then they reported this matter to Qábús, who was mightily amazed thereat and said, "Bring him before me." So Abú 'Alí ibn Síná was brought before Qábús[2].

Now Qábús had a copy of Abú 'Alí's portrait, which Sulṭán Yamínu'd-Dawla had sent to him. (٨٠) "Art thou Abú 'Alí?" enquired he. "Yes, O most puissant Prince," replied the other. Then Qábús came down from his throne, advanced several paces to meet Abú 'Alí, embraced him, sat beside him on a cushion before the throne, heaped favours upon him, and enquired of him graciously, saying, "That most illustrious and accomplished man and most perfect philosopher must without fail explain to me the rationale of this treatment." "O Sire," answered Abú 'Alí, "When I inspected his pulse and urine, I became convinced that his complaint was love, and that he had fallen thus sick through keeping his secret. Had I questioned him, he would not have told me the truth; so I placed my hand on his pulse while they repeated in succession the names of the different districts, and when it came to the region of his beloved, love stirred him, the movements of his pulse altered, and I knew that she was a dweller in that quarter. Then I bade them name the streets, and when he heard the street of his beloved the same thing occurred again, so that I knew the name of the street also. Then I bade them mention the names of the households in that street, and the same phenomenon occurred when the house of his beloved was named, so that I knew the house also. Then I bade them mention the names of its inhabitants, and when he heard the name of his beloved, he was greatly affected, so that I knew the

[1] Compare the precisely similar narrative in the first story of the first book of the *Mathnawí* of Jalálu'd-Dín Rúmí, and also a passage in the section of the *Dhakhíra-i-Khwárazm-sháhí* (Book vi, Guftár i, Juz' 2, ch. 3) dealing with the malady of love, of which this is a translation :—"Now the lover's pulse is variable and irregular, especially when he sees the object of his affections, or hears her name, or gets tidings of her. In this way one can discover, in the case of one who conceals his love and the name of his beloved, who is the object of his passion, and that in the following way. The physician should place his finger on the patient's pulse, and unexpectedly order the names of those persons amongst whom it may be surmised that his sweetheart is to be found to be repeated, whereupon it will appear from the patient's behaviour who his beloved is, and what her name is. Avicenna (upon whom be God's Mercy) says: 'I have tried this plan, and have succeeded by it in finding out who the beloved object was.'" Avicenna's actual words are quoted from the *Qánún* on pp. ٢٤٩–٢٥٠ of the Persian notes.

[2] We have it on Avicenna's own authority that he arrived in Jurján just too late to see Qábús, who had been deposed and cast into prison, where he was soon afterwards put to death in 403/1012–1013. (See pp. ٢٥٠–٢٥١ of the Persian notes.)

name of his sweetheart also. Then I told him my conclusion, and he could not deny it, but was compelled to confess the truth."

Qábús was greatly astonished at this treatment and was filled with wonder, and indeed there was good reason for astonishment. "O most glorious, eminent and excellent one," said he, "both the lover and the beloved are the children of my sisters, and are cousins to one another. Choose, then, an auspicious moment that I may unite them in marriage." So Master Abú Alí chose a fortunate hour, and in it the marriage-knot was tied, and lover and beloved were united, and that handsome young prince was delivered from an ailment which had brought him to death's door. And thereafter Qábús maintained Abú 'Alí in the best manner possible, and thence he went to Ray, and finally became minister to the Sháhinsháh 'Alá'u'd-Dawla[1], as indeed is well known in the history of Abú 'Alí ibn Síná's life.

ANECDOTE XXXVII.

The author of the *Kámilu's-Ṣiná'at*[2] was physician to 'Aḍudu'd-Dawla[3] in Párs, in the city of Shíráz. Now in that (٨١) city there was a porter who used to carry loads of four hundred and five hundred maunds on his back. And every five or six months he would be attacked by headache, and become restless, remaining so for ten days or a fortnight. One time he was attacked by this headache, and when seven or eight days had elapsed, and he had several times determined to destroy himself, it finally happened that one day this great physician passed by the door of his house. The porter's brothers ran to meet him, did reverence to him, and, conjuring him by God Most High, told him about their brother's condition and headache. "Show him to me," said the physician. So they brought him before the physician, who saw that he was a big man, of bulky frame, wearing on his feet a pair of shoes each of which weighed a maund and a half. Then the physician felt his pulse and asked for and examined his urine; after which, "Bring him with me into the open country," said he. They did so, and on their arrival there, he bade his servant take the porter's turban from his head, cast it round his neck, and twist it tight. Then he ordered another servant to take the shoes off the porter's feet and strike him twenty blows on the head, which he accordingly did. The porter's sons lamented loudly, but the physician was a man of consequence

[1] He was the son of Dushmanziyár, ruler over Iṣfahán from A.H. 398 to 433 (A.D. 1007–1041), and is commonly known as Ibn Kákawayhi or Kákúya.

[2] See Brockelmann's *Gesch. d. Arab. Litt.*, vol. i, p. 237, No. 19. His name was 'Alí ibnu'l-'Abbás al-Majúsí, and he died in A.H. 384 (A.D. 994). For some account of his life and work see Note XXVII at the end, and also p. 79 *supra*, n. 2 *ad calc.*

[3] The second prince of the House of Búya, reigned A.H. 338–372 (A.D. 949–982).

and consideration, so that they could do nothing. Then the physician ordered his servant to take hold of the turban which he had twisted round his neck, to mount his horse, and to drag the porter after him round the plain. The servant did as he was bid, and made him run far afield, so that blood began to flow from his nostrils. "Now," said the physician, "let him be." So he was let alone, and there continued to flow from him blood stinking worse than carrion. The man fell asleep amidst the blood which flowed from his nose, and three hundred *dirhams*' weight of blood escaped from his nostrils ere the haemorrhage ceased. They then lifted him up and bore him thence to his house, and he never woke, but slept for a day and a night; and his headache passed away and never again returned or required treatment.

Then 'Aḍudu'd-Dawla questioned the physician as to the rationale of this treatment. "O King," he replied, "that blood in his brain was not a matter which could be eliminated by an aperient of aloes[1], and there was no other method of treatment than that which I adopted."

(٨٢) ANECDOTE XXXVIII.

Melancholia is a disease which physicians often fail to treat successfully, for, though all diseases arising from the black bile are chronic, melancholia is a pathological condition which is especially slow to pass. Abu'l-Ḥasan ibn Yaḥyá[2] in his work entitled the "Hippocratic Therapeutics" (*Mu'álaja-i-Buqráṭí*), a book the like of which hath been composed by no one on the Art of Medicine, hath enumerated the leaders of thought, sages, scholars and philosophers who have been afflicted by this disease.

My master the Shaykh Abú Ja'far ibn Muḥammad Abú Sa'd[3] [al-Nashawí][4], commonly known as Ṣarakh[5], related to me, on the authority of the Imám Shaykh Muḥammad ibn 'Aqíl al-Qazwíní, on the authority of the Amír Fakhru'd-Dawla Abú Kálanjár the Búyid as follows:

"One of the princes of the House of Búya was attacked by melancholy, and was in such wise affected by the disease that

[1] *Aydraj* or *Yáru* is a compound medicine of a purgative or alterative character. The kind called *fíqrá* (from the Greek πικρά) has aloes as its principal active ingredient.

[2] See Brockelmann's *Gesch. d. Arab. Litt.*, vol. i, p. 237, and p. ٢٠٢ of the Persian notes. He gives his own name in full as Abu'l-Ḥasan Aḥmad ibn Muḥammad aṭ-Ṭabarí. He was court physician to the Búyid prince Ruknu'd-Dawla from A.H. 332 (A.D. 943–4) onwards. MSS. of the work cited exist at Oxford, Munich, and in the India Office.

[3] A. has Sa'dí.

[4] This *nisba* occurs only in L.

[5] So all texts, صرخ, a form hitherto unexplained.

he imagined himself to have been transformed into a cow. All day he would cry out to this one and that one saying, 'Kill me, so that a good stew may be prepared from my flesh'; until matters reached such a pass that he would eat nothing, and the days passed and he continued to waste away, and the physicians were unable to do him any good.

"Now at this juncture Abú 'Alí (Avicenna) was prime minister, and the Sháhinsháh 'Alá'u'd-Dawla Muḥammad ibn Dushmanziyár[1] favoured him greatly, and had entrusted into his hands all the affairs of the kingdom, and left all matters to his judgement and discretion. And indeed since Alexander the Great, whose minister was Aristotle, no King had had such a minister as Abú 'Alí. And during the time that he was minister, he used to rise up every morning before dawn and write a couple of pages of the *Shifá*[2]. Then, when the true dawn appeared, he used to give audience to his disciples, such as Kiyá Ra'ís Bahmanyár[3], Abú Manṣúr ibn Zíla[4], 'Abdu'l-Wáḥid Júzjání[5], Sulayman of Damascus, and me, Abú Kálanjár. We used to continue our studies till the morning grew bright, and then perform our prayers behind him; and as soon as we came forth we were met at the gate of his house by a thousand mounted men, comprising the dignitaries and notables, as well as such as had boons to crave or were in difficulties. Then the minister would mount, and this company would attend him to the Government Offices. By the time he arrived there, the number of horsemen (۸۳) had reached two thousand. And there he would remain until the noon-tide prayer, and when he retired for refreshment a great company ate with him. Then he took his mid-day siesta, and when he rose up from this he would perform his prayer, wait on the King, and remain talking and conversing with him until the afternoon prayer; and in all matters of state importance there was no third person between him and the King.

"Our object in narrating these details is to shew that the minister had no leisure time. Now when the physicians proved unable to cure this young man, the case was represented to that puissant Prince 'Alá'u'd-Dawla, and his intercession was sought, so that he might bid his minister take the case in hand. So

[1] See Note XXX at end.

[2] One of Avicenna's most celebrated works. See the *British Museum Arabic Catalogue*, p. 745[a], and the *Supplement* to the same, No. 711, pp. 484–485.

[3] Abu'l-Ḥasan Bahmanyár ibn Marzubán al-Ádharbáyjání al-Majúsí. He was one of Avicenna's most notable disciples, and died about A.H. 458 (A.D. 1066). See pp. ۲۰۲–۲۰۳ of the Persian notes.

[4] Abú Manṣúr al-Ḥusayn ibn Muḥammad ibn 'Umar ibn Zíla al-Iṣfahání. He died in A.H. 440 (A.D. 1048–49). See p. ۲۰۳ of the Persian notes.

[5] His *kunya* was Abú 'Ubayd and his father's name Muḥammad. He attached himself to Avicenna in Jurján in A.H. 403 (A.D. 1012–1013) and continued with him as long as he lived, *viz.* for about 25 years. He not only inspired and encouraged Avicenna during his lifetime, but collected and arranged his works after his death.

'Alá'u'd-Dawla spoke to him to this effect, and he consented. Then said he, 'Give good tidings to the patient, and say, "the butcher is coming to kill thee!"' When the patient was told this, he rejoiced. Then the minister mounted his horse, and came with his usual retinue to the gate of the patient's house, which he entered with two others. Taking a knife in his hand, he said, 'Where is this cow, that I may kill it?' The patient made a noise like a cow, meaning, 'It is here.' The minister bade them bring him into the middle of the house, bind him hand and foot, and throw him down. When the patient heard this, he ran forward into the middle of the house and lay down on his right side, and they bound his feet firmly. Then Abú 'Alí came forward, rubbing the knives together, sat down, and placed his hand on the patient's ribs, as is the custom of butchers. 'O what a lean cow!' said he; 'it is not fit to be killed: give it fodder until it gets fat' Then he rose up and came out, having bidden them loose his hands and feet, and place food before him, saying, 'Eat, so that thou mayst speedily grow fat.' They did as Avicenna had directed and set food before him, and he ate. After that they gave him whatever draughts and drugs Avicenna prescribed, saying, 'Eat well, for this is a fine fattener for cows,' hearing which he would eat, in the hope that he might grow fat and they might kill him. So the physicians applied themselves vigorously to treating him as the minister had indicated, and in a month's time he completely recovered and was restored to health."

All wise men will perceive (٨٤) that one cannot heal by such methods of treatment save by virtue of extreme excellence, perfect science, and unerring acumen[1].

ANECDOTE XXXIX.

In the reign of Maliksháh and during part of the reign of Sanjar there was at Herát a philosopher named Adíb Isma'íl, a very great, learned and perfect man, who, however, derived his income and livelihood from his receipts as a physician[2]. By him many rare cures of this class were wrought.

One day he was passing through the sheep-slayers' market. A butcher was skinning a sheep, and from time to time he would thrust his hand into the sheep's belly, take out some of the warm fat, and eat it. Khwája Isma'íl, noticing this, said to a

[1] This story also occurs in a versified form in Jámí's *Silsilatu'dh-Dhahab*. The text will be found in Note XXVIII at the end.

[2] This story in substantially the same form is told of Thábit ibn Qurra in al-Qifṭí's *Ta'ríkhu'l-Ḥukamá* (ed. Lippert), pp. 120–121, and in the *Ṭabaqátu 'l-Aṭibbá* of Ibn Abí Uṣaybi'a (ed. Cairo), vol. i, pp. 216–217. From the account there given Mírzá Muḥammad has restored (in brackets) a sentence which has fallen out in the *Chahár Maqála*.

green-grocer opposite him, "If at any time this butcher should die, inform me of it before they lay him in his grave." "Willingly," replied the green-grocer. When five or six months had elapsed, one morning it was rumoured abroad that such-and-such a butcher had died suddenly without any premonitory illness. The green-grocer also went to offer his condolences. He found a number of people tearing their garments, while others were consumed with grief, for the dead man was young, and had little children. Then he remembered the words of Khwája Isma'íl, and hastened to bear the intelligence to him. Said the Khwája, "He has been a long time in dying." Then he took his staff, went to the dead man's house, raised the sheet from the face of the corpse, [felt his pulse, and ordered some one to strike the soles of his feet with the staff. After a while he said to him, "It is enough." Then he] began to apply the remedies for apoplexy, and on the third day the dead man arose, and, though he remained paralytic, he lived for many years, and men were astonished, because that great man had foreseen that the man would be stricken by apoplexy.

ANECDOTE XL.

The Shaykhu'l-Islám 'Abdu'lláh Anṣárí[1] (may God sanctify his spirit!) conceived a fanatical hatred of the above-mentioned man of science, (٨٠) and several times attempted to do him an injury, and burned his books. Now this fanatical dislike arose from religious motives, for the people of Herát believed that he could restore the dead to life, and this belief was injurious to the common people[2].

Now the Shaykh fell ill, and in the course of his illness developed a hiccough for the cure of which all the methods of treatment tried by the physicians availed nothing. They were in despair, and finally sent a sample of his urine to the Khwája under the name of another, and requested him to prescribe. When Khwája Isma'íl had inspected it, he said, "This is the urine of so-and-so, who has developed a hiccough which they are unable to cure. Bid him tell them to pound together an *istár*[3] of the skins of pistachio-kernels, and an *istár* of the sugar called *'askarí*, and administer [the mixture] to him, so that he may recover; and give him also this message: 'You should study science, and not burn books.'"

[1] Concerning this celebrated mystic see pp. ٢٠٠–٨ of the Persian notes, and Note XXXI at the end. He was born in A.H. 396 (A.D. 1006) and died in A.H. 481 (A.D. 1089). He was the author of numerous works, some of which are extant, including the well-known Persian quatrains in which he calls himself *Pír-i-Anṣár*, *Pír-i-Hirí*, and *Anṣárí*. Though a mystic, he was a fanatical Ḥanbalí.

[2] Instead of عوامّ را, the reading adopted in the text, B. and L. have دعوی را, "to [his own] pretensions."

[3] A weight consisting of 4½ *mithqáls*.

So they made a powder of these two ingredients, and the patient ate it, and immediately the hiccough ceased, and the patient was relieved.

ANECDOTE XLI.

In the time of Galen one of the notables of Alexandria was attacked by pain in the finger-tips, and suffered great restlessness, being debarred from all repose. They informed Galen, who prescribed an unguent to be applied to his shoulders. As soon as they did as Galen commanded, the patient's pain ceased and he was cured. The physicians were astonished, and questioned Galen, saying, "What was [the rationale of] this treatment which thou didst adopt?" He replied, "The nerve which supplies the aching finger-tips has its origin in the shoulder. I treated the root and the branch was cured."

ANECDOTE XLII.[1]

Some traces of leprosy appeared on the chest of Faḍl ibn Yaḥyá al-Barmakí (the Barmecide), whereat he was greatly distressed, and put off going to the hot bath until night-time in order that no one might become aware of this. Then he assembled his courtiers and said, "Who is considered to-day the most skilful physician in 'Iráq, Khurásán, Syria and Párs, (٨٦) and who is most famous in this respect?" They replied, "Paul the Catholicos in Shíráz." He therefore sent a messenger and brought the Catholicos from Párs to Baghdád. Then he sat with him privately, and by way of proving him said, "There is something amiss with my foot; you must devise some treatment for it." The Catholicos said, "You must abstain from all milky foods and pickles and eat pea-soup with the flesh of chickens a year old, with sweets made of the yolk of eggs with honey. When the arrangements for this diet have been completely established, I will prescribe the proper drugs." "I will do so," said Faḍl; but that night he ate everything, according to his custom. They had prepared thick broth flavoured with carroway seed, all of which he consumed; neither did he abstain from highly-flavoured relishes or spiced beans cooked in oil[2].

Next day the Catholicos came and asked to inspect the patient's urine. When he looked at it his face flushed, and he said, "I cannot treat this case. I forbade thee pickles and milky foods, but thou dost partake of carroway broth and dost not

[1] This anecdote occurs only in C., but is given in the printed text, which is based on that MS.

[2] The description of these dishes, so far as it goes, is given on p. ٢٠٨ of the Persian notes.

avoid relishes and preserves[1], so that the treatment cannot succeed." Then Faḍl ibn Yaḥyá applauded the acumen and discernment of that great man, and revealed to him his real complaint, saying, "It was for this that I summoned thee, and what I did was for a proof."

Then the Catholicos applied himself to the treatment of the case, and did all that was possible in this matter. When some time had elapsed and there was no improvement, the Catholicos writhed inwardly, for this had appeared no great matter, yet it was thus protracted. At last one day when he was sitting with Faḍl ibn Yaḥyá, he said, "Honoured Sir, I have tried every available remedy without effect. Perchance thy father is displeased with thee. Satisfy him, and I will remove this disease from thee."

So that night Faḍl arose, went to [his father] Yaḥyá, fell at his feet, and asked for his forgiveness. His old father forgave him, [and the Catholicos continued to treat him after the same sort as before, and he began to improve, and ere long was completely cured].

Then Faḍl asked the Catholicos, "How didst thou know that the cause of my complaint was my father's displeasure?" The Catholicos answered, "I tried every known remedy without effect. So I said to myself, 'This great man has received a blow from some quarter.' (٨٧) I looked about, but could find no one who lay down at night dissatisfied and afflicted through thee; on the contrary, many were those who lived in comfort through thy alms, gifts and marks of favour. At length I was informed that thy father was vexed with thee, and that there had been an altercation between thee and him, and I knew that [thine ailment] arose from this. So I adopted this treatment and it passed away, and my conjecture was not at fault."

After this Faḍl ibn Yaḥyá enriched the Catholicos and sent him back to Párs.

ANECDOTE XLIII.

In the year A.H. 547 (=A.D. 1152–3)[2], when a battle took place at the gates of Awba[3] between the King of the World Sanjar ibn Malikshâh and my master 'Alá'u'd-Dunyá wa'd-Dín al-Ḥusayn ibnu'l-Ḥusayn (may God immortalise their reigns and domains!), and the Ghúrid army sustained so grievous a reverse, I wandered about Herát in the guise of a fugitive, because I was connected with the House of Ghúr, against whom enemies uttered all

[1] For the meaning of *anbaját* (pl. of *anba* or *anbaja*), see p. ٢٠٩ of the Persian notes.

[2] L. has "447," both in figures and writing, an evident error, since Sanjar reigned A.H. 511–552, and 'Alá'u'd-Dín Ḥusayn "Jahán-súz" A.H. 544–556. A. omits the figures, and only has "in the year forty-seven."

[3] See p. 74 *supra* and note 3 *ad calc.*

manner of railing accusations, rejoicing malignantly over their reverse. In the midst of this state of things, I chanced one night to be in the house of a certain great man. When we had eaten bread, I went out to satisfy a need. That nobleman by reason of whom I came to be there happened to praise me during my absence, saying, "Men know him as a poet, but, apart from his skill in poetry, he is a man of great attainments, well skilled in astrology, medicine, polite letter-writing, and other accomplishments."

When I returned to the company, the master of the house shewed me increased respect, as do those who are in need of some favour, and in a little while came and sat by me, and said, "O so-and-so, I have one only daughter, and, save her, no other near relative, and she is my treasure. Lately she has fallen a victim to a malady such that during the days of her monthly courses ten or fifteen maunds[1] of sanguineous matter come from her, and she is greatly weakened. We have consulted the physicians, several of whom have treated her, but it has availed nothing, for if this issue be checked, she is attacked with pain and swelling in the stomach, and if it be encouraged, it is increased in amount, and she is much weakened, so that I fear lest her strength may wholly fail." "Send me word," said I, "when next this state occurs."

When (AA) ten days had passed, the patient's mother came to fetch me, and brought her daughter to me. I saw a girl very comely, but despairing of life and stricken with terror. She at once fell at my feet, saying, "O my father! For God's sake help me, for I am young, and have not yet seen the world." The tears sprang to my eyes, and I said, "Be of good cheer, this is an easy matter." Then I placed my fingers on her pulse, and found it strong, and her colour and complexion normal, while most of the ten indications were present, such as a robust habit of body, a strong constitution, a healthy temperament, a clear complexion, a favourable age, season and climate, suitable habit, propitious accessories and skill. Then I summoned a phlebotomist and bade him open the basilic vein in both her arms; and I sent away all the women. The bad blood continued to flow, and, by pressure and manipulation, I took from her a thousand *dirhams'* weight of blood, so that she fell down in a swoon. Then I bade them bring fire, and prepared roasted meat beside her, and put a fowl on the spit, until the house was filled with the steam of the roasting meat, and it entered her nostrils. Then she came to her senses, moved, groaned, and asked for a drink. Then I, prepared for her a gentle stimulant agreeable to her taste, and treated her for a week until the loss of blood was

[1] B. has *sirs*.

made good, and that illness passed away, and her monthly courses resumed their normal condition. And I called her my daughter, and she called me her father, and to-day she is to me as my other children.

CONCLUSION.

My purpose in composing this treatise and inditing this discourse is not to flaunt my merits or recall my services, but rather to guide the beginner, and also to glorify my master, the august, divinely favoured, triumphant and victorious King Ḥusámu'd-Dawla wa'd-Dunyá wa'd-Dín, defender of Islám and the Muslims, Lord of hosts in the worlds, pride of kings and sovereigns, exterminator of heathens and infidels, subduer of heretics and innovators, guardian of the days, protector of the people, forearm of the Caliphate, beauty of the church, glory of the state, organizer of the Arabs and Persians, noblest of the world, *Shamsu'l-Ma'álí, Maliku'l-Umará*, Abu'l-Ḥasan 'Alí ibn (٨٩) Mas'úd ibnu'l-Ḥusayn *Naṣíru Amíri'l-Mú'minín* (may God continue his glory and increase his progress in prosperity!), by whose high station the Kingly Function is magnified, and for whose service Fortune hastens!

May God (blessed and exalted is He!) continue to embellish the Empire with his beauty, and the Kingdom with his perfection! May the eyes of my Lord's son, that divinely aided, victorious and triumphant Prince *Shamsu'd-Dawla wa'd-Dín* be brightened by his excellent conduct and heart! May the Divine Protection and Royal Favour be as a buckler to the majestic statures and virtuous forms of both! And may the heart of my Lord and Benefactor, that august, learned, just, divinely-aided, victorious and triumphant King *Fakhru'd-Dawla wa'd-Dín, Bahá'u'l-Islám wa'l-Muslimín*, King of the kings of the Mountains, be gladdened, not for a period but for ever, by the continuance of both[1]!

[1] For an account of the House of Shansab or Kings of Ghúr and their genealogy, see Note I at the end. Fakhru'd-Dín Mas'úd, whom the author praises in the concluding sentence of his book, was the first of the Kings of Bámiyán and the father of Shamsu'd-Dín Muḥammad and Ḥusámu'd-Dín Abu'l-Ḥasan 'Alí, of whom the latter was our author's special patron.

FINIS.

NOTES

Mírzá Muḥammad has elucidated his critical edition of the *Chahár Maqála* by copious and valuable Persian notes following the text (pp. ۹۰–۲۰۹). Instead of translating them *in extenso*, it has seemed better to incorporate the shorter ones as footnotes on the pages to which they refer, and to distribute the longer ones, with considerable rearrangement and condensation, under the topics of which they treat. A little fresh matter has been added by the translator, especially in the Fourth Discourse dealing with Medicine, and a great deal more by Mírzá Muḥammad, who carefully read and richly annotated the proofs in slip. For the astrological notes (XXIV and XXXII) contributed by Mr Ralph Shirley and Mr W. Gornold the translator desires to express his deep gratitude.

NOTES

I. The Dynasty of Ghúr or House of Shansab.

(Text, pp. 1–2; Persian notes, pp. 90–2.)

The kings of Ghúr, under whose patronage our author flourished, claimed descent from Ḍaḥḥák (Dahák, Azhidaháka) the legendary tyrant of ancient Persia, who, after a reign of a thousand years, was finally overthrown by Firídún. Shansab, the more proximate ancestor from whom they derived their name, is said to have been contemporary with the Prophet's cousin and son-in-law 'Alí ibn Abú Ṭálib, to have accepted Islám at his hands, and to have received from him a standard and recognition of his rule. It was a source of pride to the family that during the Umayyad period they refused to conform to the order for the public cursing in the pulpits of the House of 'Alí.

Our principal source of information concerning this dynasty is the *Ṭabaqát-i-Náṣirí*[1], but the history of Herát entitled *Rawḍátu'l-Jannát* by Mu'ínu'd-Dín of Isfizár also contains a pretty full account of them. This, however, was composed nearly three centuries later (in the latter part of the fifteenth century), and, moreover, exists only in manuscript.

The independent sway of the House of Shansab endured only about 67 years (A.D. 1148–1215)[2], from the time when they shook off the yoke of the House of Ghazna to the time when they succumbed to the power of the Khwárazmsháhs. They were divided into two branches, who ruled respectively over Ghúr with their capital at Fírúz-kúh, and over Ṭukháristán with their capital at Bámiyán. The relationship existing between the chief members of the dynasty mentioned in this book is shewn in the following table.

- 'Izzu'd-Dín Ḥusayn
  - 'Alá'u'd-Dín Ḥusayn, called *Jahán-súz*, the "World-consumer"
  - Bahá'u'd-Dín Sám
    - Ghiyáthu'd-Dín
    - Shihábu'd-Dín (or Mu'izzu'd-Dín)
  - Fakhru'd-Dín Mas'úd
    - Shamsu'd-Dín Muḥammad
    - Ḥusámu'd-Dín 'Alí

Of these 'Alá'u'd-Dín Ḥusayn of Fírúz-kúh was the most powerful and important, and raised the glory of his House to its highest point. To avenge the death of his two brothers Quṭbu'd-Dín Muḥammad and Sayfu'd-Dín Súrí he made war on Bahrámsháh, entered and occupied his capital Ghazna, and looted, massacred and burned it for seven days, thus earning the title of *Jahán-súz*, the "World-consumer." He reigned from A.H. 545 to 556 (A.D. 1150–1161).

[1] Published in the *Bibliotheca Indica*, and translated by Major H. G. Raverty with copious notes. Sections xvii–xix (pp. 300–507) of vol. i of the translation are devoted to this dynasty.

[2] See Stanley Lane-Poole's *Mohammadan Dynasties*, pp. 291–294.

Fakhru'd-Dín Mas'úd, first of the Bámiyán line, brother of Ḥusayn *Jahán-súz* and father of our author's special patron Ḥusámu'd-Dín 'Alí, outlived the year 558/1163, in which, according to the *Ṭabaqát-i-Náṣirí*[1], he made war on his nephews Ghiyáthu'd-Dín and Shiháb [or Mu'izz]u'd-Dín. The title *Maliku'l-Jibál* ("King of the Mountains") given to him in the text was common to all the rulers of this dynasty.

Shamsu'd-Dín Muḥammad, son of the above-mentioned Fakhru 'd-Dín and second of the Bámiyán line, survived at any rate until the year 586/1190, when he aided his cousins Ghiyáthu'd-Dín and Shiháb [or Mu'izz]u'd-Dín in their struggle against Sulṭán-sháh ibn Íl-arslán ibn Atsiz Khwárazm-sháh[2].

Ḥusámu'd-Dín Abu'l-Ḥasan 'Alí, brother of the above-mentioned Shamsu'd-Dín, was our author's patron to whom the *Chahár Maqála* is dedicated, and who must therefore have been living in 551–2/1156–7 when it was written. He is only mentioned in the *Ṭabaqát-i-Náṣirí* (p. 104) amongst the children of Fakhru'd-Dín Mas'úd, and further particulars of his life are lacking.

II. The meaning of Ṭamgháj or Tapghách.

(Text, p. 9; Persian notes, pp. 92–4.)

Ṭamgháj is generally explained as the name of a city or district in China or Chinese Turkistán. In illustration of this view Mírzá Muḥammad cites three passages from Arabic writers and some verses by the Persian poet Mukhtárí. An-Nasawí, the biographer of Sulṭán Jalálu'd-Dín Khwárazm-sháh[3], says that it is the custom of the Great Khán to spend the summer "in Ṭamgháj, which is the centre of China, and its environs"; and this statement is quoted by Abu'l-Fidá (who, however, writes the word Ṭúmḥáj or Ṭúmkháj) in his Geography. Al-Qazwíní in his *Átháru'l-Bilád*[4] describes Ṭamgháj as "a great and famous city in the land of the Turks, comprising many villages lying between two mountains in a narrow defile by which only they can be approached." Finally Mukhtárí of Ghazna, in the course of a panegyric on Arslán Khán of the Kháníyya dynasty of Transoxiana, speaks of "nimble Ṭamghájí minstrels, quick at repartee."

It seems possible, however, that Ṭamgháj and Ṭafghách[5] are merely variants of the Eastern Turkish word *Tapghách*, meaning "worshipful," "renowned," and used repeatedly in the sense of "Chinese" in the Orkhon inscriptions of the eighth century of our era. In this case the title "Ṭamgháj (or Ṭapghách) Khán" commonly assumed by rulers of the Kháníyya dynasty really signifies "the worshipful Khán," not "the Khán of Ṭamgháj"; and the prevalent belief that there was a country called Ṭamgháj arose from a misunderstanding, and from a false analogy with such titles as Khwárazm-sháh, which does actually mean "King of Khwárazm." Mírzá Muḥammad, however, in a lengthy and learned

[1] Ed. Calcutta, pp. 29 *et seqq*.

[2] Ibnu'l-Athír (ed. Tornberg), xiii, 28; *Ṭabaqát-i-Náṣirí*, p. 52; *Lubábu'l-Albáb* (ed. Browne), i, 321.

[3] Ed. Houdas, pp. 4–5.

[4] Ed. Wüstenfeld, p. 275.

[5] For this form see the Persian notes to the text, pp. 151, l. 3, 189, l. 12, *etc*.

note which he has been good enough to send me, proves that the name Ṭamgháj was applied by early Muhammadan writers to a definite and real city, identified by him on the strongest evidence with Khán Báligh ("Cambaluc") or Pekin, also called چونکدو ("the Middle Capital") and دایدو ("the Great Capital").

See also F. W. K. Müller's *Uigurica I* (Berlin, 1908), p. 13, n. 1 *ad calc.*

III. Writers adduced as models of style.

(Text, p. 13; Persian notes, pp. 95-101.)

The **Ṣáḥib Abu'l-Qásim Isma'íl ibn 'Abbád aṭ-Ṭálaqání** died in 385/995-6. Yáqút, who consecrates a long notice to him in his *Irshádu'l-Aríb*, or "Dictionary of Learned Men[1]," says that there are two places called Ṭálaqán, one in Khurásán, and the other, from which the Ṣáḥib came, between Qazwín and Abhar. Mírzá Muḥammad, however, in a long manuscript note on this passage, proves conclusively that he was a native of Iṣfahán.

Shamsu'l-Ma'álí Qábús ibn Washmgír ibn Ziyár, Prince of Ṭabaristán, was put to death by his son Minúchihr and nobles in 403/1012-3. Of him also Yáqút gives a fairly lengthy notice[2]. He corresponded with the Ṣáḥib above mentioned, and was very celebrated for his skill in this form of composition. Many of his letters were collected by Abu'l-Ḥasan 'Alí ibn Muḥammad al-Yazdádí, and extracts are given by Muḥammad ibn Isfandiyár in his *History of Ṭabaristán* as well as by Yáqút. I have recently acquired a MS. of Yazdádí's compilation entitled *Kamálu'l-Balágha* (the "Perfection of Eloquence").

Abu'l-Faraj Qudáma ibn Ja'far ibn Qudáma ibn Ziyád al-Baghdádí was born and brought up a Christian, but was converted to Islám by the Caliph al-Muktafí, and died in 337/948-9. A short notice of him also occurs in Yáqút's *Irshád*[3], where some dozen of his works are enumerated, of which three, the *Kitábu'l-Kharáj*, the *Naqdu 'n-Nathr* and the *Kitábu'sh-Shi'r* are noticed by Brockelmann (vol. i, p. 228). Ḥarírí mentions him in his *Maqámát* as a model of eloquence.

The **Maqámát-i-Ḥamídí** were composed in 551/1156-7 by the Qáḍí Abú Bakr 'Umar ibn Maḥmúd, entitled Ḥamídu'd-Dín al-Maḥmúdí al-Balkhí, who died in 559/1163-4. This work has been lithographed at Kánpúr (Cawnpore) in 1268/1851-2, and at Ṭihrán in 1290/1873-4. There is a very fine MS. of the 13th century of the Christian era in the British Museum (**Add. 7620**).

The mention of the *Maqámát* of Ḥamídí in this place is of great importance in fixing the date of composition of the *Chahár Maqála* as posterior to 551/1156-7, for since Sulṭán Sanjar, who is repeatedly (*e.g.* pp. 40 and 87 of the text) referred to as still living, died in 552/1157-8, it is evident that this date lies between these two limits (A.H. 551-552; A.D. 1156-1157).

[1] Vol. ii, pp. 273-343 of Prof. D. S. Margoliouth's edition in the "E. J. W. Gibb Memorial" Series (vi, 2, London, Luzac and Co., 1909).

[2] *Ibid.*, vol. vi, pp. 143-152.

[3] *Ibid.*, vol. vi, pp. 203-205.

Abú 'Alí Muḥammad ibn Muḥammad ibn 'Abdu'lláh at-Tamímí al-Bal'amí was minister to the Sámání King Manṣúr I ibn Núḥ ibn Naṣr (reigned A.H. 350–366; A.D. 961–976), for whom he translated Ṭabarí's great history from Arabic into Persian. This Persian version was lithographed at Lucknow in 1291/1874 (800 pages), and a French translation of it by Hermann Zotenberg was published in Paris in four volumes (1867–1874). This Bal'amí (Abú 'Alí) is often confused with his father Abu'l-Faḍl, who also bore the name of Muḥammad, was minister to Isma'íl the Sámání, and died in 329/940–1, while the son, with whom we are here concerned, died in 386/996. Bal'am, from which both derive their *nisba*, is said to be a town in Asia Minor. See Sam'ání's *Ansáb* (Gibb Series, vol. xx, f. 90[a]), where, however, an alternative statement represents Bal'am as a district in the village of Baláshjird near Merv.

Aḥmad ibnu'l-Ḥasan al-Maymandí, entitled **Shamsu'l-Kufát**, was for twenty years minister to Sulṭán Maḥmúd of Ghazna and his son Mas'úd, and died in 424/1033. He was a noted stylist, and caused all official documents to be written in Arabic, not, as had previously been the case, in Persian. His biography is given by al-'Utbí, Abu'l-Faḍl Bayhaqí, 'Awfí in his *Lubábu'l-Albáb*, Ibnu'l-Athír, the *Átháru'l-Wuzará* of Sayfu'd-Dín al-'Aqílí and the *Dastúru'l-Wuzará* of Khwándamír. For the references see the footnotes on pp. 98–9 of the Persian text.

Abú Naṣr Muḥammad ibn Manṣúr ibn Muḥammad al-Kundurí, entitled **'Amídu'l-Mulk**, was for a long while Prime Minister to the Saljúqs Ṭughril Beg and Alp Arslán, and was finally put to death at the instigation of his yet more celebrated successor the Niẓámu'l-Mulk in 456/1064, or, according to Sam'ání (*Ansáb*, f. 488[b]), about 460/1067–8.

Muḥammad [ibn] 'Abduh is mentioned again on p. 24 of the text as one of the secretaries of Bughrá Khán of the Khániyya (Turkish) dynasty of Transoxiana. He flourished in the latter part of the fourth and beginning of the fifth centuries of the *hijra*, and his poems are frequently cited in evidence by Rashídu'd-Dín Waṭwáṭ in his *Ḥadá'iqu's-Siḥr*, or "Gardens of Magic," a well-known work on Rhetoric.

The **'Abdu'l-Ḥamíd** here mentioned is probably **'Abdu'l-Ḥamíd ibn Yaḥyá ibn Sa'íd**, who was secretary to Marwán II, the last Umayyad Caliph (A.H. 127–132; A.D. 744–750), and perished with his master in the year last mentioned. It is he to whom allusion is made in the Arabic proverb: "The art of polite letter-writing opened with 'Abdu'l-Ḥamíd and closed with Ibnu'l-'Amíd."

By the **Sayyidu'r-Ru'asá** it is almost certain that allusion is made to Abu'l-Maḥásin Muḥammad ibn Faḍlu'lláh ibn Muḥammad, who bore this title, and who was one of Malikshāh's under-secretaries and favourites. He was subordinate to **Sharafu'l-Mulk Abú Sa'd Muḥammad ibn Manṣúr ibn Muḥammad**, his chief in the same Ministry, and both were notable secretaries and officials of the Saljúq dynasty. See al-Bundárí's *History of the Saljúqs* (ed. Houtsma), p. 59.

Ibn 'Abbádí, called by Ibnu'l Athír (ed. Tornberg, xi, 77, 78, 88, 103) "the Preacher" (*al Wá'iẓ*), died at 'Askar Mukram in Rabí' ii, 547 (July, 1152). See Ibn Khallikán (Cairo ed., iii, 539–540 = de Slane's translation, iii, 365–366). A long notice of his father Ardashír is given in the *Mirátu'z-Zamán* sub anno 496 (A.D. 1102–3).

By **Abíwardí** is meant **Abu'l-Muẓaffar Muḥammad ibn Aḥmad ibn Muḥammad al-Qurashí al-Umawí al-Abíwardí**, a notable poet and philologist who died in 507/1113–4 at Iṣfahán. Yáqút gives a long notice of him in his *Irshádu'l-Aríb* (ed. Margoliouth, vol. vi, pp. 341–358).

By **Ghazzí** is meant **Abú Isḥáq Ibráhím ibn Yaḥyá ibn 'Uthmán ibn Muḥammad al-Kalbí**, a notable Arabic poet who travelled widely in Persia and sung the praises of the nobles of Khurásán, where his poetry, as Ibn Khallikán informs us (de Slane's translation, vol. i, pp. 38–43), thus obtained a certain circulation. He died at Balkh in 524/1130. Rashídu'd-Dín Waṭwáṭ frequently quotes him in his *Ḥadá'iqu's-Siḥr*. There is in the Bibliothèque Nationale at Paris a fine manuscript of his *Díwán* (**Fonds Arabe 3126**) transcribed at Karkh, a quarter of Baghdád, in 590/1194. Other more eminent poets of Ghazza in Palestine bore the *nisba* al-Ghazzí, but this one, being nearly contemporary with our author and well known in Khurásán, is to him the most famous.

Abu'l-Qásim 'Alí ibn Muḥammad al-Iskáfí of Níshápúr, with whom Anecdotes II and III are concerned, completed his studies in his native town and at an early age entered the service of Abú 'Alí ibn Muḥtáj-i-Chaghání, one of the Amírs in the service of the House of Sámán, who made him one of his chief secretaries and held him in high honour. He achieved a great reputation as a stylist, and repeated but unsuccessful attempts were made to secure his services at the Sámánid Court at Bukhárá. Finally, in 334/945–6, his master Abú 'Alí rebelled against his over-lord Núḥ I ibn Naṣr the Sámánid, but was finally defeated near Bukhárá and compelled to flee to his own country. Amongst those of his followers who were taken prisoner was Iskáfí, whom Núḥ imprisoned at Quhandiz near Bukhárá. Wishing to prove him and ascertain his real sentiments, Núḥ caused a forged letter, couched in the most flattering terms and purporting to be from a certain notable at the Court, to be sent to him, the letter expressing a hope that he would enter the service of Abu'l-'Abbás i-Chaghání, the brother of his late master Abú 'Alí. Iskáfí, possibly suspecting a snare, simply wrote at the foot of the letter in Arabic: "*O Lord! This prison is more acceptable to me than that whereunto they invite me*[1]." When this was shewn to Amír Núḥ he was greatly delighted and at once released Iskáfí from prison, conferred on him a robe of honour, and made him chief assistant-secretary to Abú 'Abdu'lláh in the department of Foreign Correspondence, of which he subsequently became chief. When Amír Núḥ died in 343/954–5, his son and successor 'Abdu'l Malik continued and even increased the honours conferred by Núḥ on Iskáfí, who, however, did not long survive the opening of the new reign. His death was

[1] *Qur'án* xii, 33.

mourned by many poets, including Hazímí of Abíward, three of whose verses are quoted in the Persian notes (pp. 102–3). Tha'álibí says in the *Yatímatu'd Dahr* (vol. iv, pp. 29–33) that Iskáfí had much greater skill in official than in private and friendly correspondence, and that, like the celebrated writer al-Jáḥiẓ, he was as strong in prose as he was weak in verse.

There can be little doubt that the anecdote of the forged letter mentioned above forms the historical basis of a well-known story in the *Gulistán* of Sa'dí (ed. Platts, pp. 35–6; Book I, Story 25). The same anecdote is given by Yáqút in his notice of Iskáfí in the *Irshádu'l-Aríb* (ed. Margoliouth, vol. v, pp. 329–331).

IV. Historical errors in Anecdote II.

(Text, pp. 13–15; Persian notes, pp. 103–105.)

This anecdote furnishes several striking instances of the glaring anachronisms and historical inaccuracies which too often deface the otherwise admirable work of our author.

(1) Iskáfí could not possibly have been secretary to Núḥ II ibn Manṣúr, who reigned from A.H. 366 to 387 (A.D. 976–997), since, as we have seen, he died soon after the accession of 'Abdu'l-Malik in 343/954–5. Nor can we suppose that we are confronted with a mere scribe's error as to the name of the reigning king, since the whole point of the story lies in the king's name being Núḥ.

(2) Alptagín died, according to different authorities, in 351/962–3, 352/963, or 354/965, while Núḥ II ibn Manṣúr did not ascend the throne until 366/976–7, so that to represent the former as living in the reign of the latter is an evident anachronism. The author has probably either confused this king with his father Manṣúr I ibn Núḥ (reigned from 350/961–2 until 366/976–7), against whom Alptagín actually rebelled, and even conquered Ghazna (not Herát, as the author erroneously asserts); or (and this is perhaps more probable) has confused Alptagín with Abú 'Alí Símjúr, who raised a formidable rebellion against Núḥ II ibn Manṣúr.

(3) It is true that in 383/993–4 the above-mentioned Núḥ summoned Subuktagín from Zábulistán to help him, but not against Alptagín, who at this date had been dead thirty years; and not in conjunction with but against Abú 'Alí Símjúr, who had long been in rebellion against him.

(4) It is almost certain that by "Abu'l-Ḥasan 'Alí ibn Muḥtáj al-Kasháni...the Chief Chamberlain" our author means the famous general Amír Abú 'Alí Aḥmad ibn Muḥtáj aṣ-Ṣagháni (*i.e.* of Chagháníyán), who, however, died in 344/955–6, *i.e.* 22 years before Núḥ II succeeded to the throne, and 39 years before Subuktagín led his army into Khurásán in 383/993–4.

According to that great scholar Abú Rayḥán al-Bírúní[1], the occasion when this verse of the *Qur'án* (xi, 34) was so aptly quoted was quite different, *viz.* by Abú Aḥmad Khalaf ibn Aḥmad the ruler of Sijistán

[1] *Al-Áthάru'l-Báqiya* (ed. Sachau), p. 332.

(or Sístán) in reply to a threatening letter addressed to him by Núḥ II ibn Manṣúr the Sámánid; and this is no doubt the correct version of the story, since al-Bírúní was as remarkable for his accuracy as our author is for his carelessness, and, moreover, wrote more than a century and a half earlier.

V. Historical errors in Anecdote III.

(Text, pp. 15–17; Persian notes, pp. 105–106.)

In this anecdote also our author is guilty of two historical errors.

(1) He supposes that Mákán's rebellion took place in the reign of Núḥ II ibn Manṣúr, whereas it really occurred in the reign of his great-grandfather Naṣr II ibn Aḥmad ibn Isma'íl, and Mákán was defeated and killed in 329/940–1, some 37 years before Núḥ's accession.

(2) The general who defeated Mákán was not Tásh, as our author states, but the Amír Abú 'Alí Aḥmad ibn Muḥtáj.

VI. Anecdote V. The Ṣáḥib Isma'íl ibn 'Abbád.

(Text, pp. 17–18; Persian notes, pp. 107–109.)

The Ṣáḥib Isma'íl ibn 'Abbád is, as we have seen, described by the best authorities as "of Ṭálaqán" (*Ṭálaqání*), not "of Ray" (Rází). Al-Máfarrúkhí, author of a notable but rare history of Iṣfahán, claims him as a native of that city, and cites verses composed by him during a campaign in Jurján which lend colour to this assertion[1]. Al-Máfarrúkhí wrote his history between A.H. 465 and 485 (A.D. 1072–1092) in Arabic, and there is a MS. of it (Or. 3601) in the British Museum, while I possess another from the library of the late Sir Albert Houtum-Schindler. It was translated into Persian by Muḥammad ibn 'Abdu'r-Riḍá al-Ḥusayní about 730/1329–30 and dedicated to Ghiyáthu'd-Dín Muḥammad ibn Rashídu'd-Dín Faḍlu'lláh. Of this Persian version (of which I have since myself obtained a MS. formerly in the possession of Sir A. Houtum-Schindler) I published an abridged translation with extracts in the *J.R.A.S.* for 1901, also obtainable as a separate reprint.

VII. Fabrics and Materials mentioned in Anecdote VII.

(Text, pp. 19–21; Persian notes, pp. 110–111.)

Mírzá Muḥammad has kindly communicated to me the following shorter version of this anecdote from the *Kitábu'l-Kináya wa't-Ta'ríḍ* of ath-Tha'álibí (Berlin Arabic MS. No. 7337, Petermann II, 59, f. 146[a]), who wrote about a century and a half earlier than our author:

و يُرْوى أنّ بوران بنت الحسن بن سهل لمّا زُفّتْ الى المأمون حاضت من هيبة الخلافة فى غير وقت الحيض فلمّا اخلا بها المأمون و مدّ يده الى تكّتها قرأتْ أَتَى أَمْرُ ٱللّٰهِ فَلَا تَسْتَعْجِلُوهُ ففطن لها و تعجّب من حُسْنِ كنايتها و آزداد إعجابًا بها ؛

[1] *Cf.* p. 103 *supra*.

Three of the precious fabrics mentioned in this story are included in the glossary added by Mírzá Ḥabíb of Iṣfahán to his edition of the *Díwán-i-Albisa* (Constantinople 1303/1885–6) of Niẓámu'd-Dín Maḥmúd Qárí of Yazd, the poet of clothes. *Aṭlas* "is called by the Franks 'satin'." *Aksún* is "a black brocade (*díbá*), like *dabíqí* (a fine silken stuff) worn by the great for ostentation." *Nasíj* is "silk inwoven with gold." See Yule's *Marco Polo* (ed. 1875), vol. i, pp. 65, 67, 276 and 285.

Of the remainder the exact nature is more doubtful. Mírzá Muḥammad makes the following remarks (notes, p. 110):

Mumazzaj appears to mean a garment made of gold 'mixed' with some other substance. This fabric is mentioned by Ibnu'l-Athír *sub anno* 512/1118–9 (ed. Tornberg, vol. x, p. 382).

Miqráḍí is some precious fabric of which the exact nature is not clear, but it is also mentioned, with the addition of the epithet *Rúmí* (Greek or of Asia Minor) in a quaint passage in al-Máfarrúkhí's History of Iṣfahán (see the last note), cited on p. 110 of the Persian notes, where a dying nobleman requests that his shroud shall be made of this material, not, as the bystanders suggest, of plain linen, because he is unwilling to appear before God less sumptuously clad than it had been his habit for sixty years to appear before his fellow-men.

On the nature of *Ma'diní* and *Malikí* no information is obtainable, nor on *Tamím*, which the editor of the Ṭihrán lithographed edition has seen fit to emend to *Tumam* (pl. of *Tumma*), meaning a handful of wool or hair plucked from a sheep or other animal, an emendation neither plausible nor appropriate to the context, although the aforesaid editor mentions it with especial pride and satisfaction in his concluding note.

VIII. Another historical error in Anecdote VIII.

(Text, pp. 21–2; Persian notes, p. 111.)

In this story the author has, according to Mírzá Muḥammad, confused Sulṭán Mas'úd with Sulṭán Sanjar, for all the historians agree that it was against the former, not the latter, member of the House of Saljúq that the Caliph al-Mustarshid marched forth from Baghdád. When the two armies met near Kirmánsháh most of the Caliph's troops deserted to Mas'úd, and he himself was taken prisoner. On his arrival at Marágha he fell a victim to the Assassins of Alamút in 529/1134–5.

IX. The Gúr-Khán and the Qára-Khitá'í dynasty.

(Text, p. 22; Persian notes, pp. 112–113.)

The battle to which reference is here made took place in 536/1141–2, and is generally known as the Battle of Qaṭawán[1], this place being a suburb or quarter of Samarqand. The Muslims are said to have lost 100,000 men (of whom 12,000 were "turbaned," *i.e.* belonged to the learned or clerical classes), and Sulṭán Sanjar's wife was taken prisoner. The power of this dynasty of unbelieving Turks, known as Qára-Khitá'í and Gúr-Khání, which endured for more than eighty years, dates from this battle. They were finally overthrown by Sulṭán 'Alá'u'd-Dín Muḥammad in alliance with the Tartar Kúchluk Khán in 607/1210–11.

[1] See Ibnu'l-Athír (ed. Tornberg), vol. xi, p. 57.

For more than two centuries which elapsed between the fall of the Sámánid and the rise of the Mongol power there existed in Transoxiana a Muslim Turkish dynasty variously known as "Ílak-Khaní," "Khání" and "Afrásiyábí." These the Qára-Khitá'ís suffered to remain, only requiring of them the payment of tribute and the acceptance of a political resident (*Shaḥna*) at their Court. From most of the Khwárazm-sháhs also they received tribute until overthrown by them in 607/1210–11 as mentioned above.

This collapse of the Qára-Khitá'í power proved, in fact, to be a great calamity for the Khwárazm-sháhs in particular and the Muslims in general, for thereby was broken down a barrier which had hitherto effectively protected them from the Mongols and other predatory heathens who dwelt further to the north and east, and so was prepared that great catastrophe which shortly afterwards laid waste the Muslim world; a fact emphasized by Ibnu'l-Athír (ed. Tornberg, xii, p. 235) in a passage translated in the second volume of my *Literary History of Persia*, p. 430.

The word *Gúr-Khán*[1] (otherwise *Kúr-Khán*, *Kú-Khán*, *Úz-Khán*, *Úr-Khán* or *Or-Khán*) was a generic title of these Kings, not the proper name of any one of them. Ibnu'l-Athír says: "*Ku* in the Chinese language is a title given to the greatest of their Kings, while *Khán* is a title of the Kings of the Turks, so that it [the compound *Ku-Khán*] means 'Greatest of Kings'." In the *Ta'ríkh-i-Jahán-gusháy* (vol. ii, p. 86) and in the *Ta'ríkh-i-Jahán-árá* also it is explained as *Khán-i-Khánán*, *i.e.* "Khán of Kháns" or "Great Khán"; and on the same authority the name of this particular *Gúr-Khán* is said to have been Qúshqín Ṭáyqú. Dr Babinger has kindly called my attention to a note on Ibn 'Arabsháh's explanation of *Gúr-Khán* by S. de Sacy in the *Mémoires de l'Académie* for 1822, p. 476.

X. Atmatigín, Amír Bayábání and Átsiz.

(Text, p. 22; Persian notes, p. 114.)

The correct form and signification of the first and second of these three names is uncertain, and the MSS. differ in their readings. The first has been found by Mírzá Muḥammad in the History of Bukhárá of Muḥammad ibn Zufar ibn 'Umar, composed in 574/1178–9, only 38 years after the Battle of Qaṭawán, but here also the MSS. differ, the British Museum MS. (Add. 2777, f. 28ᵃ) having "Aymantigín" or "Ímantigín," and the Bibliothèque Nationale MS. (Suppl. Pers. 1513, f. 23ᵇ) "Alítigín." It is evidently one of the numerous Turkish names ending in *tigín* (like Subuktigín, Alptigín, *etc.*) but the first element remains doubtful. The same uncertainty affects "the son of the Amír Bayábání, on whose identity no satisfactory light has yet been thrown."

[1] Mírzá Muḥammad cites two passages which show, by the word-plays wherein lies their point, that by the Persians at any rate the pronunciation *Gúr-Khán* was adopted. Kháqání says:

نه بر سنجر شبیخون برد اوّل گورخان آخر'

شبیخون زد اجل تا گورخانه شد شبستانش'

See also vol. ii, p. 93 of the *Ta'ríkh-i-Jahán-gusháy*:

و کورخان را گور خانمان شد'

The name Átsiz, also Turkish, is compounded of *át* (Western Turkish *ád*) "name," and the privative *siz* "without," and consequently means "nameless." According to Ibn Khallikán it was customary amongst the Turks when a man lost several sons in childhood to give this name, which was supposed to be a protection, to a newly-born son in the hope that he might survive.

XI. The House of Burhán (*Ál-i-Burhán*).

(Text, p. 22, *bis*; Persian notes, pp. 114–121.)

The "Sons of Burhán," or Banú Máza, were one of the great families of Bukhárá, celebrated for their splendour and bounty, and were hereditary leaders of the Ḥanafí school of Sunní doctrine which prevailed in Transoxiana. During the later Qará-Khitá'í period they held an almost regal position, and paid tribute to that dynasty. Qazwíní in his *Átháru 'l Bilád* (ed. Wüstenfeld, p. 343), composed in 674/1275–6, mentions 'Umar ibn 'Abdu'l-'Azíz ibn Marwán as the head of the house in his time, and it still flourished in the reign of Úljáytú (Khudá-banda) the Mongol (A.H. 703–716; A.D. 1303–1316), after which all trace of it is lost. Mírzá Muḥammad has collected from various sources a mass of information about fourteen of the most eminent members of this family, which he embodied in the notes contributed by him to my edition of 'Awfí's *Lubábu'l-Albáb* (vol. i, pp. 332–6), and which he has reproduced in his notes to the *Chahár Maqála*. These are as follows.

(1) The Imám Burhánu'd-Dín 'Abdu'l-'Azíz ibn Máza of Bukhárá, the first member of the family to attain celebrity.

(2) His son Ḥusámu'd-Dín 'Umar ibn 'Abdu'l-'Azíz, born in Ṣafar 483 (April 1090) and put to death in 536/1141–2 after the Battle of Qaṭawán by the Gúr-Khán, as mentioned by our author, and hence called "the Martyr." See Ibn Quṭlúbugha's *Táju't-Tarájim fí Ṭabaqáti'l-Ḥanafiyya* (ed. Flügel, Leipzig, 1862), p. 34, No. 139, where five or six of his works are enumerated.

(3) Táju'l-Islám Aḥmad ibn 'Abdu'l-'Azíz, who succeeded his brother above mentioned, as recorded by our author, and enjoyed the favour and confidence of the Gúr-Khán.

(4) Shamsu'd-Dín Ṣadr-i-Jahán Muḥammad, son of Ḥusámu'd-Dín "the Martyr," who in 559/1163-4 saved Bukhárá from being looted by the Qarluq Turks, and whose praises were sung by Súzaní in verses of which seven are given as a specimen on pp. 116–7 of the Persian notes.

(5) Ṣadru's-Ṣudúr Ṣadr-i-Jahán Burhánu'd-Dín 'Abdu'l-'Azíz, another son of Ḥusámu'd-Dín "the Martyr," to whom Muḥammad ibn Zufar ibn 'Umar in 574/1178–9 dedicated his Persian version of an-Narshakhí's Arabic History of Bukhárá, composed in 332/943–4 for the Sámánid King Núḥ ibn Naṣr. Instances of his magnanimity and generosity are given by 'Awfí in his vast, but unfortunately unpublished, collection of stories, the *Jawámi'u'l-Ḥikáyát wa Lawámi'u'r-Riwáyát*, of which two are given in the Persian notes (pp. 117–8).

(6) Burhánu'd-Dín Maḥmúd ibn Táju'l-Islám Aḥmad, author of the *Dhakhíratu'l-Fatáwá* (also called *adh-Dhakhíratu'l-Burhániyya*) mentioned by Ḥájji Khalífa.

(7–10) Burhánu'd-Dín Muḥammad Ṣadr-i-Jahán ibn Aḥmad, brother of the above; his two sons Maliku'l-Islám and 'Azízu'l-Islám, and another brother, Iftikhár-i-Jahán. The first of these four was practically King of Bukhárá and paid tribute to the Khitá'ís, as indicated by a passage in an-Nasawí's Biography of Sulṭán Jalálu'd-Dín Mankobirní[1]. In 603/1206–7, while on his way to Mecca, he was received with great respect at Baghdád, but on his return there, on account of his behaviour towards the pilgrims, he incurred such unpopularity that he earned for himself the nick-name of *Ṣadr-i-Jahannam* (the "Chief" or "President of Hell"). In 613–614/1216–17, when 'Alá'u'd-Dín Muḥammad Khwárazm-sháh set out on his campaign against the Caliph an-Náṣir li-Díni'lláh, as a precautionary measure he deported these four persons (Burhánu'd-Dín Muḥammad and his brother and two sons) from Bukhárá to Khwárazm. Two years later (in 616/1219), when Khwárazmsháh's mother Turkán Khátún decided to flee thence for fear of the Mongol advance, she put all four of them to death, together with other hostages resident at her capital[2].

(11) Ṣadr-i-Jahán Sayfu'd-Dín Muḥammad ibn 'Abdu'l-'Azíz (son of No. 5), who is repeatedly mentioned as still living in 'Awfí's *Lubábu'l-Albáb*, which was written in 618/1221.

(12) Burhánu'l-Islám Táju'd-Dín 'Umar ibn Mas'úd ibn Aḥmad ibn 'Abdu'l-'Azíz ibn Máza (grandson of No. 3, nephew of Nos. 6, 7 and 8, and cousin of Nos. 9 and 10). He was one of the teachers and masters of 'Awfí, who makes mention of him also in the *Lubáb* (ed. Browne, vol. i, pp. 169–174).

(13) Niẓámu'd-Dín Muḥammad, son of the above, also mentioned by 'Awfí (i, 176), who spent some days with him at the town of Ámú[3] on the Oxus about 600/1203–4.

(14) Another Burhánu'd-Dín (pedigree unspecified) is mentioned by 'Alá'u'd-Dín 'Aṭá Malik-i-Juwayní in connection with the rebellion of Tárábí in 636/1238–9[4].

The latest historical reference to any member of this family occurs in the *Ta'ríkh-i-Jahán-árá* of the Qáḍí Aḥmad-i-Ghaffárí, who states that Úljáytú (Khudá-banda, reigned A.D. 1303–1316) was impelled to embrace the Shí'a doctrine by his disgust at the unseemly altercations of two Sunní theologians of different schools, Khwája 'Abdu'l-Malik the Sháfi'í, and Ṣadr-i-Jahán of Bukhárá the Ḥanafí. The title, place of

[1] This passage is cited in the Persian notes, p. 118, fourth line from the end to p. 119, l. 6. It occurs on pp. 23–4 of the edition of M. O. Houdas (Paris, 1891), and on pp. 41–2 of his French translation (Paris, 1895).

[2] *An-Nasawí* (ed. Houdas), p. 39 = pp. 66–7 of the French translation.

[3] See Yáqút's *Mu'jamu'l-Buldán*, vol. i, pp. 69–70, and G. le Strange's *Lands of the Eastern Caliphate*, p. 434. The town is also called *Ámul* by the Arabs, like the better-known town of that name in Mázandarán.

[4] See Mírzá Muḥammad's edition of the *Ta'ríkh-i-Jahán-gushdy*, vol. i, p. 88 ("E. J. W. Gibb Memorial" Series, xvi, 1).

origin, and theological school of the last-named all point to the conclusion that he belonged to the *Ál-i-Burhán.*

The following genealogical table indicates the relationship of the members of this family mentioned above. In each case the corresponding number is given for reference to what precedes, the proper name is given in full, and the title in an abbreviated form, where *'A.* = *'Azíz ; B.* = *Burhán ; D.* = *Dín ; Ḥ.* = *Ḥusám ; If.* = *Iftikhár ; Is.* = *Islám ; J.* = *Jahán ; M.* = *Malik ; N.* = *Niẓám ; S.* = *Sayf ; Ṣ.* = *Ṣadr ; Sh.* = *Shams ;* and *T.* = *Táj.*

- Máza
  - (1) B. D. 'Abdu'l-'Azíz
    - (2) Ḥ. D. 'Umar "the Martyr"
      - (4) Sh. D. Ṣ. J. Muḥammad
      - (5) Ṣ. J. B. 'Abdu'l-'Azíz
        - (11) Ṣ. J. S. D. Muḥammad
    - (3) T. Is. Aḥmad
      - (6) B. D. Maḥmúd
      - (7) B. D. Muḥammad
      - (8) If. J.
        - (9) M. Is.
        - (10) 'A. Is.
      - Mas'úd
        - (12) B. Is. T. D. 'Umar
          - (13) N. D. Muḥammad

XII. Bughrá Khán and Ílak Khán in Anecdote XI.

(Text, p. 24 ; Persian notes, pp. 121-3.)

Our author makes an error here in substituting the name of Bughrá Khán for that of Ílak Khán, who was Sulṭán Maḥmúd's contemporary. Bughrá Khán was the first King known to history of the Afrásiyábí or Khání Turkish dynasty of Transoxiana. The origin of this dynasty and the period at which they embraced Islám is involved in obscurity. Bughrá Khán's proper name is said by Ibnu'l-Athír[1] to have been Hárún ibn Sulaymán ; but, by Ibn Khaldún, Hárún ibn Farrukhán (? Qará-Khán) 'Alí, and Sir Henry Howorth in his article on the *Afrásiyábí Turks*[2] prefers the latter; but as Bughrá Khán appears to have struck no coins, the question remains uncertain. Bughrá Khán was his Turkish title ; his Islamic title (probably conferred by the Caliph) was Shihábu'd-Dawla. His territories marched with China and included most of Eastern Turkistán, with the cities of Káshghar and Balásághún, which latter was his capital. He fought several campaigns against the Sámánid Kings, in the last of which he took their capital Bukhárá, but died on his homeward march in 383/993-4[3], five or six years before Sulṭán Maḥmúd ascended the throne of Ghazna.

He was succeeded by his nephew (or, according to Howorth, his brother) Ílak Khán, whose proper name appears to have been Náṣiru'l-Ḥaqq Naṣr Ílak ibn 'Alí ibn Músá ibn Satuq, while his coins, bearing dates ranging from A.H. 390 to 400 (A.D. 1000 to 1010) were

[1] Ed. Tornberg, ix, 68.
[2] *J.R.A.S.* for 1898, pp. 467-502.
[3] Ibnu'l-Athír, *sub anno* (ed. Tornberg), ix, 70.

struck at Bukhárá, Khujand, Farghána, Úzkand, Ṣaghániyán, Samarqand, Úsh and Íláq, *i.e.* in all the chief cities of Transoxiana and Turkistán[1]. He reigned for twenty years (A.H. 383–403 = A.D. 993–1013), overthrew the authority of the Sámánids in Transoxiana, and quarrelled with Sulṭán Maḥmúd over the partition of their territories, which were finally divided between them.

XIII. Aḥmad ibn 'Abdu'lláh al-Khujistání.

(Text, p. 26; Persian notes, pp. 123–4.)

Khujistán is a district dependent on Bádghís and situated in the mountains of Herát. This Aḥmad was originally an Amír in the service of the Ṭáhirids, but on their collapse he joined the Ṣaffárids, and finally exercised authority over the greater part of Khurásán. Finally he fought and defeated the Ṣaffárid 'Amr ibn Layth at Níshápúr, struck money in his own name, and was contemplating the conquest of 'Iráq, when he was murdered by some of his own servants after exercising more or less independent authority for eight years (A.H. 260–8; A.D. 874–82).

In the *Ta'ríkh-i-Guzída*[2] Sámán, the ancestor of the Sámánid Kings, is represented as the person thus affected by these verses; but, apart from the improbability that Persian verse existed in his time, at any rate in the form in which it is known to us, Ḥanẓala, the author of these verses, flourished under the Ṭáhirid dynasty, of which the founder was contemporary with Asad the son of Sámán.

XIV. Poets and writers mentioned in Anecdote XII.

(Text, pp. 27–8; Persian notes, pp. 125–56.)

Sallámí.—Abú 'Alí as-Sallámí al-Bayhaqí of Níshápúr died in 300/912–3. According to ath-Tha'álibí (*Yatíma*, iv, 29) he was attached as secretary to Abú Bakr Muḥammad ibn al-Muẓaffar ibn Muḥtáj and his son Abú 'Alí Aḥmad. He wrote many books, of which the most famous is the "history" referred to in the text, *viz.* the History of the Governors of Khurásán, which was used by Ibn Khallikán, especially in his notice of Ya'qúb ibn Layth the Ṣaffárid. A short notice of Sallámí occurs in Ibn Funduq's History of Bayhaq, composed in 563/1167–8 in Persian, of which a good MS. (Or. 3587) exists in the British Museum. The text of this article is given in the original by Mírzá Muḥammad on p. 125 of the Persian notes.

Sharíf-i-Mujallidí of Gurgán.—This poet is mentioned in 'Awfí's *Lubáb* (vol. i, pp. 13–14), where he is called Abú Sharíf Aḥmad ibn 'Alí, and where this same verse is cited.

Rúdakí (or -gí).—One of the oldest and most authentic notices of this ancient and celebrated Persian poet occurs in the *Ansáb* of Sam'ání[3], who says that he derived his pen-name (*takhalluṣ*) from his native place

[1] See Sir Henry Howorth's paper referred to in the last paragraph.

[2] Ed. Jules Gantin (Paris, 1903), pp. 20–21; Gibb Memorial facsimile ed. (xiv, 1), p. 379.

[3] The text, given on pp. 125–6 of the Persian notes, occurs on f. 262ᵃ of the "E. J. W. Gibb Memorial" edition (vol. xx, published in 1912).

Rúdak, a district situated near Samarqand. His full name was Abú 'Abdu'lláh Ja'far ibn Muḥammad; he was "the first to produce good poetry in Persian," and he died in 329/940–1. See the late Dr Hermann Ethé's monumental paper *Rûdagî, der Sâmânîdendichter*[1]. The vocalization **Rawdhakí** also occurs, with the addition of the names of the poet's grandfather (Ḥakím), great-grandfather ('Abdu'r-Raḥmán), and great-great-grandfather (Ádam). See my *Hand-list of Muḥammadan Manuscripts* (Cambridge, 1900), No. 701, pp. 125–6.

Abu'l-'Abbás as-Ribanjaní's full name was Faḍl ibn 'Abbás. See 'Awfí's *Lubáb*, vol. ii, p. 9. Ribanjan (the correct reading is due to the late Professor de Goeje) is a city near Sughd and Samarqand, given by Yáqút in the corrupt form "Rabaykhan." It is also mentioned in the *Ansáb* of as-Sam'ání (Gibb Series, vol. xx, ff. 23[b] and 248[b]) as *Arbinjan* and *Rabinjan*. Mírzá Muḥammad has furnished me with a fresh reference to this Abu'l-'Abbás in the *Thimáru'l-Qulúb* (Cairo ed., p. 147) of ath-Tha'álibí, where some Persian verses (a good deal corrupted in the printed text) from an unlucky *qaṣída* which he composed on the occasion of a festival in the thirty-first and last year of the reign of his patron Naṣr ibn Aḥmad the Sámánid (A.H. 331 = A.D. 942–3) are cited.

Abu'l-Mathal of Bukhárá is mentioned in the *Lubáb* (ii, 26) and in Asadí's *Glossary* (ed. P. Horn, p. 28). The vocalization "Mathal" is proved by a verse of Minúchihrí's in which mention is made of ten old Persian poets, all of whom are identified by Mírzá Muḥammad, who cites the verse (pp. 127–9 of the Persian notes). Of these the most interesting is Shahíd of Balkh, who resembles 'Umar Khayyám in this, that his real fame as a philosopher has amongst his countrymen been eclipsed by his fame as a poet, though he was much more notable in the former than in the latter capacity. He is mentioned in the *Fihrist*, p. 299, as a doughty antagonist of Abú Bakr Muḥammad ibn Zakariyyá ar-Rází (the great physician), who wrote a treatise in refutation of some of his opinions. Yáqút also mentions him in his article on *Jahúdhának* near Balkh, the village in which he was born, while Tha'álibí reckons him as one of the four greatest men produced by that ancient city. The correct reading in this last case is given in the Paris MS. of the *Yatímatu'd-Dahr*; in the printed text it appears as "Sahl ibnu'l-Ḥasan" instead of "Shahídu ibnu'l-Ḥusayn." That he predeceased Rúdakí, who died in 329/940–1, is proved by a verse in which that poet laments his death. He is casually mentioned, as Mírzá Muḥammad points out to me, in two passages in Yáqút's "Dictionary of Learned Men" (Gibb Series, vi, 1, pp. 143 and 149), and an article on him was included in the lost fourth volume of this work. 'Awfí also relates a short and rather pointless story about him in the *Jawámi'u'l-Ḥikáyát* (Brit. Mus. MS. Or. 2676, f. 235[b]).

Abú Isḥáq-i-Júybárí's personal name, according to the *Lubáb* (ii, 11) and Asadí's *Glossary* (p. 17), was Ibráhím, and his father's name was Muḥammad. The Júybár from which he derived his *nisba* was apparently situated near Bukhárá.

[1] *Gottinger Nachrichten*, 1873, pp. 663–742.

Abu'l-Ḥasan Ághají was one of the nobles of the Sámánid Court whose praises were sung by Daqíqí[1]. This celebrated poet, as appears from Awfí's *Lubáb* (i, 31–2) and Asadí's *Lughat* (p. 17), was contemporary with Núḥ II ibn Manṣúr the Sámánid, who reigned from A.H. 366 to 387 (A.D. 976–997). Ághájí's full name was Abu'l-Ḥasan 'Alí ibn Ilyás al-Ághájí (or al-Ághjí) of Bukhárá. His title *Ághájí* (or one of its several variants) appears to be a Turkish word meaning a chamberlain or personal servant of a king, serving as an intermediary between him and his subjects[2]. There is a notice of him in ath-Tha'álibí's Supplement[3] to his *Yatímatu'd-Dahr*, from which we learn that he was fond of translating his own Persian verses into Arabic verse. How he understood the art of verse-translation may be seen by comparing the Persian verses in 'Awfí's *Lubáb*, i, 32, ll. 1–4 with the Arabic rendering on p. 130, ll. 5–6, of the Persian notes to the *Chahár Maqála*.

About **Ṭaḥáwí** (so in all three MSS.) nothing is known[4]. For **Khabbází** of Níshápúr, see 'Awfí's *Lubáb*, ii, 27, where, however, except that he is included amongst the poets of the Sámánid period, no particulars are given. The modern *Majma'u'l-Fuṣaḥá* (i, 199) makes him a contemporary of Rúdagí, Kisá'í, *etc.*, and gives the date of his death as A.H. 342 (A.D. 953–4), but on what authority is not stated.

Abu'l-Ḥasan al-Kisá'í was born, as stated by himself in one of his poems[5], on Wednesday, Shawwál 26, A.H. 341 (March 16, 953), and had attained the age of fifty when he wrote it. How much longer he lived is unknown. The late Dr Hermann Ethé wrote a valuable monograph on him (*Die Lieder des Kisa'i*) in the *Sitzungsberichte d. Münchener Akad.* (*philos.-philol. Classe*) for 1874, pp. 133–153.

Abu'l-Ḥasan 'Alí Bahrámí of Sarakhs was not only a poet but composed several reputable works on Prosody and Rhyme, such as the *Gháyatu'l-'Arúḍayn*, *Kanzu'l-Qáfiya* and *Khujista*, often cited by Shams i-Qays in his *Mu'jam fí Ma'áyíri Ash'ári'l-'Ajam*[6]. His date is not exactly known, and the statements of the *Majma'u'l-Fuṣaḥá* (i, 173) tend rather to obscure than to elucidate it.

Zínatí, called 'Alawí "the descendant of 'Alí," was one of the court poets of Ghazna under Sulṭán Maḥmúd and his son Mas'úd, and is twice mentioned by Abu'l-Faḍl of Bayháq in his *Ta'ríkh-i-Mas'údí* (Ṭihrán ed., pp. 125 and 276) as receiving a handsome present for his verse.

[1] The only authority for this statement is the passage in 'Awfí's *Lubáb* cited in the next line, and, as Mírzá Muḥammad now thinks, it is not certain that it will bear so precise an interpretation.

[2] For the evidence for this see a note by Mírzá Muḥammad in my edition of Awfí's *Lubáb*, i, 297–8.

[3] There is a fine MS. of this *Tatimma*, or Supplement, in the Bibliothèque Nationale at Paris (**Fonds Arabe, 3308**). Unfortunately it still remains unpublished.

[4] He is, perhaps, identical with the *Ṭukhárí* (or native of Ṭukháristán) mentioned in the *Majma'u'l-Fuṣaḥá* as Khabbází's contemporary.

[5] The first eight verses are cited in the Persian notes, pp. 131–2. The whole *qaṣída* is given in 'Awfí's *Lubáb*, ii, 38–9.

[6] Vol. x of the "E. J. W. Gibb Memorial" Series.

The full name of **Buzurjmihr** of Qáyin was Amír Abú Manṣúr Qasím ibn Ibráhím, and he flourished during the same period as the above-mentioned Zínatí. Abú Manṣúr ath-Tha'álibí mentions him in the *Tatimma*[1], or Supplement to his *Yatímatu'd-Dahr*, as one of the bilingual poets, who wrote both in Arabic and Persian, and quotes some of his Arabic verses, including some very shrewd satires on a miser.

By **Muẓaffarí** is meant Muẓaffar of Panjdih (see 'Awfí's *Lubáb*, ii, 63–65). Dr Paul Horn in his edition of Asadí's *Lughat* has misread "Marwí" (of Merv) as "Hirawí" (of Herát), and has confused this poet with a later namesake who died in A.H. 728 (A.D. 1327–8).

The proper name of **Manshúrí** was Abú Sa'íd Aḥmad ibn Muḥammad of Samarqand (see 'Awfí's *Lubáb*, ii, 44–46). He is mentioned by Rashídu'd Dín Waṭwáṭ in the *Ḥadá'iqu's-Siḥr* as especially skilful in composing verses of the kind called *Mulawwan*, capable of being scanned in two or more metres.

Mas'údí was one of the court poets of Sulṭán Mas'úd of Ghazna, whose anger he incurred, as we learn from Bayhaqí's history[2], by some admonitory verses in which he (with a foresight justified by subsequent events) warned his sovereign against the growing power of the Saljúq Turks.

Qaṣárámí was one of the panegyrists of Sulṭán Abú Aḥmad Muḥammad ibn Maḥmúd of Ghazna. He is mentioned by Asadí in his *Lughat* (p. 27). His name remains unexplained, nor is it known to what this *nisba* refers.

Abú Ḥaníía-i-Iskáf[3] was one of the court poets of Sulṭán Ibráhím ibn Mas'úd of Ghazna (reigned A.H. 451–492 = A.D. 1059–1099), and is repeatedly so described, in terms of the warmest eulogy, by Abu'l-Faḍl-i-Bayhaqí (ed. Ṭihrán, pp. 276–281, 387–391 and 633–636). 'Awfí, therefore, can hardly be correct in including him amongst the poets of Sulṭán Sanjar the Saljúq (A.H. 511–552 = A.D. 1117–1157). The account of him given in the *Majma'u'l-Fuṣaḥá* is full of the most astonishing confusions and chronological errors, fully set forth by Mírzá Muḥammad at the conclusion of his long note (pp. 136–140 of the Persian text) on this poet.

Ráshidí is not mentioned by any of the biographers, but somewhat detailed references are made to him by his contemporary and rival Mas'úd-i-Sa'd-i-Salmán (see below) in two of his *qaṣídas* cited by Mírzá Muḥammad in the Persian notes (pp. 140–142).

Abu'l-Faraj-i-Rúní was a younger contemporary of the two poets above mentioned, for he survived into the reign of Sulṭán Ibráhím's son Mas'úd III (A.H. 492–508 = A.D. 1099–1114), so that the biographer Taqiyyu'd-Dín-i-Káshí is evidently mistaken in placing his death in

[1] See p. 115 *supra*, n. 3 *ad calc.* [2] Ṭihrán lithographed ed., p. 601.

[3] This is the form given here and in 'Awfí's *Lubáb* (ii, 175–6), but Abu'l-Faḍl Bayhaqí, his contemporary and friend, calls him "Iskáfí," which is probably the correct form. (*Ta'ríkh-i-Bayhaqí*, ed. Ṭihrán, pp. 276–281.) Iskáf, according to as-Sam'ání, is a suburb of Baghdád, but, on the face of it, it is not likely that our Iskáfí can have been directly connected with that city.

A.H. 489 (A.D. 1096). Rúna, from which he took his *nisba*, was a place near Lahore, not, as asserted in the *Ta'ríkh-i-Guzída*, in Kháwarán of Khurásán, nor, as the *Majma'u'l-Fuṣaḥá* states, near Nishápúr.

Mas'úd-i-Sa'd-i-Salmán.—On this poet Mírzá Muḥammad wrote a long critical notice, based on a careful study of his poems, which I translated into English and published in the *J.R.A.S.* for 1905 (pp. 693–740) and 1906 (pp. 11–51). The substance of this, which he has summarized in the Persian notes (pp. 142–150 and 178–182) to this text, is here given in a still more condensed form. The poet's family came originally from Hamadán in Persia, but he himself was born at Lahore, of which, in several passages in his poems, he speaks as his native place. Five Kings of the House of Ghazna were the objects of his panegyrics, to wit Ibráhím, Mas'úd III, Shírzád, Arslán and Bahrámsháh, whose reigns extended over a period of 96 lunar or 93 solar years (A.H. 451–547 = A.D. 1059–1152). His special patron was Sulṭán Ibráhím's son Maḥmúd, who was made governor of India in A.H. 469 (A.D. 1076–7), an event which the poet asserts to have been foreshadowed fifty years earlier by the great astronomer al-Bírúní in his *Tafhím*[1]. This is the earliest date explicitly mentioned by Mas'úd-i-Sa'd. He was probably born about A.H. 440 (A.D. 1048–9) and died about A.H. 515 (A.D. 1121–2). In A.H. 480 (A.D. 1087–8) he shared the suspicion and disgrace into which his master fell and was imprisoned in different fortresses for ten years. At the end of this period he was set free at the intercession of Abu'l-Qásim, one of Sulṭán Ibráhím's courtiers, and returned to his father's estate in India. In A.H. 492 (A.D. 1098–9) Sulṭán Ibráhím died and was succeeded by his son Mas'úd III, who conferred the government of India on his son Shírzád, with whom he sent Qiwámu'l-Mulk Abú Naṣr Hibatu'lláh of Párs as commander-in-chief and adviser. This man, being an old friend of the poet, made him governor of Jálandar, a dependency of Lahore; but soon afterwards fell into disfavour in which his clients were involved, and Mas'úd-i-Sa'd was again imprisoned in the fortress of Maranj for another period of eight or nine years. Finally, about A.H. 500 (A.D. 1106–7), he was released at the intercession of Thiqatu'l-Mulk Ṭáhir ibn 'Alí ibn Mushkán. Being now sixty years of age and worn out by his long confinements, he retired from public life and spent the remainder of his days in seclusion. Many contemporary poets, such as 'Uthmán Mukhtárí of Ghazna, Mu'izzí and Saná'í (who first collected and edited his poetry) bear witness to his pre-eminence in their art.

Jamálu'd-Dín **Muḥammad ibn Náṣir** al-'Alawí and his brother Sayyid Ḥasan ibn Náṣir of Ghazna were two well-known poets of the court of Bahrámsháh, as was also Shihábu'd-Dín **Sháh 'Alí Abú Rijá.** See 'Awfí's *Lubábu'l-Albáb*, vol. ii, pp. 267–282.

There is a faint probability that **Aḥmad-i-Khalaf** may have been the son of Khalaf ibn Aḥmad, the ruler of Sístán, a probability enhanced by the fact that the latter bore the *kunya* of Abú Aḥmad, although there is no other record of the existence of such a son.

[1] See the verses from this interesting poem cited on pp. 144–5 of the Persian notes, and note 1 at the foot of the latter.

'Uthmán ibn Muḥammad **Mukhtárí** of Ghazna died in A.H. 544 (A.D. 1149–1150) or A.H. 554 (A.D. 1159). He was the panegyrist of Arslán and his brother and successor Bahrámsháh of the House of Ghazna, whose reigns extended from A.H. 509–552 (A.D. 1115–1157); of Arslánsháh the Saljúq of Kirmán (A.H. 494–536 = A.D. 1100–1141); and of Arslán Khán Muḥammad of the Turkish Kháníyya dynasty of Transoxiana (A.H. 495–524 = A.D. 1101–1130). Mírzá Muḥammad (p. 151 of the Persian notes) calls attention to some extraordinary chronological errors in the notice of this poet in the *Majma'u'l-Fuṣaḥá*, and some arbitrary alterations of the text of certain poems into which these errors have misled the author.

Abu'l-Majd **Majdúd** ibn Ádam **as-Saná'í** of Ghazna, the well-known mystical poet, author of the *Ḥadíqatu'l-Ḥaqíqa* and an extensive *Díwán*, died, according to the most correct statement, in A.H. 545 (A.D. 1150–1). The date given by Jámí in his *Nafaḥátu'l-Uns* (p. 697), *viz.* A.H. 525 (A.D. 1131), is certainly much too early, since Saná'í composed verses on the death of Mu'izzí, which took place in A.H. 542 (A.D. 1147–8).

Najíbí of Farghána (of whom further mention is made in Anecdote XIX) was one of the court poets of Khiḍr Khán ibn Ṭafgháj Khán (of the Kháníyya dynasty of Transoxiana) who succeeded to the throne in A.H. 472 (A.D. 1079–1080) and died after a brief reign. **'Am'aq of Bukhárá**, poet-laureate of the same king, died, according to Taqiyyu'd-Dín of Káshán, in A.H. 543 (A.D. 1148–9). Abú Muḥammad 'Abdu'lláh (or 'Abdu's-Sayyid) **Rashídí of Samarqand, Najjár-i-Ságharjí** (from Ságharj, a village of Sughd), **'Alí Pánídhí** and **Pisar-i-Darghúsh** were poets attached to the same court, of whom little or nothing is known.

Abu'l-Maḥámid Maḥmúd ibn 'Umar **al-Jawharí** (the Jeweller) aṣ-Ṣá'igh (the Goldsmith) of Herát was contemporary with Farrukh-zád, Sulṭán of Ghazna (A.H. 444–451; A.D. 1052–9). A notice of him is given in 'Awfí's *Lubáb* (ii, 110–117).

The Dihqán **'Alí Shaṭranjí** of Samarqand, another poet of Transoxiana, is said by the *Majma'u'l-Fuṣaḥá* to have been a pupil of the celebrated satirist Súzaní, who died, according to Taqiyyu'd-Dín of Káshán, in A.H. 569 (A.D. 1173–4).

Manṣúr ibn 'Alí **al-Manṭiqí** of Ray, whose verses are repeatedly cited in evidence by Rashídu'd-Dín Waṭwáṭ in his *Ḥadá'iqu's-Siḥr*, was one of the poets attached to the Ṣáḥib Isma'íl ibn 'Abbáḍ (*Lubáb*, ii, 16–18).

Abú Zayd Muḥammad ibn 'Alí **al-Ghaḍá'irí** of Ray was a contemporary of 'Unṣurí and his circle, and died, according to the *Majma'u'l-Fuṣaḥá*, in A.H. 426 (A.D. 1034–5). His *nisba*, Ghaḍá'irí, is explained[1] as meaning "potter," "tile-maker," *ghaḍá'ir* being the plural of *ghaḍára*, a kind of sticky, greenish clay used for making pottery. The form Ghaḍá'irí (not Ghaḍárí, as the *Majma'u'l-Fuṣaḥá* has it) is proved cor-

[1] See the *Ansáb* of as-Sam'ání (Gibb Series, vol. xx), f. 409b.

rect by verses of the poet himself and of his contemporary 'Unṣurí (see Persian notes, p. 153). Minúchihrí, it is true, uses the form Ghaḍárí, but apparently only from the requirements of his metre.

Bundár of Ray, chiefly notable for his *Fahlawiyyát*, or verses in dialect[1], was a contemporary of the Ṣáḥib Isma'íl ibn 'Abbád and of Majdu'd-Dawla-i-Daylamí, and therefore flourished between A.H. 387 and 420 (A.D. 997 and 1029).

Though all the MSS. have **Farrukhí of Gurgán** it seems probable that it should be **Fakhrí**, *i.e.* Fakhru'd-Dín As'ad of Gurgán, author of the well-known romantic poem on the loves of Wís and Rámín. The only well-known Farrukhí, to whom Anecdote XV is devoted, was from Sístán.

Abu'l-Ḥasan Muḥammad ibn Isma'íl **al-Lámi'í** al-Jurjání **ad-Dihistání** was one of the poets of Malikshá̄h the Saljúq and his celebrated Minister Niẓámu'l-Mulk, and was the contemporary of Burhání, the father of Mu'izzí.

"Bábá" **Ja'far of Hamadán** was a friend of Bábá Ṭáhir, and contemporary with Sulṭán Ṭughril the Saljúq. See vol. ii of my *Lit. Hist. of Persia*, p. 260.

The only other mention of **Dur-Fírúz-i-Fakhrí** at present noticed occurs in al-Máfarrúkhí's "Beauties of Iṣfahán," composed in the fifth century of the *hijrá* (eleventh of the Christian era), where he is described as contemporary and is given the *kunya* of Abu'l-Faḍl.

'Abdu'l-Malik **Burhání** of Níshápúr, entitled *Amíru'sh-Shu'ará*, who died at Qazwín early in the reign of Malikshá̄h, was the father of the more celebrated **Mu'izzí**, whose early struggles are described in Anecdote XVI and who was accidentally shot by Sulṭán Sanjar in A.H. 542 (A.D. 1147–8).

The Dih-Khudá **Abu'l-Ma'álí of Ray** was the panegyrist of Mas'úd ibn Muḥammad ibn Malikshá̄h the Saljúq (reigned A.H. 527–547; A.D. 1133–1152), and died, according to the *Majma'u'l-Fuṣaḥá*, in A.H. 541 (A.D. 1146–7). See 'Awfí's *Lubáb*, ii, 228–236.

The Amír **'Amíd** Kamálu'd-Dín of Bukhárá, known as **Kamálí**, was skilled in music as well as poetry, and was one of the favourites of Sulṭán Sanjar. See 'Awfí's *Lubáb*, i, 86–91.

By **Shihábí** Shihábu'd-Dín Aḥmad ibnu'l-Mu'ayyad an-Nasafí as-Samarqandí appears to be meant. The *Majma'u'l-Fuṣaḥá* quotes several of his *qaṣídas* in praise of Ruknu'd-Dín Qilij Ṭamghá̄j Khán Mas'úd, of the Kháni̇yya dynasty, who reigned from A.H. 488–494 (A.D. 1095–1101)

Abu'l-Qásim Ziyád ibn Muḥammad **al-Qamarí al-Jurjání** was a contemporary of Shamsu'l-Ma'álí Qábús ibn Washmgír, who was killed in A.H. 403 (A.D. 1012–1013). See 'Awfí's *Lubáb*, ii, 19–20.

[1] See my edition of Dawlatshá̄h, pp. 42–3; *Majálisu'l-Mú'minín* (Ṭihrán lith. ed., A.H. 1268); *Ta'ríkh-i-Guzída* (Gibb Series, xiv, 1), p. 816; and the *Mu'jam* of Shams-i-Qays (Gibb Series, x), pp. 145 and 146.

The only other mention of **Ráfi'í of Níshápúr** occurs in the *Majma'u'l-Fuṣahá*, from which it appears that he was a contemporary of Sulṭán Maḥmúd of Ghazna (A.H. 388–421 ; A.D. 998–1030).

XV. The Vengeance of Sulṭán 'Alá'u'd-Dín Ḥusayn Jahán-súz.

(Text, p. 29 ; Persian notes, pp. 156–9.)

By "those two Kings, the Prince-martyr and the Laudable Monarch" are meant Quṭbu'd-Dín Muḥammad ibn 'Izzu'd-Dín Ḥusayn *Maliku'l-Jibál* and his brother Sayfu'd-Dín Súrí, the brothers of Sulṭán 'Alá'u'd-Dín Ḥusayn. Quṭbu'd-Dín, whose capital was Fírúz-kúh, had quarrelled with his brothers and gone to Ghazna, where Bahrámsháh at first treated him as an honoured guest, but subsequently, his suspicion being aroused by intriguers, poisoned him. Sayfu'd-Dín on hearing this marched on Ghazna with a large army. Bahrámsháh fled to India, and Sayfu'd-Dín occupied the city, took possession of the throne, and soon disbanded a great part of his army. On the approach of winter, when the roads to Ghúr were blocked with snow and the arrival of reinforcements was impossible, Bahrámsháh, at the instigation of his subjects, suddenly returned to Ghazna, took captive Sayfu'd-Dín and his followers, and put them to death in the year A.H. 544 (A.D 1149–1150).

Sulṭán 'Alá'u'd-Dín Ḥusayn, furious at the loss of a second brother, sent a threatening quatrain[1] to the Chief Judge of Ghazna, and, assembling a large army from Ghúr and Gharjistán, marched on Ghazna and proceeded to make good his threats. Having thrice defeated Bahrámsháh and compelled him again to retire to India, he occupied Ghazna, and for seven days and nights gave it up to slaughter, pillage and destruction. He killed the men, took captive the women and children, and caused the bodies of all the Kings of Ghazna, except those of Sulṭán Maḥmúd, Mas'úd and Ibráhím, to be exhumed and burned. During the seven days of massacre and pillage he was drinking and making merry in the Royal Palace of Ghazna, and at the end of this period, when he put a stop to the slaughter, he ordered his minstrels to sing some rather fine and spirited verses which he had composed for the occasion[2]. After spending another week in mourning for his brothers, he returned to Ghúr with their effects, destroying on his way all the fine buildings erected by Sulṭán Maḥmúd of Ghazna. On reaching Fírúz-kúh he composed another fine but arrogant piece of poetry[3] which he bade his minstrels sing. These events took place in A.H. 545 (A.D. 1150–1), the year of his accession to the throne, or in the following year. Two or three years later, in A.H. 547 (A.D. 1152–3), he was himself defeated and taken prisoner at Awba near Herát, by Sulṭán Sanjar the Saljúq, together with our author, who refers to this event in Anecdote XXXI.

The chief authority for the history of the Kings of Ghúr is the *Ṭabaqát-i-Náṣirí* of the Qáḍí Minháju'd-Dín 'Uthmán ibn Siráju'd-Dín Muḥammad, who was their contemporary (born 589/1193 and survived the year 658/1260). This valuable history has been published in the *Bibliotheca Indica* Series, but the late Major H. G. Raverty's English

[1] Persian notes, p. 157, ll. 7–8.
[2] *Ibid.*, p. 157, l. 18—p. 158, l. 5.
[3] *Ibid.*, p. 158, l. 11—p. 159, l. 2.

translation (2 vols. containing lxiv+1296+xxvi+272 pp., London, 1881) is even more valuable, being based on a careful and extensive collation of fresh MSS., and furnished with numerous notes, critical, historical and geographical. The first six of the twenty-three sections comprised in the work are only given in brief epitome, but this is of little consequence, as they deal with matters which can be better studied in older Arabic histories.

XVI. Notes on Anecdote XIII.

(Text, pp. 31–4; Persian notes, p. 160.)

This anecdote about Rúdakí and his improvisation is very well known and occurs in nearly all the biographies of poets, but nowhere so fully as here. A very interesting point, to which I have elsewhere called attention[1], is the wide divergence of opinion as to the merit of the verses existing between the author of this work and Dawlatsháh, who lived some three centuries later, indicating a complete change in the canons of taste during this period, and, it must be admitted, a change for the worse. The late Dr Hermann Ethé's monograph, published in the *Göttinger Nachrichten* for 1873 (pp. 663–742), remains the best and fullest account of Rúdakí, concerning whom some further particulars have already been given (pp. 113–114 *supra*).

The true explanation of the name of the stream *Jú-yi-Múliyán* has been discovered by Mírzá Muḥammad in Narshakhí's *History of Bukhárá*. This work, originally composed in Arabic in A.H. 332 (A.D. 943–4), was translated into Persian first by Abú Naṣr-i-Qabáwí in A.H. 522 (A.D. 1128), and again by Muḥammad ibn Zufar in A.H. 574 (A.D. 1178–9). It is this second translation which was published at Paris in 1892 by the late M. Charles Schefer, and from which the information in question is derived. In a section entitled "Account of the Jú-yi-Múliyán and its qualities" the author writes as follows[2]:

"In old times these estates of the Jú-yi-Múliyán belonged to King Ṭughsháda, who gave a portion of them to each one of his sons and sons-in-law. Amír Isma'íl the Sámání (may God have mercy upon him!) bought these estates from Ḥasan ibn Muḥammad ibn Ṭálút, who was a captain of [the Caliph] al-Musta'ín ibnu'l-Mu'taṣim, and made palaces and gardens in the Jú-yi-Múliyán, most of which he conferred on the *Mawálís*[3], and which are still endowments. His heart was always preoccupied about his *Mawálís* (clients), until one day he was gazing from the fortifications of Bukhárá towards the Jú yi-Múliyán. His father's client, Símá'u'l-Kabír, whom he greatly loved and held in high honour, was standing before him. Amír Isma'íl said, 'Will it ever be that God Most High will bring it to pass that I may buy these estates for you, and grant me life to see these estates yours, for they are of greater value than all the other estates of Bukhárá, and pleasanter and of better climate?' And God Most High vouchsafed to him to buy them all and give them to his *Mawálís*, so that the place was named *Jú-yi-Mawáliyán*, which was commonly called *Jú-yi-Múliyán*."

[1] *Lit. Hist. of Persia*, vol. i, pp. 16–17. See also my article on *The Sources of Dawlatsháh, etc.*, in the *J.R.A.S.* for January, 1899 (pp. 37–69).

[2] The original passage is quoted on p. ١٦٠ of the Persian notes.

[3] *Mawálí* being itself the plural of *Mawlá* (a client), *Mawáliyán*, a Persian plural of an Arabic plural, appears to be a solecism.

XVII. Note on Anecdote XIV.

(Text, pp. 34–6; Persian notes, 161–2.)

'Alí ibn Qaríb, known as "the Great Chamberlain" (*Hájib-i-Buzurg*) was one of the principal nobles of Sulṭán Maḥmúd of Ghazna. On the death of this monarch, he raised his younger son the Amír Abú Aḥmad Muḥammad to the throne. A quarrel shortly arose between him and his brother Sulṭán Mas'úd, who was then at Iṣfahán. The latter marched on Ghazna, and when he reached Herát 'Alí ibn Qaríb deposed Abú Aḥmad Muḥammad and imprisoned him in the Castle of Kúhshír near Ghazna. On Dhu'l-Qa'da 3, A.H. 421 (Nov. 2, 1030) he waited at Herát on Sulṭán Mas'úd, who, however, seized him and his brother the Chamberlain Mankítarák and cast them both into prison, after which they were no more heard of.

XVIII. Note on the House of Muḥtáj of Chagháníyán.

(Text, p. 36; Persian notes, pp. 163–6.)

The noble and influential House of Muḥtáj, which had its home at Chagháníyán in Transoxiana, produced many notable men during the Sámání and Ghaznawí periods. Concerning some of the most famous of these Mírzá Muḥammad has collected from various sources the following particulars.

(1) Abú Bakr Muḥammad ibnu'l-Muẓaffar ibn Muḥtáj was given the chief command of the armies of Khurásán by the Amír Naṣr II ibn Aḥmad the Sámání in A.H. 321 (A.D. 933), which position he held until the latter part of his life, when, being attacked by a chronic illness, he resigned in favour of his son Abú 'Alí Aḥmad, died in A.H. 329 (A.D. 941), and was buried at Chagháníyán.

(2) This son, Abú 'Alí Aḥmad, defeated and killed Mákán ib Kákúy the Daylamí in A.H. 329 (A.D. 941), and it was on this occasion that the celebrated despatch of his secretary Abu'l-Qásim Iskáfí (alluded to in Anecdote III, pp. 16–18 *supra*) was penned. He extended the Sámánid authority over Jurján, Ṭabaristán, Zanján, and Kirmánsháh. In A.H. 333 (A.D. 944–5) the Amír Núḥ I ibn Naṣr II ibn Aḥmad dismissed him from the Government of Khurásán, whereupon he rebelled, deposed the Amír (who fled to Samarqand), overran Khurásán, and captured Bukhárá. Finally in A.H. 344 (A.D. 955–6) he fell a victim to the plague at Ray and was buried with his father at Chagháníyán.

(3) Abu'l-'Abbás Faḍl ibn Muḥammad, brother of the above, who appointed him in A.H. 333 (A.D. 944–5) Governor of the Jabal province (modern 'Iráq-i-'Ajam). He subdued Dínawar and Niháwand. When his brother rebelled against the Sámánids, as above mentioned, he supported them, in spite of which he incurred their suspicion in A.H. 336 (A.D. 947–8) and was imprisoned at Bukhárá, after which all future trace of him disappears.

(4) Abu'l-Muẓaffar 'Abdu'lláh ibn Aḥmad, son of No. 2, who, in A.H. 337 (A.D. 948–9), when his father made peace with Amír Núḥ I the Sámánid, was sent as a hostage to Bukhárá, where he dwelt as an honoured guest until he was killed by a fall from his horse in A.H. 340 (951–2), and was buried at Chagháníyán.

(5) Abú Manṣúr ibn Aḥmad, another son of No. 2, who appointed him Governor of Chagháníyán in A.H. 340 (A.D. 951–2) when he himself was made Governor of Khurásán.

(6) Abu'l-Muẓaffar Ṭáhir ibn Faḍl, nephew of No. 2 and son of No. 3, was Governor of Chagháníyán until his death in A.H. 377 (A.D. 987–8). He was himself a poet and a generous patron of poets, Manjík of Tirmidh being one of his *protégés*. See 'Awfí's *Lubáb*, i, pp. 27–29.

(7) Fakhru'd-Dawla Abu'l-Muẓaffar Aḥmad ibn Muḥammad, the person to whom reference is here made in the *Chahár Maqála*, is believed by Mírzá Muḥammad to have been a son or grandson of the above mentioned Abú 'Alí. Daqíqí preceded Farrukhí as his panegyrist, a fact to which the latter alludes in three verses not included in the portion of the *qaṣída* here quoted, but given on pp. 165–6 of the Persian notes.

Of Farrukhí's "admirable description of the poetic art" six verses, besides the one given in the text, are cited on p. 166 of the Persian notes. The editor's learned demonstration of the identity of *Khuttal* and *Khatlán*, of which place the former is the Arabic and the latter the Persian name, is mentioned in note 2 at the foot of p. 44 *supra*. The details of the proof must be sought in the Persian notes, pp. 166–8.

XIX. Note on Ṭughánsháh, and the arbitrary methods of some Persian editors.

(Text, p. 43; Persian notes, pp. 170–3.)

As pointed out in note 1 at the foot of p. 48 *supra*, this Ṭughánsháh the son of Alp Arslán the Saljúq is a totally different person from the Ṭughánsháh ibn Mu'ayyad Áy-Ába with whom the author of the *Majma 'u'l-Fuṣaḥá* and others have rashly identified him, regardless of the fact that Azraqí (as shewn by three conclusive proofs on p. 173 of the Persian notes) must have been dead long before the latter ascended the throne in A.H. 569 (A.D. 1173–4). The curious thing about the first Ṭughánsháh (the Saljúq, to whom reference is here made) is that he is not mentioned by any of the historians of this period[1] except our author Niẓámí of Samarqand in this passage and in 'Awfí's *Lubáb* (ii, 87–8), and nearly all that we know about him is derived from Azraqí's poems in his honour. The author of the *Majma'u'l-Fuṣaḥá*, starting from the misconception to which allusion has been made, has deliberately and arbitrarily falsified the text of Azraqí's poems to make it support his erroneous theory, and has changed (vol. i, p. 145) "Ṭughánshah ibn Muḥammad" into "Ṭughánshah ibn Mu'ayyad." On these reprehensible methods Mírzá Muḥammad justly remarks (pp. 172–3 of the Persian notes *ad calc.*):—

"Such arbitrary emendations are not only an encouragement to ignorance, but a betrayal of the trust committed to us by men of yore. For it is evident that their books, compositions, writings and harangues are a precious heritage which our forefathers have bequeathed to us

[1] Dawlatsháh, Ḥájji Khalífa and the *Haft Iqlím* do, indeed, speak of an older Ṭughánsháh praised by Azraqí, but all the statements they make about him are incorrect. See the Persian notes, p. ۱۷۳, second paragraph.

in trust, and which we in turn should transmit to our descendants untampered with and unaltered. For should it once be allowed that from the time of Firdawsí until now, a period of nearly a thousand years, everyone should emend the verses of the *Sháh-náma* in accordance with his own whims and fancies, no trace or sign would now remain of this Royal Treasure, this Mine of Jewels and Coral, which constitutes the greatest literary glory of Persia, and is the guarantee of the perpetuation of our national tongue.

"I actually heard a certain Persian scholar in Paris say: 'My late father, besides having no rival in all sciences and accomplishments, possessed a special talent wherein no one could equal him. This was that any manuscript work of an ancient writer, from the beginning, end or middle of which some leaves had been lost, used to be given to my father, who, in the course of one or two nights, would supply the missing portion with a composition of his own in the same style and cast as the rest of the book, and would add it to the original; and it so closely resembled the other chapters and sections of the book that no scholar or savant could decide whether these leaves formed part of the original book or were an addition to it.'

"May God guide us into the Way of Rectitude!"

Note XX. Azraqí (Anecdote XVII).

(Text, p. 43; Persian notes, pp. 174–178.)

Abú Bakr Zaynu'd-Dín ibn Isma'íl al-Warráq ("the book-seller") of Herát, poetically surnamed Azraqí, would appear from a verse in one of his poems (p. 174 of the Persian notes) to have borne the proper name of Ja'far. His father Isma'íl was the contemporary of Firdawsí, who, when he fled from Sulṭán Maḥmúd's wrath, was for six months in hiding in his house at Herát.

Most of Azraqí's panegyrics are in praise of two Saljúq princes, Ṭughánsháh ibn Alp Arslán, mentioned in the last note, and Amíránsháh ibn Qáwurd. This Qáwurd was the first of the Saljúq rulers of Kirmán, but, as his son Amíránsháh did not ascend the throne, the date of his death is not recorded, though he predeceased his brother Sulṭánsháh, who died A.H. 476 (A.D. 1083–4).

Taqiyyu'd-Dín of Káshán gives A.H. 527 (A.D. 1132–3) as the date of Azraqí's death, which, however, must have taken place at least forty years earlier. For in the first place 'Awfí says that "he was antecedent to Mu'izzí," and secondly he makes no mention in his poems of Maliksháh or Sanjar or their nobles and ministers, which omission would be almost inconceivable if he lived in their time. Thirdly, Azraqí's father was the contemporary of Firdawsí, who died sometime before A.H. 421 (A.D. 1030), and it is evidently extremely improbable that he could have had a son who was still living a century later. It is probable that Azraqí died before A.H. 465 (A.D. 1072–3).

Rashídu'd-Dín Waṭwáṭ in his *Ḥadá'iqu's-Siḥr* ("Gardens of Magic") criticizes Azraqí for his far-fetched and fantastic comparisons, and especially comparisons to non-existent things, so that, for example, he compares burning charcoal to a sea of musk with golden waves.

Ḥájji Khalífa and many of the biographers ascribe to Azraqí th *Sindibád-náma* and the *Alfiyya wa Shalfiyya*. This is an error, for th former of these two books was of Persian or Indian origin, and wa composed in pre-Islamic days, as clearly appears from the statement of Mas'údí in the *Murúju'dh-Dhabab*[1] and of the *Fihrist*[2]. Of thi *Sindibád-náma* the Pahlawí text was extant in the time of the Amí Núḥ II ibn Manṣúr the Sámánid (A.H. 366–387; A.D. 976–997), b whose command it was translated into Persian by Khwája 'Amíd Abu'l Fawáris-i-Qanáwazí, whose translation, however, appears to be entirel lost. This translation was, however, revised and re-edited in a mor ornate form about A.H. 600 (A.D. 1203–4) by Bahá'u'd-Dín Muḥammad.. aẓ-Ẓahírí of Samarqand, who was secretary to Sulṭán Ṭamgháj Khán o the Khániyya dynasty of Transoxiana. Of this recension one manuscrip exists in the British Museum, from the preface of which Mírzá Muḥamma derived the information here given. It was apparently the older Persia prose translation of Qanáwazí which Azraqí versified or intended t versify; a task which he evidently found far from easy, for in a passag of a *qaṣída* addressed to Ṭughánsháh (quoted on p. 177 of the Persia notes) he says:—

> "*O Prince, whoever regards the counsels of Sindibád*
> *Knows well that to compose poetry thereon is difficult:*
> *I will render its ideas a help to learning*
> *If thy fortune, O King, helps my mind.*"

This versified translation of Azraqí, if ever completed, seems to hav been entirely lost, though a later anonymous verse translation compose in A.H. 776 (A.D. 1374–5) is preserved in the India Office Library[3] This, however, in Mírzá Muḥammad's opinion, is of very poor literar quality.

The *Alfiyya wa Shalfiyya* is another ancient book which existe long before Azraqí's time. The *Fihrist* mentions two recensions, greater and a lesser; and the *Ta'ríkh-i-Bayhaqí*[4] mentions a summer house which Prince Mas'úd had built for himself secretly in th Bágh-i-'Adnání on the walls of which were painted the pictures illustra tive of the *Alfiyya*. This book may have been versified or re-edited b Azraqí, but was certainly not his original work.

Note XXI. Another instance of the Author's inaccuracy.

(Text, p. 45; Persian notes, pp. 182–4.)

It is an extraordinary and inexplicable thing that Niẓámí of Samar qand, in recounting what professes to be a personal reminiscence, shoul commit several grave historical and chronological errors. *First*, the rea name and genealogy of Qutulmush were Shihábu'd-Dawla [not -Dín] ib Isrá'íl ibn Saljúq, and he was first cousin to Ṭughril, the first of th Great Saljúqs, and father of Sulaymán, the first of the Saljúqs of Rúm In A.H. 456 (A.D. 1064) he rebelled against Ṭughril's nephew Alp Arslán and was killed in battle near Ray. Sulṭán Muḥammad, the grandson o Alp Arslán, was born in A.H. 473 (A.D. 1080–1), seventeen years afte

[1] Ed. B. de Meynard, i, 162 and iv, 90.
[2] Ed. Flügel, pp. 304–5.
[3] See Dr H. Ethé's *Catalogue*, No. 1236.
[4] Ṭihrán ed., p. 116.

the death of Qutulmush, who therefore obviously could not have rebelled against him. *Secondly*, Qutulmush was not the son-in-law of Sulṭán Muḥammad, but the first cousin of his great-grandfather. *Thirdly*, the title of Qutulmush was Shihábu'd-Dawla, not Shihábu'd-Dín. *Fourthly*, he did not bear the name Alp Ghází. *Fifthly*, the battle in which he was killed was near Ray, not Hamadán; and *sixthly*, it took place nearly a century before Niẓámí of Samarqand wrote the *Chahár Maqála*.

We are driven to suppose that in this passage the original text has been tampered with. The real Alp Ghází was the nephew of Sulṭán Ghiyáthu'd-Dín Muḥammad of Ghúr, and fell in battle with Sulṭán Muḥammad Khwárazmsháh near Herát in A.H. 600 (A.D. 1203–4), fifty years after the *Chahár Maqála* was written. There were two kings called Ghiyáthu'd-Dín Muḥammad, the one of Ghúr, mentioned immediately above, who died in A.H. 599 (A.D. 1202–3) and was actually related to the real Alp Ghází; and the other the grandson of Alp Arslán the Saljúq, to whom this anecdote refers, and who died in A.H. 511 (A.D. 1117–8).

Note XXII. The Kháqání, Khání or Afrásiyábí Kings.

(Text, p. 46; Persian notes, pp. 184–189.)

This Turkish Muslim dynasty, also called Ílak-Khání, ruled for nearly 230 years (A.H. 380–609 = A.D. 990–1212) over Transoxiana, supplanting the Sámánid and succumbing to the Khwárazmsháhí power. They were sometimes practically independent, while at other times they paid tribute to the Saljúqs, Qará-Khitá'ís or Khwárazmsháhs. Their history is confused and obscure, nor is it precisely known when their power arose or when they embraced Islám. Hárún ibn Sulaymán, better known as Bughrá Khán Ílak, and entitled Shihábu'd-Dawla, conquered Bukhárá in A.H. 383 (A.D. 993), and is the first of the dynasty mentioned in history. His lieutenant Shamsu'd-Dawla Naṣr ibn 'Alí ibn Músá ibn Sutuq, better known as Ílak Khán, again subdued Bukhárá in A.H. 389 (A.D. 999) and finally extinguished the Sámánid power in Transoxiana. The last of the line was Nuṣratu'd-Dín Qilij Arslán Kháqán 'Uthmán ibn Qilij Ṭamgháj Khán Ibráhím, who was killed in A.H. 609 (A.D. 1212–3) by Sulṭán 'Alá'u'd-Dín Muḥammad Khwárazmsháh.

The first historian of this dynasty appears to have been the Imám Sharafu'z-Zamán Majdu'd-Dín Muḥammad ibn 'Adnán as-Surkhakatí, uncle of Núru'd-Dín Muḥammad 'Awfí, the author of the often-quoted *Lubábu'l-Albáb* and of the vast collection of anecdotes entitled *Jawámi'u'l-Ḥikáyát wa Lawámi'u'r-Riwáyát*. This history, dedicated to Sulṭán Qilij Ṭamgháj Khán, the last ruler but one of the dynasty, is mentioned by Ḥájji Khalífa, and 'Awfí quotes from it in the seventeenth chapter of the fourth part of his *Jawámi'u'l-Ḥikáyát*, composed about A.H. 630 (A.D. 1232–3). Except for this quotation (of which the text is cited on pp. 185–6 of the Persian notes) this work appears to be entirely lost. The chief extant sources of information about them are as follows:—

(1) Scattered references in such Arabic general histories as Ibnu'l-Athír and Ibn Khaldún.

(2) The *Ta'ríkh-i-Jahán-árá* of the Qáḍí Aḥmad-i-Ghaffárí has a short chapter on this dynasty[1], which, though it adds little to the particulars given by the above-mentioned historians, has the advantage of gathering the details under one head and giving them a connected arrangement.

(3) A rare general history in Persian, of unknown authorship, entitled *Majma'u't-Tawáríkh*[2], contains a chapter of seven large pages on this dynasty, here called "the House of Afrásiyáb."

(4) A long note by Major H. G. Raverty on pp. 900–911 of his English translation of the *Ṭabaqát-i-Náṣirí* (vol. ii, London, 1881).

(5) An article by Sir Henry Howorth on the *Afrásiyábí Turks* in the *J.R.A.S.* for 1898, pp. 467–502. For this excellent article he obtained new materials from a Turkí MS from Eastern Turkistán entitled *Tadhkira-i-Bughrá Khán*.

(6) Scattered references in such special histories as 'Utbí's *Ta'ríkh-i-Yamíní*, the *Ta'ríkh-i-Bayhaqí*, Narshakhí's *Ta'ríkh-i-Bukhárá*, 'Imádu'd-Dín's and Abú Bakr ar-Ráwandí's histories of the Saljúqs, the *Ta'ríkh-i-Jahángusháy* of Juwayní, 'Awfí's *Lubábu'l-Albáb* and *Jawámi'u'l-Ḥikáyát*, the *Ṭabaqát-i-Náṣirí*, and this book, *etc.*, the history of this dynasty being intermixed to some extent with that of the Ghaznawís, Saljúqs and Khwárazmsháhs.

(7) The verses of certain contemporary poets who were their panegyrists, such as Rashídí and Súzaní of Samarqand, Mukhtárí of Ghazna, Raḍiyyu'd-Dín of Níshápúr, 'Am'aq of Bukhárá, Shams-i-Ṭabasí, *etc.*

In none of these books, however, except 'Awfí's *Lubáb*, is mention made of Qilij Ṭamghái Khán Ibráhím, the last ruler but one of the dynasty. He was a great patron of poetry and learning. Raḍiyyu'd-Dín, the poet just mentioned, has especially celebrated his generosity to men of letters, and several notable prose works were dedicated to him, amongst others the *Sindibád-náma*[3] and the *A'ráḍu'r-Riyásat fí Aghraḍi's-Siyásat*[4] of Bahá'u'd-Dín aẓ-Ẓahírí of Samarqand, and another work by the same author entitled *Sam'u'ẓ-Ẓahír fí Jam'i'ẓ-Ẓahír*[5].

Note XXIII. Five notable Astronomers.

(Text, pp. 54–5; Persian notes, pp. 193–206.)

Abú Rayḥán Muḥammad ibn Aḥmad al-Bírúní (or *Bêrúní* or *Bayrúní*[6]) was born in a suburb or outer district (*bírún*) of Khwárazm

[1] Or. 141 of the British Museum, ff. 132a–134b.
[2] Suppl. Persan 1331 in the Bibl. Nationale of Paris, ff. 132b–136a.
[3] See p. 125 *supra*.
[4] See Ḥájji Khalífa, *s.v.*, and 'Awfí's *Lubáb*, i, 91. There is a MS. of the work in the Leyden Library.
[5] See *Ḥ. Kh.*, *s.v.*, and the *Lubáb*, i, 91.
[6] Sachau quotes the *Ansáb* of as-Sam'ání in favour of this latter pronunciation, but in the *facsimile* of this work published by the "E. J. W. Gibb Memorial" (vol. xx, f. 98b) the passage in question has *bi'l-kasri* (with the *i* vowel) instead of *bi'l-fatḥi* (with the *a* vowel).

(Khiva)[1] on Dhu'l-Ḥijja 3, A.H. 362 (Sept. 4, A.D. 973), and died (probably at Ghazna) on Rajab 2, A.H. 440 (Dec. 11, A.D. 1048) at the age of 77 lunar years and 7 months. He was one of the greatest men of science produced by Persia, and in him, as Dr Sachau says, "there is much of the modern spirit and method of critical research," in which respect "he is a phenomenon in the history of Eastern learning and literature" As a writer his industry equalled his learning. In A.H. 427 (A.D. 1035–6), when he had reached the age of 65 lunar (63 solar) years, he drew up for a correspondent a list of his writings, which has been fortunately preserved to us, and of which the original Arabic text is included by Sachau in the German Introduction to his edition of *al-Átháru'l-Báqiya* (pp. xxxviii–xlix). This list comprises over a hundred works, arranged in 13 classes as follows:—

I.	Geometry, Astronomy, *etc.* ...	18	works
II.	Geography	15	,,
III.	Arithmetic	8	,,
IV.	Light	4	,,
V.	The Astrolabe	5	,,
VI.	Times and Seasons	5	,,
VII.	Comets	5	,,
VIII.	Stations of the Moon	12	,,
IX.	Astrology	7	,,
X.	Persian and other tales ...	13	,,
XI.	Religion	6	,,
XII.	Books of which the author retained no copy	5	,,
XIII.	Unfinished books	10	,,
	Total:	113	

He also enumerates 25 other works written by three other men of learning and ascribed to him, *viz.* 12 by Abú Naṣr Manṣúr ibn 'Alí ibn 'Arráq; 12 by Abú Sahl 'Ísá ibn Yaḥyá al-Masíḥí; and one by Abú 'Alí al-Ḥasan ibn 'Alí al-Jílí. Further, Ḥájji Khalífa enumerates 15 more of al-Bírúní's works not appearing in the above list, though some of them are no doubt included in it under slightly different titles, while others are probably wrongly ascribed to our author. In Europe he is chiefly known by his "Chronology of Ancient Nations" (*al-Átháru'l-Báqiya 'ani'l-Qurúni'l-Kháliya*) and his work on India, editions and translations of both of which we owe to the learning and industry of Dr Edward Sachau. The former, unfortunately, presents many serious *lacunae*: "Many most essential parts," says Dr Sachau[2], "both large and small, are missing, *e.g.* the chapter on Zoroaster, a most deplorable loss, arising probably from Muslim bigotry." On Nov. 12, 1912, however, I received a letter from my colleague Professor Bevan in which he wrote:—"I have just received from Salemann in St Petersburg an article which he has

[1] Mírzá Muḥammad points out to me that the original capital city of Khwárazm was Káth on the eastern bank of the Oxus. Later (and probably already in al-Bírúní's time) its place was taken by Urgánj or Gurgánj (called in Arabic Jurjániyya) on the western bank. The modern city of Khiva is situated some distance to the south-west of the older Urgánj.

[2] Preface to the English translation, p. xiii.

published in the *Bulletin de l'Académie Impériale*. You will be glad to hear that another MS. of al-Bírúní's *al-Âthâru'l-Bâqiya* has turned up and enables us to supply most of the gaps in Sachau's edition, in particular the sections on Zoroaster and Bardaiṣán."

Al-Qifṭí has no article on al-Bírúní in his "History of the Philosophers," and only once refers to him. Ibn Abí Uṣaybi'a gives him a short notice in his "Lives of the Physicians" (ii, pp. 20–21). The short articles consecrated to him by Ẓahíru'd-Dín Abu'l-Ḥasan ibn Abu'l-Qásim (wrote about the middle of the twelfth century of our era) and by Shamsu'd-Dín Muḥammad ibn Maḥmúd ash-Shahrazúrí (early thirteenth century) are quoted in full by Sachau[1]. There is also a long notice of him in the modern Persian *Náma-i-Dánishwarán* (vol. i, pp. 37–49) composed in A.H. 1294 (A.D. 1877), which is of little authority and does not add much to our knowledge.

Abú Ma'shar Ja'far ibn Muḥammad ibn 'Umar al-Balkhí was one of the most celebrated astronomers of the third century of the *hijra* (ninth of the Christian era), and, according to al-Qifṭí[2], the greatest authority on the history of the ancient Persians. He dwelt in Baghdád, in the western part, and was originally a traditionist; and his fanaticism led him to insult and molest Ya'qúb ibn Isḥáq al-Kindí, the "Philosopher of the Arabs," and to stir up the common people against him. Finally al-Kindí induced some of his friends to draw his attention to, and arouse his interest in Mathematics and Geometry, so that he came to seek instruction from al-Kindí, and was reconciled with him. He soon passed on (at the age of forty-seven) to the study of Astronomy. On one occasion he was scourged by command of the Caliph al-Musta'ín (reigned A.H. 248–251; A.D. 862–5) because of a prognostication which he had made and which proved too correct. Thenceforth he used to say: "I guessed right and was punished." He died on Ramaḍán 28, A.H. 272 (March 8, A.D. 886). Al-Qifṭí enumerates 38 of his works, of which such as are still extant are enumerated by Brockelmann (i, 221–2).

Abú Sa'íd Aḥmad ibn Muḥammad ibn 'Abdu'l-Jalíl as-Sajzí was a notable mathematician and astronomer of the fourth century of the *hijra*. Amongst his numerous works is the *Jámi'-i-Sháhí*, or "Royal Compendium," containing 15 treatises on astronomical subjects; of which there is a fine MS. in the British Museum[3]. In the course of this work, written at Shíráz, where he apparently spent most of his life, he refers to the years A.H. 351 (A.D. 962) and A.H. 380 (A.D. 990). The Bibliothèque Nationale at Paris possesses a beautiful MS.[4], containing 41 mathematical and astronomical tracts, transcribed by him in Shíráz during the years A.H. 358–361 (A.D. 969–972). The colophons of such of these tracts as have them are given by Mírzá Muḥammad on pp. 200–201 of the Persian notes. Including the 15 tracts comprised in the *Jámi'-i-Sháhí*, 29 of his treatises are extant in European libraries[5], besides the *Ṣad Báb* mentioned in the text, and a dissertation on the Astrolabe.

[1] German Introduction to the text, pp. lii and liii.
[2] *Ta'ríkhu'l-Ḥukamá*, ed. Lippert, p. 152.
[3] See Rieu's *Arabic Suppl.*, pp. 528–530.
[4] Fonds Arabe 2457.
[5] See Brockelmann, i, 219.

Kiyá Abu'l-Ḥasan Kúshyár ibn Labbán ibn Bá-shahrí al-Jílání (of Gílán) was a notable astronomer who flourished in the latter part of the fourth century of the *hijra*. In his *Mujmalu'l-Uṣúl*[1] he alludes to the year 321 of Yazdijird (A.H. 342 = A.D. 953–4), and in another passage of the same work[2] to A.Y. 361 (A.H. 383 = A.D. 993–4), so that his active life appears to have lain between these two limits, and the date given by Ḥájji Khalífa (A.H. 459 = A.D. 1066–7) under *Zíj-i-Kushyár* is certainly too late. See also Brockelmann, i, 222–3.

Abú Yúsuf Ya'qúb ibn Isḥáq . . al-Kindí, entitled "the Philosopher of the Arabs," traced his descent from Ma'di-Karib, and belonged to an Arabian family equally notable for ancient and noble lineage and honourable achievements. How our author can have represented him as a Jew is incomprehensible. The story about him and Abú Ma'shar, however, derives some confirmation from the *Fihrist*[3]. He composed some 270 works on Logic, Philosophy, Geometry, Arithmetic, Music, Astrology and Medicine, of which about a score are extant in European libraries[4]. The date of his death is not known, but he flourished in the reigns of al-Ma'mún and al-Mutawakkil (A.H. 198–247; A.D. 813–861). It is not clear on what authority Dr Heinrich Suter[5] gives A.H. 260 (A.D. 873–4) as the date of his death. He was noted for his parsimony, and a good many pages are devoted to him in the "Book of Misers" (*Kitábu'l-Bukhalá*) of al-Jáḥiẓ[6]. A number of his sayings in praise of this unattractive quality are quoted on p. 206 of the Persian notes from Ibn Abí Uṣaybi'a's "Lives of the Physicians" (vol. i, pp. 208–9).

Note XXIV. Certain astrological terms.

(Text, pp. 56, 59 and 62; Persian notes, pp. 206–8.)

In these anecdotes about astrologers and their predictions there occur a few technical terms which can be properly understood only by those (few in these days) who have made Astrology the special object of their studies. Amongst such is Mr Ralph Shirley, editor of the *Occult Review*, who has most kindly supplied me with the valuable notes which I have placed after the explanations derived from Arabic and Persian works.

1. *Khaby* and *Ḍamír* (خَبْی و ضمیر).

The explanation of these terms, which I have translated by "divination and thought-reading," is given by Abú Rayḥán al-Bírúní in a passage of his *Tafhím*, quoted by Mírzá Muḥammad in the Persian notes (pp. 206–7), of which the translation is as follows:—

[1] Brit. Mus. MS. Add. 7490, f. 22[b].

[2] *Ibid.*, f. 4[a]. For a description of this fine MS. see Rieu's *Arabic Supplement*, pp. 513–9.

[3] Ed. Flügel, p. 277.

[4] See Flügel's *Al-Kindí genannt der Philosoph der Araber*, in the *Abhandlung f. die Kunde des Morgenlandes*, vol. i, part 2 (Leipzig, 1857); the long notice in al-Qiftí's *Ta'ríkhu'l-Ḥukamá*, pp. 366–378; and Brockelmann, i, 209–210.

[5] In his *Die Mathematiker und Astronomen der Araber und ihre Werke* (Leipzig, 1900).

[6] Cairo ed. of 1323/1905–6, pp. 64–76.

"Q. 'What are *khaby* and *ḍamír*?'

"A. '*Khaby* is that which is hidden in the fist; and *ḍamír* is that one should think of something and [that the operator should] find it out by questioning.'

"Herein are astrologers speedily put to shame, and their mistakes are more frequent than their successes."

2. *Sahmu's-Sa'ádat* and *Sahmu'l-Ghayb* (سهم السعادة و سهم الغيب).

A full explanation of these terms, which I have translated "Part of Fortune" and "Part of the Unseen," is given in vol. i of the *Dictionary of the Technical Terms used in the Sciences of the Musalmáns*[1], pp. 698–9. After defining the pronunciation and ordinary meaning ("arrow") of *sahm*, and its special sense in Geomancy and Geometry, the article proceeds:—

"With astronomers the term *sahm* means a definite portion of the zodiacal heaven. According to them, these 'Parts' (*sahm-há*) are many, *e.g.* the 'Part of Fortune' (or 'Happiness': *Sahmu's-Sa'ádat*), also called by them the 'Part of the Moon'; and the 'Part of the Unseen' (*Sahmu'l-Ghayb*), the 'Part of Days' (*Sahmu'l-Ayyám*), the 'Part of Men-servants and Maid-servants' (*Sahm-i Ghulámán wa Kanízakán*), and so forth. So by day they compute the 'Part of Happiness' from the Sun to the degree of the Moon, and add to it (that is to the degrees between the Sun and the Moon) the degree of the Ascendant. Then from the Ascendant's total they subtract thirty each [for the Sign of the Ascendant and the adjoining Sign], and what remains will be the degree of the position of the 'Part of Happiness.' And by night they compute from the degree of the Moon to the degree of the Sun, and add thereto the degree of the Ascendant.

"*Example.* Ascendant 10° in Aries; the Sun 20° in Leo; the Moon 15° in Libra, leaving 40° [from the position of the Sun in Leo] to [the beginning of] Libra. [To this] we add the 15° [already] traversed by the Moon [in Libra], which gives us 55°. To this we add the degree of the Ascendant, which gives us 65°. Of these we give 30° to Aries and 30° to Taurus, and the 5° remaining to Gemini. So the place of the 'Part of Happiness' will be the fifth degree of Gemini."

Pisces *Aries*
Aquarius *Taurus*
Capricorn *Gemini*
Sagittarius *Cancer*
Scorpio *Leo*
Libra *Virgo*

"As for the 'Part of the Unseen,' by day they compute it from the Moon and by night from the Sun, adding thereto the degree of the Ascendant, and subtracting thirty each from the Ascendant, as before; then what remains over is the place of the 'Part of the Unseen.'"

Then follow directions on similar lines for calculating the other 'Parts,' *viz.* the 'Part of Days' (*Sahmu'l-Ayyám*), the 'Part of Men-servants

[1] Published in the *Bibliotheca Indica*, Calcutta, 1862.

and Maid-servants,' the 'Part of Wealth and Friends' (*Sahm-i-Mál u Aṣdiqá*), the 'Marriage of Women' (*Tazwíj-i-Zanán*), and the 'Parts' of the Five Planets, Saturn, Jupiter, Mars, Mercury and Venus."

3. *Kad-khudá* and *Hayláj* (کدخدا و هیلاج).

These terms are applied in Astrology to two indications of the length of life of the child. According to Abú Rayḥán al-Bírúní[1], "the *Hayláj* is one of five things: *first*, the Master of the day- or night-shift (*Ṣáḥib-i-Nawbat-i-rúz yá shab*); *secondly*, the Moon by day and the Sun by night; *thirdly*, the Degree of the Ascendant; *fourthly*, the 'Part of Fortune'; *fifthly*, the House of the Conjunction or Opposition which shall have taken place before birth. One of these five things they call the *Hayláj* when it is conjoined with its own proper conditions described in books on Astrology, and the sum total they call *Haydlij* or *Haylájat*.

"The *Kad-khudá* ('Master of the House') is the star which dominates the place of the *Hayláj* in this sense, that it is the Lord of the Mansion wherein the *Hayláj* is actually situated, or the Lord of its exaltation (*Ṣáḥib-i-Sharaf*), or the Lord of some other of its Parts which stand in relation to that position.

"If the *Hayláj* be one which has no *Kad-khudá*, then they leave it out and seek another of the five *Hayálij* which has one; and if none of them has a *Kad-khudá*, then the quality of being a *Hayláj* belongs to the Degree of the Ascendant.

"*Example of the Hayláj and Kad-khudá.* If at the time of the birth of the child (by day) the Moon be in 19° of Aries, then the Moon will be one of the five *Hayálij* (subject to the concurrence of the other proper conditions which are set forth in books of Astrology). Then, in this hypothetical example, the *Kad-khudá* will be the Sun, for the Sun dominates the place of the *Hayláj*, that is to say is the Lord of its altitude, for the exaltation (*sharaf*) of the Sun is in 19° of Aries. And if, in this hypothetical example, the degree of the Ascendant is in 19° of Aries, this degree of the Ascendant will be the *Hayláj*, and again the Sun will be the *Kad-khudá*, and so on.

"So from the admixture and combination of the sum-total of the *Hayláj* and the *Kad-khudá*, they deduce (as they imagine) the duration of the child's life, its length or brevity, and its happiness or infelicity.

"The derivation of the word *Hayláj* is unknown[2]."

Mr Ralph Shirley's observations are contained in three letters, dated May 22, May 31 and October 25, 1920, the first addressed to Professor Margoliouth, to whom my enquiries were originally addressed, the others to myself, the last one after reading the proofs containing the anecdotes to which this note refers.

[1] These particulars were derived by Mírzá Muḥammad from the British Museum MS. of the *Tafhím*, Add. 7697, ff. 146ᵃ and 154ᵃ, and from Kushyár's *Mujmalu'l-Uṣúl*, Add. 7490, ff. 28-9.

[2] It is said to be from the Greek ὑλικός; see Sédillot's *Prolegomena*, p. ١٤٩ of the text. See also Schefer's *Chrestomathie Persane*, vol. i, p. 102 *ad calc.*

(*Extracts from first letter.*)

"The hyleg (*hayláj*) in astrology is the vital point, or 'giver of life.' This is considered to be either the sun, or the moon, or the ascendant. In order to be hyleg, the sun or moon must occupy either the 9th, 10th, or 11th houses, or else the ascendant or 7th house. If, *e.g.*, the sun occupies one of these positions and the moon does not, then the sun is hyleg or life-giver. If, on the other hand, they both occupy such a position, then the one that is most predominant or most elevated, would be hyleg, *i.e.*, if the sun occupied the 10th house and the moon the 11th, the sun would be hyleg, and *vice versa.* If neither sun nor moon occupy any of these positions, it is usual to take the ascending degree as hyleg, but some of the old astrologers would regard the dominant planet as hyleg under such circumstances. It must not be supposed from this that when the sun is hyleg the moon has therefore no influence on the constitution. The moon in any case has to do with the digestion and various matters of this kind, and the sun is in any case the ruler of the heart and therefore always important. The sun, however, might be violently afflicted though the health might not be seriously endangered, if it did not occupy the position of hyleg. The same would apply to the moon. I think, other things being equal, the moon is to be regarded as having more influence with a woman and the sun with a man. Alcohoden is merely another name for hyleg, but is not used nowadays.

"As regards the other words, I have never heard of them. I have however little doubt that the last, *sahmu's-sa'ádat*, is the Arabic term for the 'Part of Fortune.' Some old astrologers attached a good deal of importance to this, without, I imagine, much justification. The 'Part of Fortune' is that part of the horoscope where the moon would be if the sun were exactly rising. The 'Part of Fortune' was supposed to refer to the wealth and property of the 'native.' Ptolemy laid great stress on it, but the author of the Text-book of Astrology remarks that 'it must be rejected from a rational system of genethlialogy.'

"'Part of Mystery' (*sahmu'l-ghayb*) conveys no meaning, and I do not think anything can be found corresponding to this in the astrological books at present available. The only suggestion I can make is that it might conceivably be the opposite point in the horoscope to the 'Part of Fortune.' But this is pure conjecture and may be entirely on the wrong track. It looks as if the Arabs had some tradition here which does not find its place in any astrological books extant."

(*Extract from second letter.*)

"Thank you for yours of the 29th May. I think it might be a help if you sent me a copy of the book in question. I have, however, read so much on the subject of astrology that I question whether there is any likelihood of my being able to throw light on the 'Part of the Unseen.' I cannot think there is any reference to it in any known author on the subject. Astrologers of the present day look upon Neptune as the planet that gives psychic powers, and this is unquestionably correct. In the case of people who have clairvoyant gifts, *etc.*, or are mediumistic in temperament, one constantly finds Neptune and the Moon predominant in the horoscope. But it is of course impossible to suppose that the Arabian astrologers had any clue to the planet Neptune. The 'Part of Fortune' is merely the translation of the Latin *Pars Fortunae*. I cannot account for the origin of the idea, which seems quite fantastic....

"The Ascendant is the degree rising at birth; *i.e.*, at sunrise the sun would be on the ascendant. The 'Lord of the Ascendant' is the planet that rules the ascending sign of the Zodiac. The two most important positions in the horoscope are the ascendant and the mid-heaven, and any planets here are considered more powerful than any others. The Ascendant has special relation to the individual, and the mid-heaven to the fortune."

(*Extract from third letter.*)

"I am sorry to have kept your proofs so long, but I have been a good deal away from the office lately, and consequently my work has got into arrears.

"With regard to the 'Part of the Unseen,' this is evidently something kindred in nature to the 'Part of Fortune,' and as the Part of Fortune (*pars fortunae*) is always so called by astrologers, I think it would be well to use the expression 'Part' and not 'Share.' I have not yet discovered what the 'Part of the Unseen' actually is. It obviously cannot be the opposite position to that of the 'Part of Fortune,' as I see that in one instance cited in your proofs the two are in conjunction on the Ascendant."

Note XXV. 'Umar-i-Khayyám.

(Text, pp. 63–4, 65; Persian notes, pp. 209–228.)

Abu'l-Fatḥ 'Umar ibn Ibráhím al-Khayyámí, commonly called **'Umar** (or **'Omar**) **Khayyám,** is so much more celebrated in the West, especially in England and America, than in the East that Mírzá Muḥammad has, for the benefit of his own countrymen, for whom he is primarily writing, added a very long note on his biography, the sources of our information about him, and the history of the "Omar Khayyám Club" founded in London in his honour in 1892. The information contained in this note is mainly derived from Professor Valentin Zhukovski's masterly article on the "Wandering Quatrains" of 'Umar-i-Khayyám, which appeared in the *Festschrift* published in 1897 at St Petersburg in honour of the late Baron Victor Rosen, by eleven of his pupils, and entitled, in allusion to his Christian name, *al-Muẓaffariyya*. This article, written in Russian, was translated by Sir E. Denison Ross and published in the *J.R.A.S.* for 1898 (vol. xxx, pp. 349–366), and reproduced in its essentials by him in Methuen's edition of FitzGerald's *Quatrains*, and by me in vol. ii of my *Literary History of Persia*, pp. 246–9. It is therefore sufficient to summarize here the information which can be found in greater detail in those places.

Persian and Arabic Sources of Information arranged chronologically.

1. The Chahár Maqála.

This present work, the author of which was personally acquainted with 'Umar, and wrote only some thirty years after his death, contains the oldest account of him yet discovered.

2. The Kharídatu'l-Qaṣr.

(*Addition to Persian notes*, p. ٢٠٩)

This book, composed by 'Imádu'd-Dín al-Kátib al-Iṣfahání in 572/1176–7, contains a notice of 'Umar-i-Khayyám amongst the poets of Khurásán. Two MSS. of this work exist in the Leyden library (see Dozy's *Catalogue*, vol. ii, pp. 208–288), *viz.* **Warner 348**, f. 185,* and **Gol. 21b**, f. 238.

3. Kháqání.

A single reference to him occurs in a verse of the Persian poet Kháqání, who died about A.H. 595 (A.D. 1198–9).

4. The Mirṣádu'l-'Ibáḍ.

The *Mirṣádu'l-'Ibáḍ* of Shaykh Najmu'd-Dín Dáya, composed in A.H. 620 (A.D. 1223–4), contains a passage in which 'Umar is denounced as an atheist, and two of his quatrains are cited with disapproval. The text of this important passage is quoted by Mírzá Muḥammad (Persian notes, p. 211) from Zhukovski's article. I have collated this with a fine old *MS. of the *Mirṣád* transcribed in A.H. 768 (A.D. 1367), which presents the following variants, generally improvements.

211, 1, inserts کردد after معلوم; reads نورانی‌را for و روحانی‌را; inserts قالب after صورت; and reads خاك for خاکی. 211, 5, inserts و before *بمرتبه: l. 6 after نهد substitutes for وآن at the end of the line the following words:—

تا آنچ در نظر آورد در قدم آورد که ثمر نظر ایمانست و ثمرهٔ قدم عرفان '

211, 8, for معرفت reads معروف و. 211, 9, substitutes در تیه for و before, and inserts وی‌را after ضلالت; and after کفت adds و اظهار تا بینائی خود نمود. 211, 10, inserts شعر at beginning of line. 211, 12, omits [و ایضاً]. 211, 11, فکندش. Of the passage thus emended the translation is as follows:—

"And it will become apparent for what reason this pure, celestial and luminous spirit was drawn into the form of this lowly earthen mould, and also why it must part therefrom, why the spirit must sever its connection with this mould, why the form must perish, and what is the reason for the restoration of this mould at the Resurrection and the reinvestiture of the spirit therewith. Then will he [*i.e.* the enquirer] come forth from the company of '*these are like cattle, nay, they are yet more misguided*[1],' attain to the rank of [true] humanity, escape from the

[1] *Qur'án*, XXV, 46.

veil of heedlessness of '*they know the outward appearance of this present life, but are careless as to the life to come*[1],' and set his feet eagerly and joyfully in the Pilgrim's Path, so that what he acquires by vision he may translate into progress, seeing that the fruit of vision is Faith, while the fruit of progress is Wisdom. But those poor philosophers, atheists and materialists, who are debarred from these two stations, err and go astray, so that one of the most talented of them, who is known and noted amongst them for scholarship, philosophical knowledge and judgement, that is 'Umar-i-Khayyám, in the extreme of bewilderment must needs advertise his blindness in the desert of error by uttering the following verses:

'*To that circle wherein is our coming and going*
Neither beginning nor end is apparent.
No one breathes a true word in this world
As to whence is our coming and whither our going.'

'*Since* [*God the All-*] *Holder arranged the composition of* [*men's*] *natures*
Wherefore did He again cast them into decline and decay?
If these forms are ugly, whose is the fault,
And if they are good, wherefore their destruction'[2]?"

5. Shahrazúrí's Tawáríkhu'l-Ḥukamá.

This "History of the Philosophers," properly entitled *Nuzhatu'l-Arwáḥ wa Rawḍatu'l-Afráḥ*, composed by Shamsu'd-Dín Muḥammad ibn Maḥmúd of Shahrazúr between A.H. 586 and 611 (A.D. 1190 and 1214), exists in two recensions, one Arabic and one Persian[3]. Of the latter there exists, besides the MS. described by Rieu, another MS. (No. 97) in the Pote Collection in the library of King's College, Cambridge. Both versions are given in the original by Zhukovski[4], with a Russian translation of the Persian version, while Sir E. Denison Ross's English translation follows the Arabic, of which the text is reprinted on pp. 212–214 of Mírzá Muḥammad's Persian notes. The Arabic verses contained in it are, however, corrupt, and need emendation.

6. Ibnu'l-Athír.

Mention of 'Umar-i-Khayyám is made by this great historian, who wrote in A.H. 628 (A.D. 1230–1), under the year A.H. 467 (A.D. 1074–5), where he says:—

"And in it the Niẓámu'l-Mulk and Sulṭán Malikshâh assembled a number of the most notable astronomers, and fixed the *Naw-rúz* (Persian New Year's Day) in the first point of Aries, it having been hitherto at the passage of the Sun through the middle point of Pisces; and what the Sulṭán did became the starting-point of [all subsequent] Calendars. In it also was constructed the Observatory for Sulṭán

[1] *Qur'án*, XXX, 6.

[2] The second of these quatrains, which may be accounted amongst the most certainly genuine of those ascribed to 'Umar, is No. 126 in E. H. Whinfield's edition.

[3] See Sachau's Introduction to his edition of al-Bírúní's *al-Áthâru'l-Báqiya*, pp. L–LI, and Rieu's *Persian Supplement*, pp. 68–9.

[4] *Op. cit.*, pp. 327–9.

Malikshâh, for the making of which a number of notable astronomers were assembled, amongst them 'Umar ibn Ibráhím al-Khayyámí, Abu'l-Muzaffar al-Isfizárí, Maymún ibnu'n-Najíb al-Wásiṭí, and others. A great amount of wealth was expended upon it, and the Observatory remained in use until the King died in A.H. 485 (A.D. 1092–3), but after his death it was disused."

7. Al-Qifṭí's Ta'ríkhu'l-Hukamá.

The "History of the Philosophers," composed between A.H. 624 and 646 (A.D. 1227 and 1248–9) by Jamálu'd-Dín Abu'l-Ḥasan 'Alí ibn Yúsuf al-Qifṭí, and edited by Dr Julius Lippert[1], also contained a notice of 'Umar-i-Khayyám, of which a French translation is given by Woepcke in his *L'Algèbre d'Omar Alkhayyâmi*[2], while later Russian and English versions are given by Zhukovski and Ross respectively[3].

8. Ta'ríkh-i-Jahán-gushá.

In the account of the massacre of the people of Merv perpetrated by the Mongols early in the year 618/1221 one of 'Umar's quatrains is said to have been recited by Sayyid 'Izzu'd-Dín *Nassába* when he had finished counting the bodies of the victims, of whom the number exceeded 1,300,000. This history was composed in 658/1260, and the passage in question occurs in vol. i, p. 128 ("E. J. W. Gibb Memorial" Series, xvi, 1).

9. Qazwíní's Átháru'l-Bilád.

In his "Monuments of the Lands," composed in A.H. 674 (A.D 1275–6), Zakariyyá ibn Muḥammad ibn Maḥmúd al-Qazwíní gives, under his notice of the city of Níshápúr, some account of 'Umar[4] containing certain new materials which I have summarized in my *Lit. Hist. of Persia* (ii, 251–2).

10. The Jámi'u't-Tawáríkh.

I believe that I was the first to call attention[5] to an important notice of 'Umar in Rashídu'd-Dín Faḍlu'lláh's great history, compiled about the beginning of the eighth century of the *hijra* (fourteenth of the Christian era). The importance of this notice lies in the fact that it professes to be copied from an Isma'ílí biography of Ḥasan-i-Ṣabbáḥ, entitled *Sar-guzasht-i-Sayyid-ná* ("the Adventures of Our Master"), found in the library of Alamút, the Assassins' chief stronghold in Persia, where it was destroyed by Húlágú and his Mongols in the middle of the thirteenth century of our era; and that it affords a much more respectable authority than any previously adduced for the famous "Story of the Three Friends," *i.e.* the *Niẓámu'l-Mulk*, Ḥasan-i-Ṣabbáḥ, and 'Umar-i-Khayyám[6]. The chronological difficulties involved in this story, how-

[1] Leipzig, 1903. The notice of 'Umar occurs on pp. 243–4.
[2] Paris, 1851, pp. v–vi of the Preface and p. 52 of the text.
[3] See also my *Lit. Hist. of Persia*, ii, pp. 250–1.
[4] P. 318 of Wüstenfeld's edition.
[5] In a paper entitled *Yet more Light on 'Umar-i-Khayyám* which appeared in the *J.R.A.S.* for 1899 (pp. 409–411). See my *Lit. Hist. of Persia*, ii, 252–3.
[6] See, besides the passage in my *Lit. Hist. of Persia* cited in the previous note, pp. 190–193 of the same volume.

ever, render its acceptance very difficult. Mírzá Muḥammad has communicated to me the ingenious suggestion that its historical basis is to be found in a passage in Yáqút's *Mu'jamu'l Udabá* or "Dictionary of Learned Men[1]," where it is stated on the authority of Abu'l-Ḥasan ibn Abi'l-Qásim Zayd al-Bayhaqí, author of the *Masháribu't-Tajárib*, that in the year 434/1042–3 the poet 'Alí ibnu'l-Ḥasan al-Bákharzí and Abú Naṣr Muḥammad ibn Manṣúr al-Kundurí, who subsequently became famous under the title of *'Amídu'l-Mulk* as Minister to the Saljúq Sulṭáns Ṭughril Beg and Alp Arslán, were fellow-pupils of the same Imám Muwaffaq of Níshápúr at whose lectures the "Three Friends" are supposed to have become acquainted. That the framework of a story should be preserved with the substitution of more interesting or more celebrated personalities as its heroes is a very common literary phenomenon. If this has happened in the present case, the poet al-Bákharzí has simply been replaced by the poet 'Umar-i-Khayyám, and Alp Arslán's earlier Minister *'Amídu'l-Mulk* by his later Minister *Niẓámu'l-Mulk*, the Imám Muwaffaq remaining in both versions.

11. Ta'ríkh-i-Guzida.

This well-known history, composed in 730/1329–1330, also contains a brief notice of 'Umar and cites one of his quatrains. ("E. J. W. Gibb Memorial" Series, xiv, 1, pp. 817–818.)

12. Firdawsu't-Tawáríkh.

This work, the "Paradise of Histories," composed in A.H. 808 (A.D. 1405–6) by Mawláná Khusraw of Abarqúh, contains an account of 'Umar-i-Khayyám of which the Persian text is reproduced from Zhukovski's article on pp. 217–219 of the Persian notes. and of which the substance is given in my *Lit. Hist.*, ii, 254.

13. The Ta'ríkh-i-Alfí.

This late work, composed, as its title implies, in A.H. 1000 (A.D. 1591–2)[2] for the Emperor Akbar by Aḥmad ibn Naṣru'lláh of Tatta in India, contains a very entertaining anecdote concerning 'Umar-i-Khayyám's belief in Metempsychosis, which is given in English on pp. 254–5 of vol. ii of my *Lit. Hist. of Persia*, and of which the text will be found on pp. 219–220 of the Persian notes.

The above list is far from exhaustive, but contains all the older and more authentic as well as the more interesting of the modern notices of this famous man.

'Umar-i-Khayyám's Scientific Works.

These include—

(1) His treatise on Algebra, of which the Arabic text accompanied by a French translation was published at Paris in 1851 by F. Woepcke.

(2) On the difficulties of Euclid's Definitions, of which a manuscript is preserved at Leyden (No. 967). See also Brockelmann, i, 471.

[1] "E. J. W. Gibb Memorial" Series, vi, 5, p. 124.
[2] It extends, however, only to the year 997/1588–9.

(3) The *Zíj*, or Calendar, of Malikshâh, to which, as noticed above (*s.v.* Ibnu'l-Athír), 'Umar contributed.

(4) A brief treatise on Natural Philosophy.

(5) A Persian treatise on Being, composed for Fakhru'l-Mulk[1] ibn Mu'ayyad, of which a MS. (**Or. 6572**, f. 51) is preserved in the British Museum. In another MS. (**Suppl. Pers. 139**, No. 7) in the Bibliothèque Nationale in Paris, described by M. E. Blochet in his *Catalogue des Manuscrits Persans* (Paris, 1905, vol. i, p. 108), the name of the person to whom this work is dedicated is given as Fakhru'd-Dín Mu'ayyadu'l-Mulk, whom Mírzá Muḥammad is inclined to identify with the son of the Niẓámu'l-Mulk who bore this latter title. This treatise, according to a manuscript note by M. Blochet, has been translated by M. Christensen and published in the *Monde Oriental* (Copenhagen, 1905).

(6) A treatise on Growth and Obligation (*Kawn wa Taklíf*).

(7) Methods for ascertaining the respective proportions of gold and silver in an amalgam or admixture containing both. A MS. of this (No. 1158) exists in the library of Gotha.

(8) A treatise entitled *Lawázimu'l-Amkina* on the Seasons and on the causes of the diversity of climate in different places.

The Quatrains.

How many of the *Rubá'iyyát* or Quatrains attributed to 'Umar-i-Khayyám are really his it is impossible to determine, since no very ancient manuscript collection of them has yet been discovered[2]; but Zhukovski has enumerated more than fourscore which are ascribed on at least equally good authority to other poets[3]. Although they have repeatedly been lithographed in Persia and India, they enjoy, thanks to Edward FitzGerald's translation, a far greater celebrity in the West, and especially in England and America, than in the land of their origin, where no one would think of ranking 'Umar as a poet in the same category as Firdawsí, Sa'dí or Ḥáfiẓ. The causes of 'Umar's popularity in the West are manifold. *First*, he had the supreme good fortune to find a translator like FitzGerald. *Secondly*, the beauty of his quatrains depends more on their substance than on their form, whereas the converse

[1] Perhaps Fakhru'l-Mulk ibn Niẓámu'l-Mulk, the Prime Minister of Sulṭán Barkiyáruq.

[2] The oldest MS. (**Bodl. No. 525**) was copied in A.H. 865 (A.D. 1460–1) nearly three centuries and a half after 'Umar's death. The text of this, in *facsimile* and in print, with literal prose translation, was published by Mr Edward Heron Allen (London: H. S. Nichols, Ltd.) in 1898. Mírzá Muḥammad informs me that a year or two before the War (*i.e.* in 1912 or 1913) there was offered for sale by an Armenian dealer in Paris a very fine autograph MS. of the *Mú'nisu'l-Aḥrár* of the Persian poet Muḥammad ibn Badr-i-Jájarmí, transcribed in the year 740/1339–1340. It comprised about 600 leaves, and contained extensive selections from the works of some two hundred of the most celebrated Persian poets from the earliest times down to the date of compilation. Amongst these poems were included some twenty of 'Umar-i-Khayyam's quatrains, which were copied by Mírzá Muḥammad into a note-book. I do not know what has become of this precious manuscript.

[3] For a list of these see my *Lit. Hist. of Persia*, ii, 256–7.

holds good of much Persian poetry. *Thirdly*, their gentle melancholy, half sceptical mysticism and graceful pessimism are congenial to an age which, like his own, has come to the conclusion that science can answer almost every question save that which most intimately concerns our own hopes and happiness

The information given by Mírzá Muḥammad in the latter part of his note (pp. 222–7) about the European renderings of 'Umar-i-Khayyám and his admirers and imitators, and especially about the Club called by his name, though new to most Persian readers, is familiar to all in this country who take an interest in such matters, and may be found in great detail in Nathan Haskell Dole's "Multi-Variorum edition" (Macmillan, London, 1898).

Note XXVI. On certain medical terms in the Preface to the Fourth Discourse.

(Text, pp. 68–9; Persian notes, p. 230.)

The Pulse (*Nabḍ*) is very fully discussed in all Arabic and Persian works on Medicine, *e.g.* the **Firdawsu'l-Ḥikmat** of 'Alí ibn Rabban aṭ-Ṭabarí, *Naw' iv, Maqála xii, chs.* 6–9 (Brit. Mus. **Arundel Or. 41**, ff. 163ᵃ–165ᵇ); the **Kámilu'ṣ-Ṣiná'at**, also called **al-Kitábu'l-Malikí**, of 'Alí ibnu'l-'Abbás al-Majúsí, *Part I, Maqála vii, chs.* 2–11 (Cairo ed. of 1294/1877, vol. i, pp. 254–281); the **Qánún** of Avicenna, *Book I, Fann ii, Ta'lím iii, Jumla* 1 (19 sections), pp. 62–8 of the Rome edition of A.D. 1593 (= ff. 49ᵇ–53ᵇ of the Latin translation printed at Venice in 1544); and the Persian **Dhakhíra-i-Khwárazmsháhí**, *Book II, Guftár iii, chs.* 1–23.

As our author chiefly follows Avicenna, we may conveniently do the same, though indeed the general views of all these writers appear to be almost identical. Each pulsation consists of four factors or elements, two movements (*ḥarakat*), a diastole (*inbisáṭ*) and a systole (*inqibáḍ*), and two pauses (*sukún*) separating the two movements. The ten kinds or genera (*jins*) of pulse are determined by consideration of the following features:—

(1) The amount of the diastole (*miqdáru'l-inbisáṭ*, "genus quod est sumptum ex quantitate diastoles"). In this genus three elements are to be considered, length (*ṭúl*), breadth (*'arḍ*) and depth (*'umq*), each of which supplies three simple varieties of pulse, two extremes and a mean, besides composite varieties, which I shall not here enumerate. Thus we have the long (*ṭawíl*), the short (*qaṣír*, "curtus") and the intermediate (*mu'tadil*, "mediocris"); the broad (*'arîḍ*, "latus"), the narrow (*ḍayyiq*, "strictus") and the intermediate; the depressed (*mukhaffaḍ*, "profundus"), the ascending, elevated or prominent (*mushrif*, "apertus") and the intermediate.

(2) The quality of the impact on the fingers of the observer (*kayfiyyatu qar'i'l-ḥarakati'l-aṣábi'a*, "genus quod est sumptum ex qualitate percussionis venæ in digitos"). This also has three varieties, the strong (*qawí*, "fortis"), the weak (*ḍa'íf*, "debilis") and the intermediate (*mu'tadil*, "æqualis").

(3) The time or duration of each movement (*zamánu kulli ḥarakat*ⁿ, "quod ex tempore cujuscunque motionis sumptum est"). This also comprises three varieties, the quick (*sarí'*, "velox"), the slow (*baṭí'*, "tardus"), and the intermediate ("æqualis").

(4) Resistance to the touch (*qiwámu'l-álat*, "quod ex essentiâ instrumenti sumitur"). Here also we have three varieties, the soft (*layyin*, "mollis"), the hard (*ṣalb*, "durus") and the intermediate ("mediocris").

(5) Emptiness or fulness (*ḥálu má yaḥtawí 'alayhi min khalá'ihi wa 'mtilá'ihi*, "quod est sumptum ex eo quod continetur"), three varieties, the full (*mumtali'*, "plenus"), the empty (*khálí*, "vacuus") and the intermediate ("mediocris").

(6) Heat or cold (*ḥarru malmasihi wa barduhu*, "quod ex suo tactu sumptum est"), three varieties, the hot (*ḥárr*, "calidus"), the cold (*bárid*, "frigidus") and the intermediate ("temperatus").

(7) The duration of the pause (*zamánu's-sukún*, "quod est sumptum ex tempore quietis"), three varieties, the continuous (*mutawátir*, also called *mutadárik* and *mutakáthif*, "frequens," "consequens" or "spissus"), the differentiated (*mutafáwit*, also called *mutarákhí* and *mutakhalkhil*, "rarus," "lassus" or "resolutus"), and the intermediate ("mediocris").

(8) The equality or diversity of the pulse (*istiwá'u'n-nabḍi wa 'khtiláfuhu*, "quod est sumptum ex æqualitate et diversitate," "aut æquale, aut diversum seu inæquale"), two varieties, equal (*mustaw*ⁿ, "æqualis") and unequal (*mukhtalif*, "diversus").

(9) The regularity or irregularity of the pulse (*an-niẓám wa ghayru'n-niẓám*, "genus quod ex ordinatione et inordinatione sumptum est"), two varieties, regularly different (*mukhtalif muntaẓim*, "diversē ordinatus") and irregularly different (*mukhtalif ghayru muntaẓim*, "diversē inordinatus").

(10) Weight, harmony or measure (*wazn*, "quod ex pondere est sumptum"), which may be either good or bad, each of which comprises three varieties.

It will thus be seen that 37 primary varieties of pulse are recognized, but there are many secondary and composite types which it would take too long to enumerate. Speaking of the latter in the first group or genus mentioned above Avicenna says that some only are named, such as *al-'aẓím* ("magnus") and *aṣ-ṣaghír* ("parvus"), *al-ghalíẓ* ("grossus") and *ar-raqíq* ("subtilis"); and the next section but one (§ iii) treats of the different sorts of composite pulse which have proper names, such as *al-ghazálí* ("gazellans"), *al-mawjí* ("undosus"), *ad-dúdí* ("vermiculosus"), *an-namlí* ("formicans"), *etc.* Very full treatment is accorded to the whole subject, and in particular it is explained why the pulse is felt at the wrist preferably to any other place, and what precautions should be observed in feeling it. The remarks about the observing of the systole ascribed by our author to Avicenna appear to be really quoted by him from Galen: "Galenus quoque dixit 'longo tempore non fui sollicitus ex depressione: postea vero non quievi tangendo donec ex eo aliquid percepi, et postea illud complevi. Nam postea portæ pulsus mihi apertæ fuerunt'."

Next in importance to the examination of the pulse came the inspection of the urine as a means of diagnosis. This is called, as in the text, *Tafsira*, a word thus defined in the great *Dictionary of the Technical Terms used in the Sciences of the Musalmáns* (p. 1115): "This with the physicians is the vessel wherein is the patient's urine [intended] to be shewn to the physician; and it is also called *dalíl* (indication, guide). It is only called *tafsira* because it explains (*tufassir*) and makes manifest to the physician the patient's physical condition." The chief points to be observed in it are the colour (*lawn*), consistency (*qiwám*), smell (*rá'iha*), froth (*zubd*), sediment (*rusúb*), and copious or scanty quantity (*kathrat wa qillat*). Twelve sections are devoted to this subject in the *Qánún*, and twenty-nine in the *Dhakhíra-i-Khwárazmsháhí*.

The word translated "delirium" in the text is *sarsám*, so explained by Schlimmer (pp. 179 and 460), with the equivalent of Phrenitis. This latter word appears correctly as فرّانيطس (*farránítus*) in a fine old twelfth or thirteenth century MS. of the *Qánún* in my possession; but in the Rome edition of A.D. 1593 (p. 302) in the corrupt form قرانيطس (*qaránítus*)[1], and in the Latin version as "karabitus." It is defined by Avicenna as a "hot swelling (or inflammation) of the pia mater or dura mater not extending to the substance of the brain," and would therefore appear to be equivalent to meningitis.

The general doctrine of Fever and its Varieties taught by "Arabian Medicine" is most clearly and succinctly set forth in Book V of the Persian *Dhakhíra-i-Khwárazmsháhí*, of which I possess a very fine MS. transcribed in the thirteenth century of the Christian era. This Book comprises six *Guftárs*, or Discourses, of which the first, divided into four chapters, treats "of what Fever is, and of how many species, how it appears and how it passes away." The first chapter, on "What Fever is," may be translated in full on account of its brevity.

"You must know that 'Fever is an abnormal[2] heat enkindled in the heart, transmitted by the intermediary of the spirit and the blood to the blood-vessels and [thus] diffused throughout the whole body, which it heats and inflames with an inflammation whereof the harmful effects appear in all the natural functions.' This sentence formulated above is the definition (*ḥadd*) of Fever; the word 'Heat' is the genus, while the other words are the specific differentiations (*faṣl-há-yi dhátí*) whereby the definition is completed. Further you must know that the heat of Fever is not like the heat of anger, fatigue, grief and the like, because these heats harmfully affect the natural functions without the intervention of anything else, even as when water descends into the eye the hurtful effect thereof on the vision becomes apparent without the intervention of anything else; and when the heat of anger, or the like thereof, reaches that point where it will be injurious to the natural functions, it is but the cause, and the injury thereof only becomes apparent by the intervention of something else. Even so is the putridity ['ufúnat] of fever, for the

[1] This same corrupt form also occurs in most MSS. of the *Dhakhíra-i-Khwárazmsháhí*, Book VI, Guftár i, Part 1, ch. 1, where, however, the word is specifically recognized as Greek.

[2] *Gharíb*, lit. "strange."

putridity is the cause, while the hurt thereof is through the intervention of that heat which is produced from it. And the natural functions, wherein the hurt of fever becomes apparent, are such as the appetite for food and wine, digestion, rising up, sitting down, going, eating, sexual intercourse, and the like thereof."

The next (second) chapter deals with the different kinds of fever, and is too long (3 pages) to be translated in full here. The human body is compounded of three sorts of substances; (1) basic tissues such as the bones, nerves and blood-vessels; (2) the marrow of the bones, the blood, and other liquids contained in the vessels and cavities of the body, such as the phlegm, bile and black bile, known as the 'humours'; (3) the natural, animal or vital, and psychic spirits, and the vapours diffused throughout the body. This composite body the ancients have likened to a hot bath, whereof the walls, bricks and stones are represented by the bones, nerves and blood-vessels; the water by the marrow, the blood, and the humours; and the steam by the natural, animal and psychic spirits, and the vapours. When the heat of the fever attacks the basic tissues of the body, it is like the heat of the fire affecting the walls, stones and bricks of the hot bath; and this kind of fever is called 'hectic' (*diqq*). When it first attacks the humours and subsequently the basic tissues, it is like the hot water being let into the chambers of the bath and heating the walls; and this kind of fever is called 'humoristic' (*khalṭiyya*). When it attacks the spirit and the vapours, which in turn heat the humours and the tissues, it is like the hot air in the bath heating in turn the water and the walls thereof; and this kind of fever is called 'quotidian' (Pers. *tab-i-yak-rúza*; Arab. *ḥummá yawm*[in]).

This is one classification. Another is into 'simple' (*basíṭ*) and 'compound' (*murakkab*), according as one humour only is involved, or more than one. Thirteen kinds of fever are recognized, *viz.*:—

(1) That which is in itself an independent disease.

(2) That which is the symptom of some other disease.

(3) Very high fever called 'acute' (*ḥádda*).

(4) The slower and heavier fever called 'chronic' (*muzmina*).

(5) That which attacks by day.

(6) That which attacks by night.

(7) That which passes away easily.

(8) Fevers which are fierce in their onset and accompanied by alarming symptoms.

(9) Continuous fevers (*lázim* or *muṭbiqa*).

(10) Non-continuous fevers (*mufttra*).

(11) Cold fevers.

(12) Fevers accompanied by rigors (Pers. *larza*; Arab. *náfiḍ*, *ra'da*).

(13) Fevers accompanied by 'goose-skin' (Pers. *faráshá*; Arab. *qash'aríra*).

These, says the author, are the broad general divisions, each of which contains subdivisions which will be treated of in subsequent chapters. Fevers of the type called "putrid" (*'afin*, in Persian *ganda* or *púsída*) are of four kinds, corresponding to the four humours (*akhláṭ*) from the corruption of which they arise, and each of these is subdivided into two varieties, according as the corruption arises within or without the blood vessels. But since two or more of these kinds may co exist or combine, a large number of compound or composite fevers (*tab-há-yi murakkab*) arises, each presenting different and characteristic symptoms. Thus two types of intermittent fever may co-exist, or two types of continuous fever, or an intermittent with a continuous fever, so that the diagnosis may be very difficult. Generally speaking, quotidian fever (Arab. *ḥummá kull' yawm*ⁱⁿ, Pers. *tab-i-har-rúza*) arises from corruption of the phlegm (*balgham*); tertian (Arab. *ghibb*) from that of the bile (*ṣafrá*); quartan is atrabilious (*sawdáwí*) in origin; and semi-tertian (*shaṭru'l-ghibb*) is from a combination of bilious and phlegmatic disturbance. Fevers arising from corruption in the blood, on the other hand, are continuous (*muṭbiqa*, or *lázim*). If the blood become overheated in the vessels without undergoing corruption, the resulting fever is called *súnákhís* (? συνεχής). If there is corruption as well, it may affect half the blood, or less, or more, in which last case the resulting fever is called "burning" (Arab. *muḥriqa*, Pers. *súzanda*). But if all the blood be so affected, the patient will surely die. All fevers arising from the blood are continuous, whether the affection of the blood be primary or secondary. The latter may arise from a "bloody swelling" (*ámás-i-khúní*) of one of the internal organs, such as the stomach, liver, spleen, gall-bladder, bowels, lungs, diaphragm, muscles or nerves. Such secondary fever is not an independent disease but a symptom, and the treatment must therefore be directed to the cause. The aetiology of corruption of the humours is discussed in a subsequent section of the book (Book V, Guftár iii, ch. 1).

It is to be noted that in the older Arabic medical treatises, such as the *Firdawsu'l-Ḥikmat* (composed in A.D. 850), there is a tendency to use the original Greek nomenclature transcribed into Arabic characters instead of the Arabic translations which subsequently replaced these foreign forms. Thus we find quotidian fever called افيمروس (ἐφήμερος) as well as حمّى يوم; hectic fever called اقطيقوس (ἑκτικός) instead of دقّ; tertian طراطاوس (τριταῖος) instead of حمّى غبّ; and semi-tertian as اميطراطاوس (ἡμιτριταῖος) instead of شطر الغبّ.

The student's attention may also be directed to an excellent article on Fever (الحمّى) in vol. i of the *Dict. of Technical Terms, etc*, pp. 381–3, where a fourfold classification is adopted having regard to (1) causation, primary or secondary (*maraḍ* or *'araḍ*); (2) point of attack, as explained above (quotidian, hectic and putrid or humoristic); (3) simplicity or complexity; (4) occurrence or non-occurrence of rigors (*náfiḍ*).

Note XXVII. Physicians and their Works mentioned in Anecdote XXXII.

(Text, pp. 70–71; Persian notes, pp. 230–8.)

It will be convenient to arrange the medical works here mentioned under their authors, and these in turn, so far as possible, in chronological order. For the authorities to which reference is most constantly made the following abbreviations are used. By **Barhebraeus** is meant the *Mukhtaṣaru'd-Duwal* (Beyrout ed. of 1890) of Gregorius Abu'l-Faraj ibn Ahrún commonly called Ibnu'l-'Ibrí or Barhebraeus. The **Fihrist** of Abu'l-Faraj Muḥammad ibn Abí Ya'qúb Isḥáq an-Nadím al-Warráq is, of course, quoted from Flügel's (the only) edition. **Ibn Abí Uṣaybi'a** means that author's *'Uyúnu'l-Inbá fí Ṭabaqáti'l-Aṭibbá*, Cairo edition of 1299/1882, two volumes. **Qifṭí** means Jamálu'd-Dín Abu'l-Ḥasan 'Alí ibn Yúsuf al-Qifṭí's *Ta'ríkhu'l-Ḥukamá*, ed. Lippert (Leipzig, 1903). The chief European authorities quoted are **Wüstenfeld's** *Geschichte der Arabischen Aerzte und Naturforscher* (Göttingen, 1840), a small book but compact with useful information; Lucien **Leclerc's** *Histoire de la Médecine Arabe* (2 vols., Paris, 1876); Max **Neuburger's** *Geschichte der Medizin* (Stuttgart, 1908), especially vol. ii, pp. 142–228, "Die Medizin bei den Arabern," and the complementary *Literarhistorische Übersicht*; **Pagel's** *Einführung in die Geschichte der Medizin* (Berlin, 1898), ninth lecture (pp. 146–160) on Arabian Medicine; Adolf **Fonahn's** *Zur Quellenkunde der Persischen Medizin* (Leipzig, 1910); E. T. **Withington's** *Medical History from the earliest times* (London, 1894); and F. H. **Garrison's** *Introduction to the History of Medicine* (London and Philadelphia, 1917). As a rule, however, in these brief notes reference will only be made to the original Arabic sources.

1. *Bukht-Yishú'.*

Ten members of this great medical family, which for three centuries (eighth to eleventh of our era) produced some of the most eminent physicians of that time, are enumerated by Wüstenfeld (pp. 14–18, Nos. 26–35). They were Christians, as indicated by the family name, for the correct explanation of which (Bukht-Yishú' = "Jesus hath delivered") we are indebted to Noldeke[1]. The chief members of the family, with their affiliation, so far as it is known, were as follows:—

1. *Bukht-Yishú'* I
|
2. *Jurjis*[2] I (physician to al-Manṣúr, d. 152/769)
|
3. *Bukht-Yishú'* II (physician to -Mahdí, -Hádí and Hárúnu'r-Rashíd, d. 185/801)

Sons of 3:
- 4. *Jibrá'íl* (physician to Hárúnu'r-Rashíd, -Amín and -Ma'mún, d. 213/828–9)
- 5. *Jurjis* II

Sons of 4:
- 6. *Bukht-Yishú'* III (physician to -Mu'tazz, d. 256/870)
  - 8. *Yaḥyá* or *Yuḥanná*
    - 10. *Bukht-Yishú'* IV (physician to -Muqtadir, d. 329/940–1)
- 7. *'Ubaydu'llah* (physician to -Muttaqí)
  - 9. *Jibrá'íl* (physician to 'Aḍudu'd-Dawla, d. 397/1006–9)
    - 11. *Abú Sa'íd 'Ubaydu'lláh* (d. 450/1058–9)

[1] See p. 81 *supra*, n. 1 *ad calc.*

[2] Wüstenfeld (p. 14), following Ibn Abí Uṣaybi'a (i, 123), inserts a Jibrá'íl between Jurjis and Bukht-Yishú', but Qifṭí (p. 158 *etc.*) represents Jurjis I as the son, not the grandson, of Bukht-Yishú' I.

Concerning the original Bukht-Yishú' I can find out nothing, but it may be supposed that he, like his son Jurjís, was attached to the great hospital (*Bímáristán*) and medical school of his native town Jundí-Sábúr. This once famous Persian city, of which hardly a trace now remains, though its site has been identified by Rawlinson[1] as the modern Sháh-ábád, about mid-way between Dizful and Shúshtar, was originally founded by Shápúr I, and named, according to Ṭabarí[2], *Beh-az-Andêw-i-Shápúr*, or "Shápúr's 'Better than Antioch,'" a name gradually shortened to Gundê-Shápúr, or, in its Arabic form, Junday-Sábúr. "It was enlarged into a great city," says Rawlinson, "by his seventh successor Shápúr II '*Dhu'l-Aktáf*' (A.D. 309–379)...and during his reign became the see of a bishop of the Nestorian Church which had been instituted in Susiana a century before; and when Jundí-Sábúr soon afterwards rose to be the chief city of the province, the seat of the metropolitan, which had been formerly fixed at Ahwáz, or, as it is called by the Syrians, Bêth Lâpât[3], was transferred to it. The School of Jundí-Sábúr was renowned, during the reign of Anúsharwán (A.D. 531–578), through the East and West; and the city continued, to the time of the Arab conquest, one of the great capitals of Susiana. It appears to have sunk before the rising greatness of Shúshtar in the thirteenth century; and it is little mentioned in Oriental History after that time."

On the destruction of the great Persian school of Edessa in A.D 488–9 by order of the Emperor Zeno[4] many of its learned Nestorian professors and physicians sought refuge from Byzantine fanaticism under the more tolerant rule of the Sásánians at Jundí-Sábúr, and gave a fresh impulse to its activity. During the Arab invasion of Persia (A.H. 15–17; A.D. 636–8) it surrendered on terms to the Muslims[5], and its school apparently continued unmolested until the early 'Abbásid period, when the Caliph al-Manṣúr (A.H. 136–158; A.D. 754–775), being grievously ill, summoned Jurjís I, son of Bukht-Yishú' I, to Baghdád, where he remained, greatly trusted and honoured, in spite of his refusal to forsake the Christian for the Muhammadan faith, until A.H. 152 (A.D. 769), when, being himself sick unto death, he obtained the Caliph's permission to return home. From that time onwards until the middle of the eleventh century some member of the family was always one of the chief physicians of the Court at Baghdád. Lengthy notices of most of those enumerated above, with lists of their medical and other works, are given by Qifṭí, Ibn Abí Uṣaybi'a and other medical biographers. For such as do not read Arabic the information given by Wüstenfeld (pp. 14–18) and Leclerc (i, pp. 95–103) will probably suffice. It is uncertain whether the Bukht-Yishú' mentioned in the text (Anecdote XXXIII) is intended to be the father or the son of Jibrá'íl. The former died twelve years before al-Ma'mún's accession, while the latter survived him thirty-seven years.

[1] *Notes on a March from Zoháb to Khúzistán* in the *J.R. Geogr. Soc.* for 1839, vol. ix, pp. 71–72. See also Layard's remarks in vol. xvi, p. 86, of the same Journal.

[2] See Nöldeke's *Gesch. d. Pers. u. Arab. zur Zeit d. Sasaniden* (Leyden, 1879), pp. 40–42.

[3] See Nöldeke, *loc. cit.*

[4] See Dr W. Wright's *Syriac Literature*, pp. 46–47.

[5] See Baládhurí's *Futúḥu'l-Buldán* (ed. de Goeje), pp. 382–385.

An anecdote in the *Kitábu'l-Bukhalá* ("Book of Misers")[1] of al-Jáḥiẓ in which an Arab physician, Asad ibn Jání, complains that patients will not consult him because, amongst other reasons, "his language is Arabic, and it should have been the language of Jundí-Sábúr," shews how great was the repute of that famous school of Medicine in early 'Abbásid times. Exactly what this language was is uncertain. Ibn Ḥawqal[2] says that, besides Arabic and Persian, the people of Jundí-Sábúr have another speech of Khúzistán which is neither Hebrew, nor Syriac, nor Persian; while in the *Manáhiju'l-Fikar* it is said that they have a language peculiar to themselves, resembling a jargon (*raṭána*), though the Persian language is prevalent amongst them[3]. Speaking of their religion al-Muqaddasí[4] says that in his time (middle of the tenth century of the Christian era) there were few Christians and not many Jews and Zoroastrians, and that of the Muslims many were Mu'tazilites, Shí'a (especially at Ahwáz) and Ḥanbalites.

2. *Ḥunayn ibn Isḥáq al-'Ibádí.*

This was another Christian scholar, well known to mediaeval Europe under the name of Joannitius, who rendered signal services to Arabian science, together with his sons Dá'úd and Isḥáq and his nephew Ḥubaysh, all of whom were skilful and industrious translators of Greek books into Arabic. He was a Nestorian of Ḥíra, where his father was an apothecary, and early in the ninth century of the Christian era came to Baghdád, where he studied under the celebrated Yaḥyá (or Yuḥanná) Másawayh (Mesuë senior) of Jundí-Sábúr, a pupil of Jibrá'íl ibn Bukht-Yishú'. Offended at some real or fancied slight, he went off to study Greek amongst the Greeks[5], and some years later was seen by one of his former acquaintances in the guise of a long-haired wandering bard reciting Homer in the streets. Later he returned to Baghdád, having perfected his knowledge of Greek, and applied himself to the study of Arabic under Khalíl ibn Aḥmad. He then became so excellent as a translator from Greek into Arabic that Jibrá'íl ibn Bukht-Yishú' said of him, "By God, if his life be prolonged he will assuredly put Sergius[6] to shame!" He attracted the notice, and finally, after undergoing a cruel test of his professional honour[7], won the confidence of the Caliph al-Mutawakkil (A.D. 847–851), but finally succumbed to the intrigues of his rivals, was excommunicated by Bishop Theodosius, and died in A.H. 260 (A.D. 873). Wüstenfeld (pp. 28–9) enumerates 33 of his original works and a number of his translations from the Greek, including the Aphorisms (*Fuṣúl*) of Hippocrates. His son Isḥáq died in A.D. 910 or 911, and his nephew Ḥubaysh about the same time.

[1] Ed. Van Vloten (Leyden, 1900), pp. 109–110.

[2] De Goeje's *Bibl. Geogr. Arab.*, vol. ii, pp. 173–174.

[3] Ibn Abí Uṣaybi'a specially mentions that both Jurjís I (vol. i, p. 124) and his son Bukht-Yishú' (vol. i, p. 126), on being presented to the Caliphs al-Manṣúr and Hárúnu'r-Rashíd respectively, prayed for them in Arabic and Persian.

[4] De Goeje's *Bibl. Geogr. Arab.*, vol. iii, pp. 414–415.

[5] Qifṭí, pp. 174–175.

[6] Sergius of Ra's 'Ayn flourished about A.D. 536, and translated the Greek sciences into Syriac. See Wright's *Syriac Literature*, pp. 88–93.

[7] Qifṭí, p. 176.

3. *Thábit ibn Qurra of Ḥarrán.*

Thábit ibn Qurra was the chief of another group of non-Muslim scholars to whom Arabic science is deeply indebted. These were the so-called Sabeans (*Ṣábi*)[1] of Ḥarrán, a town so devoted to Greek culture that it was known as Hellenopolis. The following were the most notable members of the family:—

Qurra
|
Thábit I (d. Feb. 19, 901 A.D.)
|
Ibráhím I — *Sinán* (d. A.H. 331; A.D. 942–3)
|
Thábit II (d. A.H. 363; A.D. 973–4) — *Ibráhím* II
|
Isḥáq

Thábit ibn Qurra, to whom Qifṭí devotes a long notice (pp. 115–122), was a most prolific writer on logic, arithmetic, geometry, astronomy, medicine, etc. He was born at Ḥarrán in A.H. 221 (A.D. 836) but spent most of his life at Baghdád, where he enjoyed the favour of the Caliph al-Mu'taḍid (A.D. 892–902). Qifṭí gives a very full and authoritative list of his writings compiled by Abú 'Alí al-Muḥassin[2] ibn Ibráhím ibn Hilál aṣ-Ṣábí, including some in Syriac on the Sabean religion and on music which were never translated into Arabic. The almost miraculous cure of the butcher related in Anecdote XXXIX of this book is by Qifṭí (pp. 120–1) and Ibn Abí Uṣaybi'a (i, 216) ascribed to Thábit ibn Qurra. The *Dhakhíra* ("Thesaurus") mentioned in the text was, according to Qifṭí (p. 120), declared by Thábit's homonymous grandson to be unauthentic, though a good book enjoying a wide circulation.

4. *Abú Bakr Muḥammad ibn Zakariyyá ar-Rází.*

This famous Persian physician, known to mediaeval Europe as Bubikir, Abu-beter, Errasis, Rasis and Rhazes, was probably the greatest practitioner of the so-called Arabian Medicine who ever lived[3], and as a clinical observer far surpassed his later and more celebrated countryman Avicenna, whose reputation rests more on his philosophical than on his medical attainments, while the contrary holds good of ar-Rází. Indeed Qifṭí says (p. 271) that though he devoted a good deal of attention to Metaphysics he did not understand its ultimate aim, so that his judgement was disturbed, and he adopted untenable opinions and objectionable doctrines. In Medicine, on the other hand, he was incomparable, and

[1] The true Sabeans of Chaldaea are the *Mughtasila* of the Arabs, the so-called "Christians of St John the Baptist" of some European writers. The heathens of Ḥarrán only adopted this name in the time of al-Ma'mún for a curious reason fully explained by Chwolson in his great work *Ssabier und Ssabismus* (vol. i, ch. vi, pp. 139–157).

[2] This name, being unpointed, might equally be read "Muḥsin," but Mírzá Muḥammad, in the course of a long note, has pointed out to me that, though common in later times, Muḥsin was in early days a very rare name compared with Muḥassin; a statement which he amply substantiates.

[3] Compare the enthusiastic but judicious estimate of his talents given by Neuburger (pp. 168 *et seqq.*).

his great work the *Ḥáwí* (or "Continens" of mediaeval Europe), so far as I can judge from the portions of it accessible to me in the original Arabic, stands on an altogether different plane from the *Qánún* of Avicenna or any other Arabic system of Medicine.

The year of Rází's birth is not recorded, but he seems to have spent the first thirty years of his life in his native town of Ray (situated near the modern Persian capital Ṭihrán), from which he derived the name by which he is generally known, without becoming famous for anything except an unusual skill in music and singing. He was then seized with a desire to study Medicine and Philosophy, went to Baghdád, and there became the pupil of 'Alí ibn Rabban[1] aṭ-Ṭabarí, formerly physician to the unfortunate Persian rebel Mázyár and afterwards to the Caliph al-Mutawakkil, for whom in A.D. 850 he composed his remarkable work the "Paradise of Wisdom" (*Firdawsu'l-Ḥikmat*). Having completed his medical studies he became director first of the hospital at Ray and then at Baghdád[2]. He also devoted some attention to Alchemy, on which he composed 12 books[3], but the study brought him no luck, for, being unable to translate his theories into practice, he was struck on the head by his disappointed patron Manṣúr, governor of Ray, in consequence of which he became blind. He refused to undergo an operation on his eyes on ascertaining that the surgeon who was to perform it was ignorant of the anatomy of the eye, adding afterwards that he had looked on the world until he was tired of it.

The marvellous acumen displayed and the wonderful cures effected by him form the subject of numerous anecdotes similar in character to No. XXXV in this book in such collections of stories as the Arabic *al-Faraj ba'da'sh-Shidda* ("Joy after Sorrow") of at-Tanúkhí[4] and the Persian *Jawámi'u'l-Ḥikáyát* of 'Awfí.

Rází was a most prolific writer, and Qifṭí (pp. 274–7) enumerates more than a hundred of his works, most of which, unfortunately, are lost, while only a very few have been printed in the original, to wit his celebrated treatise on small-pox and measles[5], his work on stone in the kidneys and bladder[6], and the anatomical portion of the *Manṣúrí*[7]. Latin versions of the *Ḥáwí* ("Continens"), *Manṣúrí* ("Liber ad Almansorem"), and various smaller works were made and widely read in mediaeval Europe, and were in many cases printed during the fifteenth and sixteenth centuries. They are enumerated by Dr Ludwig Choulant in his *Handbuch der Bücherkunde für die Ältere Medicin* (Leipzig, 1841), pp. 340–5. One of the most interesting of Rází's minor works, in which he discusses the reasons why quacks often enjoy

[1] His father's name is often wrongly given as *Zayn* (زين), but he explicitly states in the Introduction to his *Firdawsu'l-Ḥikmat*, or "Paradise of Wisdom," that he was called *Rabban* (ربن), "that is to say, our master and teacher." Ibn Abí Uṣaybi'a (i, 186) explains the title in precisely the same sense.

[2] Qifṭí, p. 271.

[3] *Ibid.*, p. 272.

[4] See the edition of this work printed at the Hilál Press, Cairo, in 1903, vol. ii, p. 96. The author was born in 327/938–9 and died in 384/994–5.

[5] *De Variolis et Morbillis, arabice et latine, cura John Channing* (London, 1766).

[6] *Traité sur le Calcul dans les Reins et dans la Vessie...traduction accompagnée du texte par P. de Koning* (Leyden, 1896).

[7] *Trois Traités d'Anatomie arabes...texte et traduction par P. de Koning* (Leyden, 1903), pp. 2–89.

greater popularity than properly qualified physicians, has been translated into German by the learned Moritz Steinschneider and published in Virchow's *Archiv* (vol. xxxvi, 1865, pp. 570–586). This is entitled "Wissenschaft und Charlatanerie unter den Araben im neunten Jahrhundert," and appears to be identical with the tract described by Qifṭí (p. 274) as *Kitáb fi'l-Asbábi'l-mumayyila li-qulúbi'n-Nás 'an afáḍili'l-Aṭibbá'i ila akhissá'ihim*, on "the causes which incline men's hearts from the most eminent of physicians to the vilest of them."

Only four of Rázi's numerous works are mentioned in the *Chahár Maqála*. One of them, the *Tuḥfatu'l-Mulúk* (p. 71, l. 22 of the text), is nowhere else mentioned by this title, and cannot be identified. Another, here called the *Murshid* ("Guide"), is properly entitled *al-Fuṣúl fi'ṭ-Ṭibb* ("Aphorisms in Medicine")[1]. The two remaining works, the *Manṣúrí* and the *Ḥáwí*, are more important (especially the last named), and deserve somewhat fuller mention.

Al-Kitábu'l-Manṣúrí ("Liber ad Almansorem").

A great deal of confusion exists, even amongst Oriental writers, as to the identity of the Manṣúr to whom Rází dedicated this work, and at whose hands (as narrated above) he finally suffered such indignity. Yáqút[2] alone correctly identifies him as Manṣúr ibn Isḥáq ibn Aḥmad ibn Asad, who was appointed Governor of Ray in A.H. 290 (A.D. 903) by his cousin Aḥmad ibn Isma'íl ibn Aḥmad ibn Asad ibn Sámán, the second King of that Royal House, held that position until A.H. 296 (A.D. 908–9), and rebelled against Naṣr II ibn Aḥmad ibn Isma'íl in A.H. 302 (A.D. 914–915). All other authorities, even those generally most trustworthy, seem, as Mírzá Muḥammad points out (Persian notes, pp. 231–3 and 240–1), to have fallen into error. Thus the *Fihrist* (pp. 299–300), Qifṭí (p. 272, ll. 21–2) and Ibn Abí Uṣaybi'a (i, p. 310, l. 29) call Rázi's patron "Manṣúr ibn Isma'íl," a person unknown to history; or (Ibn Abí Uṣaybi'a in another passage, *viz.* i, p. 313, l. 20) "Manṣúr ibn Isma'íl ibn Kháqán, lord of Khurásán and Transoxiana"; or (Ibn Abí Uṣaybi'a, i, p. 317, ll. 17–18) "Manṣúr ibn Isḥáq ibn Isma'íl ibn Aḥmad." Ibn Khallikán in one passage identifies him with Abú Ṣáliḥ Manṣúr ibn Isḥáq ibn Aḥmad ibn Núḥ (which is correct if we substitute "Asad" for "Núḥ" in the genealogy), and in another falls into the same error as the author of the *Chahár Maqála* by identifying him with the sixth Sámánid ruler Manṣúr ibn Núḥ ibn Naṣr, who reigned from A.H. 350 to 366 (A.D. 961–976–7), long after the death of Rází, which is generally placed either in the year A.H. 311 (A.D. 923–4), or in A.H. 320 (A.D. 932), though one MS. of Qifṭí (p. 272) puts it as late as A.H. 364 (A.D. 974–5).

The Arabic text of the *Manṣúrí* has, so far as I know, never been published in its entirety, nor are MSS. common. For his edition of the anatomical portion of the work Dr P. de Koning made use of a MS. in the Bibliothèque Nationale at Paris (No. 2866 of de Slane's *Catalogue*). The Latin version, as already noted, has been repeatedly printed[3].

[1] See Choulant's *Handbuch*, pp. 341 and 343.

[2] *Mu'jamu'l-Buldán*, vol. ii, p. 901.

[3] See Choulant, *op. laud.*, p. 343

Al-Kitábu'l-Ḥáwí ("Continens").

This is the largest and most important of the works of Rází. It is, moreover, a posthumous work, for after Rází's death Muḥammad ibnu'l-'Amíd, the Minister of Sulṭán Ruknu'd-Dawla ibn Buwayh, bought the materials and notes left by the author from his sister for a high price and placed them in the hands of a committee of his pupils to be arranged and edited. It therefore lacked the finishing touch of the Master's hand, which fact, perhaps, accounts for its somewhat inchoate character and confused arrangement. The original Arabic text has never been published; MSS. are rare and widely scattered, and it is doubtful if those which exist in the British Museum, the Bodleian, Munich and the Escorial represent in all more than half of the entire work. The Latin version, first published in 1486, and subsequently in 1500, 1506 and 1509, is rare, and has been accessible to me only in the copy marked XV. 4. 2 in the Library of King's College, Cambridge; nor do its contents agree well either with the account of the original given in the *Fihrist* (pp. 299–302) or with the manuscript volumes which I have examined in London and Oxford.

The *Fihrist* (p. 300) and Qifṭí describe the book as comprising twelve parts, thus enumerated by the former:—

(i) The treatment of disease and of the sick.
(ii) The preservation of health.
(iii) Fractures, dislocations and surgical operations.
(iv) Materia medica and diet.
(v) Compound medicaments.
(vi) The Art of Medicine.
(vii) Apothecarium; colours, tastes and smells of drugs.
(viii) Bodies.
(ix) Weights and measures.
(x) The anatomical structure and uses of the different members.
(xi) Natural causes in Medicine.
(xii) Introduction to the study of Medicine: medical names and first principles of Medicine.

The Latin version, on the other hand (Brixiæ, October 18, 1486), comprises twenty-five parts[1] entitled as follows:—

(1) De morbis cerebri.
(2) De oculis.
(3) De auribus, naribus, lingua et gula.
(4) De asmate, peripleumonia et pleuresi.
(5) De passionibus stomachi.
(6) De evacuationibus.
(7) De passionibus cordis et epatis et splenis.

[1] But according to Choulant (p. 343) the Venice edition of A.D. 1509 is divided into 37 books. In the following table I have retained the original spelling, except in the case of ligatures and contractions.

(8) De passionibus intestinorum.
(9) De clisteribus et morbis matricis.
(10) De passionibus renum.
(11) De passionibus vesice, hernia, vermibus et cabbo(?) emorroidibus et spermate.
(12) De arthetica et varicibus.
(13) De squirros et aliis apostematibus.
(14) De eo quod dissolvit saniem.
(15) De dislocatione et minutione.
(16) De prognosticis et summa febrium.
(17) De effimera et ethica (for ectica).
(18) De quotidiana, quartana, rigore et aliis.
(19) De crisi.
(20) De urina et venenis.
(21) De simplicibus medicinis, incipiendo a Camomille usque ad Dausar.
(22) De simplicibus medicinis, incipiendo a Dausar usque ad Cordumeni.
(23) De simplicibus medicinis, incipiendo a Cordumeni complet totum.
(24) De electionibus et sophisticationibus medicinarum simplicium tabulâ.
(25) De regimine sanitatis.

Since the *Ḥáwí* or "Continens" must be regarded as the most important work of the greatest of "Arabian" physicians, access to the original text would be an essential condition of success in any detailed and comprehensive study of "Arabian" Medicine. This condition, unfortunately, is unlikely to be fulfilled, for who would undertake the labour of editing, or pay the cost of printing, for so large and so crabbed an exposition of an obsolete science? And even were the difficulty of finding an editor and a publisher overcome, it is doubtful if the manuscript materials are sufficient; if, indeed, more than half the work is still extant. Of the MSS. I have only been able to examine cursorily those in the British Museum and the Bodleian. **Laud 289** in the latter is described as containing Part (or Book) I of the work; but since it deals not only with the diseases of the Brain, but also of the Throat, Lungs and Stomach it would appear to correspond with Books I–V of the Latin translation. **Marsh 156** in the same library is described as containing Books VI and VII, but, to judge by the contents, appears rather to contain Books XVI and XVII. The third Bodleian MS., **Or. 561**, is described by Uri (ii, 162), apparently correctly, as containing Books XXIV and XXV, and deals chiefly with drugs and diet; but beginning with a glossary, alphabetically arranged, of the different organs and the diseases to which they are subject, followed by the *Kitábu ḥalli'r-Rumúz wa Saydalati'ṭ-Ṭibb* on Materia Medica, and "Rules for the use of foods and drinks for the preservation of Health," *etc.* The British Museum MS. **Arundel Or. 14** contains Books VIII, IX and X; while Books IV, V, VI and XI are said to be preserved in the Escorial: Book XII (? XIX) at Munich; and another MS. of Book IV in the Khedivial Library at Cairo. Should these identifications prove correct, Books I–VI, VIII–XI, XVI–XVII, and XXIV–XXV (*i.e.* 14 out of the 25 Books) would appear to be extant, while others, still undescribed and unidentified, probably exist elsewhere.

One very important and interesting feature of the Bodleian MS. **Marsh 156** is that six leaves of it (ff. 239^b–245^b) contain clinical reports of some two dozen of Rází's own cases which presented some unusual features rendering the diagnosis difficult. The name of the patient, the signs and symptoms of the disease, the initial and final diagnosis and treatment, with the termination of the case, are fully described with great clearness and acumen; and these cases, which certainly deserve publication, quite bear out Rází's high repute as a clinical observer[1].

5. *Abu'l-Khayr ibn Khammár.*

This was another eminent philosopher, physician and logician, born at Baghdád in A.H. 331 (A.D. 942–3), with whom the author of the *Fihrist* was personally acquainted[2]. The date of his death is unknown, but from Anecdote XXXVI it is clear that he survived the year A.H. 408 (A.D. 1017–8) in which Sulṭán Maḥmúd conquered Khwárazm. His full name was Abu'l-Khayr al-Ḥasan ibn Suwár ibn Bábá ibn Bahrám (or, according to Ibn Abí Uṣaybi'a, Bihnám), and he was a Christian, apparently of Persian ancestry. He made translations from Syriac into Arabic. Fifteen of his works are enumerated by Ibn Abí Uṣaybi'a[3], but it is uncertain whether any of them still exist.

6. *Abú Naṣr ibn 'Arráq.*

He was another contemporary of al-Bírúní, in whose name he composed twelve astronomical and mathematical tracts[4]. His full name was Abú Naṣr Manṣúr ibn 'Alí ibn 'Arráq *Mawlá Amíri'l-Mú'minín.* He was descended from the old kings of Khwárazm, who claimed descent from the legendary Kay-Khusraw, and who maintained a quasi-independent sovereignty until the tenth Christian century. The penultimate king or prince of this line, Abú Sa'íd Aḥmad ibn Muḥammad ibn 'Arráq, revised and corrected the Khwárazmian Calendar, while the last of them, Abú 'Abdi'llah Muḥammad ibn Aḥmad ibn Muḥammad ibn 'Arráq, is entitled by al-Bírúní "*Shahíd*" ("the Martyr")[5]. This, like so many other ancient and noble Persian families, seems to have been destroyed or dispersed by Sulṭán Maḥmúd of Ghazna. There is no justification for our author's assertion that Abú Naṣr ibn 'Arráq was the nephew of Khwárazmsháh.

[1] Cf. Neuburger, ii, pp. 168–175. [2] See pp. 245 and 265 of that work.

[3] *Op. cit.*, i, p. 333.

[4] See p. xlviii of the *Einleitung* of Sachau's edition of the *Átháru'l-Báqiya*, where they are enumerated; and also pp. 246–249 of the Persian notes to the *Chahár Maqála.*

[5] Al-Bírúní's references to these two kings occur on pp. 241 and 35–36 of *al-Átháru'l-Báqiya.*

7. *Abú Sahl Sa'íd ibn 'Abdu'l-'Azíz an-Nílí.*

He was a poet as well as a physician, and is consequently mentioned by Tha'álibí in his *Yatímatu'd-Dahr* as well as by Ibn Abí Uṣaybi'a in his *Ṭabaqátu'l-Aṭibbá*[1]. His brother Abú 'Abdu'r-Raḥmán was as eminent in Jurisprudence as he was in Medicine. Only two or three of his medical works (commentaries on Hippocrates and Galen, an epitome of Ḥunayn's "Questions" or *Masá'il*, and extracts from Rází's commentaries) are mentioned.

8. *'Alí ibnu'l-'Abbás al-Majúsí.*

This notable physician, known to mediaeval Europe as "Haly Abbas," and bearing, as well as al-Majúsí ("the Magian," presumably because his father or grandfather was converted to Islám from the Zoroastrian religion[2]), the *nisbas* of al-Ahwází and al-Arrajání, was the pupil of Abú Máhir Músá ibn Yúsuf ibn Sayyár and afterwards court-physician to 'Aḍudu'd-Dawla, and died in A.H. 384 (A.D. 994–5). The notices of him given by Qifṭí (p. 232) and Ibn Abí Uṣaybi'a (i, pp. 236–7) are very meagre, and he is chiefly known through his great work the *Kámilu'ṣ-Ṣiná'a* ("Perfect Practitioner") or *Kitábu'l-Malikí* ("Liber Regius"), of which there is a good edition of the original Arabic text printed at Cairo in 2 vols. in 1294/1877, besides an edition lithographed at Lahore in 1283/1866. This book enjoyed a great reputation, though it was, as Qifṭí tells us, to some extent eclipsed by Avicenna's *Qánún*, which was deemed stronger on the theoretical, though less strong on the practical side. It was translated into Latin, and this translation was printed at Venice in A.D. 1492 and again at Lyons in A.D. 1523. The title-page of the latter edition bears the following legend:—

Liber totius Medecinæ necessaria continens quem sapientissimus Haly filius Abbas discipulus abimeher moysi filii seiar edidit: regique inscripsit. unde et regalis dispositionis nomen assumpsit et a Stephano philosophiæ disciplulo ex arabicâ linguâ in Latinam satis ornatam reductus necnon a domino Michæle de Capella, artium et medecinæ doctore, fecundis sinonomis a multis et diversis autoribus ab eo collectis illustratur, summâque cum diligentiâ impressus.

Each volume, the first dealing with the theory and the second with the practice of Medicine, contains ten Discourses (*Maqálát*), which are subdivided into numerous chapters. The anatomical portion of the first volume (*Maqálas* ii and iii), comprising 53 chapters, has, as already been mentioned, been published with a French translation by Dr P. de Koning in his *Trois Traités d'Anatomie arabes* (Leyden, 1903).

[1] Vol. i, pp. 253–254.

[2] Mírzá Muḥammad (Persian notes, p. 234) thinks that he himself was a Magian, but if so how could he have been called 'Alí and his father al-'Abbás? In the Cairo edition of his *Kámilu'ṣ-Ṣiná'at* "Majúsí" has been wantonly pointed as "Mujawwisí" or "Mujawwasí," in order, I suppose, to attempt to conceal his Zoroastrian origin. Mírzá Muḥammad, however, after reading this note, has supplied me with many instances derived from such respectable authorities as aṣ-Ṣábí, Qifṭí, Ibn Khallikán, Ibn Abí Uṣaybi'a, *etc.*, of Jews, Christians and other non-Muslims bearing Muhammadan names, titles and *kunyas*.

The *Kámilu'ṣ-Ṣiná'a* is, in my opinion, far superior in style, arrangement and interest to Avicenna's *Qánún*, and the author's estimate of his predecessors, both the "Ancients" (*i.e.* the Greeks, especially Hippocrates, Galen, Oribasius and Paul of Aegina) and the "Moderns" (*i.e.* the Syrians and Arabs, such as Ahrún, Ibn Serapion, Rází, *etc.*) is admirable, as is the model description of Pleurisy which he gives as a specimen of the method he proposes to employ in the description of each disease. Dr Lucien Leclerc (*Hist. de la Médecine Arabe*, vol. i, pp. 383–8) gives a French translation of the opening portion.

9. *Abú Sahl-i-Masíḥí.*

This writer's full name is Abú Sahl 'Ísá ibn Yaḥyá al-Masíḥí (the Christian) al-Jurjání (of Gurgán, Jurján or Hyrcania), and his work, here called *Ṣad Báb* (the "Hundred Chapters"), properly bears the Arabic title of *Kitábu'l-Mi'a fi'ṭ-Ṭibb* (the "Book of the Hundred on Medicine"), or *al-Mi'atu Maqála* (the "Hundred Discourses"). Born in Jurján, the author studied chiefly at Baghdád, and was one of Avicenna's teachers, and one of the numerous men of learning who found patronage and protection at the Court of Ma'mún ibn Muḥammad Khwárazmsháh and his son Abu'l-'Abbás Ma'mún ibn Ma'mún, killed in 407/1016–7. His friend Abú Rayḥán al-Bírúní enumerates twelve books and treatises which Abú Sahl composed in his honour and dedicated or ascribed to him[1]. Wüstenfeld gives 390/1000 as the year of Abú Sahl's death, but it is not clear on what authority.

10. *Avicenna* (*Shaykh Abú 'Alí ibn Síná*).

So much has been written about this celebrated philosopher and physician that it will be sufficient here to recapitulate the chief facts of his life. These are particularly well authenticated by his autobiography, which carries the narrative down to the time of his father's death, when he was twenty-one years of age, and its continuation by his friend and pupil Abú 'Ubayd al-Júzjání[2]. An excellent summary, together with a list of nearly one hundred of his books, will be found in Brockelmann's *Gesch. d. Arab. Litt.*, vol. i, pp. 452–8, and there is an independent work on him (considered rather as a philosopher than a physician) by Baron Carra de Vaux[3]. Accounts of him, of varying degrees of completeness and accuracy, are naturally to be found in most Muhammadan biographical works composed subsequently to the eleventh century of our era. His intellectual influence, not only in the Islamic world, but, until the Renaissance, in Europe also, was immense. Brockelmann (*op. laud.*, i, 453) well says:—"He displayed an extraordinarily fruitful activity in the most varied fields of learning, especially in Philosophy and Medicine. His works, indeed, lack originality throughout; but, because they set forth in an elegant and easily intelligible form almost all the profane learning of his time, they have exercised an enduring influence on scientific studies, not only in the East, but also in Europe."

[1] See pp. xlvii–xlviii of the Preface to Sachau's edition of al-Bírúní's *Áthâru 'l-Báqiya* (Leipzig, 1876).
[2] For the Arabic text of them, see al-Qifṭí (ed. Lippert, Leipzig, 1903), pp. 413–426.
[3] *Les Grands Philosophes: Avicenna* (Paris, 1900).

Abú 'Alí al-Ḥusayn ibn 'Abdu'lláh ibn Síná (better known in the West by the Europeanized form of his name **Avicenna**, and commonly called in Persia, his native country, **ash-Shaykhu'r-Ra'ís**, "the Chief Doctor," or **al-Mu'allimu'th-Thání**, "the Second Great Teacher") was born in August, A.D. 980, in a village near Bukhárá, where he received his earlier education, the philosopher an-Nátilí and the physician 'Ísá ibn Yaḥyá being amongst his teachers. At the early age of 17 he achieved medical renown by his successful treatment of the Sámánid prince Núḥ ibn Manṣúr (reigned A.D. 976–997). On his father's death, when he was about 21 years of age, he went to Khwárazm, the circumstances of his departure from which are described in Anecdote XXXVI. Attracted to Ṭabaristán by the fame of Qábús ibn Washmgír, he arrived there, as he himself says[1], only to find that that talented but unfortunate prince had been deposed and cast into prison, where he was soon afterwards murdered (403/1012–3). Avicenna subsequently became minister to Shamsu'd-Dawla at Hamadán, where he suffered disgrace and imprisonment, but presently escaped to Iṣfahán, and entered the service of 'Alá'u'd-Dawla Abú Ja'far Muḥammad ibn Dushmanziyár of the so-called Kákawayhid dynasty[2], for whom he wrote his Persian Encyclopaedia of the Sciences called in his honour *Dánish-náma-i-'Alá'í*[3]. He died of colic on the march to Hamadán (where his tomb still exists) in 428/1037, at the age of 58 lunar years, after a short illness for which he treated himself with less than his usual success, so that it was said of him by a contemporary satirist[4]:—

رأيتُ ابن سينا يعادى الرّجال، و بالحَبْس مات أخسّ الممات،
فلم يُشف ما ناله بالشّفا، و لم يَنْجُ من مَوْته بالنّجات،

"I saw Ibn Síná (Avicenna) contending with men, but he died in prison (or, of constipation) the most ignoble death;
"What he attained by the *Shifá* (or, by healing) did not secure his health, nor did he escape death by his *Naját* (or 'Deliverance')."

In these verses there are three ingenious word-plays, for *ḥabs* means both "imprisonment" and "constipation," while two of his most famous works are entitled *Shifá* ("Healing") and *Naját* ("Deliverance").

Besides his medical and philosophical works, Avicenna wrote a good deal of fine poetry in Arabic and a few quatrains (some of which are often ascribed to 'Umar-i-Khayyám) in Persian. The latter have been collected by the late Dr Hermann Ethé[5], and of the former a considerable number are given by Ibn Abí Uṣaybi'a[6]. Of his beautiful Arabic *qaṣída* on the descent of the soul into the body a translation will be found in vol. ii of my *Literary History of Persia* (pp. 110–111). Another remarkable *qaṣída*[7] ascribed to him foretells with extraordinary prevision the Mongol invasion, the sack of Baghdád, the murder of the Caliph,

[1] See the note on p. 79, l. 23 of the text (Persian notes, pp. 250–251).
[2] See S. Lane-Poole's *Mohammadan Dynasties*, p. 145.
[3] See Rieu's *Persian Catalogue*, pp. 433–434. A lithographed edition of this book was published at Ḥaydarábád in the Deccan in 1309/1891–2.
[4] See Ibn Abí Uṣaybi'a's *Ṭabaqát*, vol. ii, p. 6.
[5] *Avicenna als persischer Lyriker* in the *Gottinger Nachrichten* for 1875, pp. 555–567.
[6] Vol. ii, pp. 10–18.
[7] *Ibid.*, pp. 16–18.

and the victory of the Egyptians led by Quṭuz al-Maliku'l-Muẓaffar over the Tartars at 'Ayn Jálút in A.D. 1260, these predictions being based on astrological considerations connected with the conjunction of Jupiter and Saturn in Capricorn "the Mansion of Saturn." Another poem contains medical advice as to the treatment of an ulcer on the forehead addressed to the Wazír Abú Ṭálib al-'Alawí, who had consulted Avicenna on this subject, in similar verses[1]. There are also some remarkable verses in praise of wine, which is compared to "blood of gold," the Christian Trinity, and the First Cause. His literary activity was prodigious and varied, extending to almost every branch of letters and learning, as may be seen by glancing at the lists of his works given by Ibn Abí Uṣaybi'a[2] and Brockelmann. Of these only three are specifically mentioned in the *Chahár Maqála*, namely the *Kitábu'l-Mabda'wa'l-Ma'ád*, quoted by Mírzá Muḥammad[3] from the British Museum MS.; the book entitled "How to guard against various mistakes in medical treatment," printed at Búláq in the margins of ar-Rází's *Manáfi'u'l-aghdhiya wa daf'u maḍárri-há* under the title of *Daf'u'l-maḍárri'l-kulliyya 'ani'l-abdáni'l-insániyya*[4]; and the *Qánún*, the largest and most famous of Avicenna's medical writings. In the preparation of the FitzPatrick lectures on "Arabian Medicine" which I delivered at the Royal College of Physicians in November 1919 and 1920, and which will I hope be published in the course of 1921, I made use of the fine but not very correct edition printed at Rome in A.D. 1593, but there is also a Búláq edition in two volumes. A good account of the various editions and Latin translations will be found in Dr Ludwig Choulant's *Handbuch der Bücherkunde für die Ältere Medicin* (Leipzig, 1841), pp. 359–368. See also Moritz Steinschneider's *Die Europäischen Übersetzungen aus dem Arabischen bis Mitte des 17 Jahrhunderts*[5] in the Index *s.v.* "Avicenna."

In Anecdote XXXVIII the narrator, Abú Kálanjár, mentions four other disciples of Avicenna, concerning three of whom Mírzá Muḥammad gives some valuable information in the Persian notes on pp. ۲۰۲–۲۰۰. Bahmanyár's full name was Abu'l-Ḥasan Bahmanyár ibn Marzubán al-Ádharbayjání al-Majúsí, and he died in 458/1066. A few of his writings exist in manuscript, and two of his metaphysical treatises were printed at Leipzig in A.D. 1851. Abú Manṣúr al-Ḥusayn ibn Muḥammad ibn 'Umar ibn Zíla al-Iṣfahání died in 440/1048–9. The assertion that he was a Zoroastrian is unsupported by evidence, and, in view of the names of his father and grandfather, appears very improbable[6]. There exist in the British Museum MSS. of two of his treatises, one on Music, entitled *al-Káfí* (Or. 2361), and the other a Commentary on Avicenna's *Story of Ḥayy ibn Yaqẓán*.

Far more important than these two was Abú 'Ubayd Abdu'l-Wáḥid ibn Muḥammad al-Júzjání, who first became acquainted with Avicenna in Jurján in 403/1012–3[7]. Avicenna was then about thirty-two years old, and

[1] Vol. ii, p. 14.
[2] *Loc. cit.*, pp. 18–20.
[3] See p. ٢٤٠ of the Persian notes.
[4] *Ibid.*, p. ٢٣٧.
[5] Published in two parts with separate pagination in the *Sitzungsberichte d. Kais. Akad. d. Wissensch.* (*Philos.-histor. Klasse*), Vienna, 1904 and 1905.
[6] Compare, however, note 2 at the foot of p. 154 *supra*.
[7] Mírzá Muḥammad has established this date from the writings of both Avicenna and al-Júzjání. See Persian notes, pp. ۲۰۳–۲۰٤ *ad calc.*

al-Júzjání was thenceforth constantly with him until his death in 428/1037, always urging him to record his knowledge in books while he lived, and preserving these writings from destruction after his death. For Avicenna, as recorded in the *Chahár Maqála* (p. 92 *supra*), distracted by the rival claims of learning, pleasure and statecraft, enjoyed little leisure and tranquillity, and when he wrote a book would often give the original to the person who had asked him to write it without keeping a copy for himself. After his death al-Júzjání sought out these scattered writings wherever they could be found and arranged and edited them, while in other cases he actually assisted in their composition. Thus the *Dánish-náma-i-'Alá'í*[1], Avicenna's most important Persian work, composed for and dedicated to 'Alá'u'd-Dawla Abú Ja'far Kákúya, was designed to treat of Logic, Metaphysics, Natural Science, Mathematics, Astronomy, Music and Arithmetic; but after his death only the first three sections could be found. The missing portions were therefore compiled and translated by al-Júzjání from the *Shifá* and other Arabic works of his master, and the lacuna thus filled. We also owe to al-Júzjání the continuation of Avicenna's autobiography from the time of their first meeting in Jurján down to his death The full text of this is given by Ibn Abí Uṣaybi'a[2] and an abridgement of it by al-Qifṭí[3].

11. *Sayyid Isma'íl Jurjání.*

This is probably the first Muslim physician who used the Persian language chiefly or exclusively in writing on scientific subjects, or at least the first whose works have come down to us. He gives his name and genealogy as follows in the Introduction to his *Dhakhíra-i-Khwárazmsháhí*[4]:—Isma'íl ibnu'l-Ḥasan ibn Muḥammad ibn Aḥmad al-Ḥusayní al-Jurjání. Fonahn[5] gives his father's name as Aḥmad instead of al-Ḥasan, his *laqab* as Zaynu'd-Dín, and his *kunya* as Abú Ibráhím; while Rieu[6] transposes Muḥammad and Aḥmad in his pedigree; and Leclerc[7] calls him Abu'l-Faḍá'il and Sharafu'd-Dín. Little is known of his life except that he came to Khwárazm (Khiva) and entered the service of Quṭbu'd-Dín Muḥammad Khwárazmsháh in 504/1110–1111, composed the four medical works (*Aghráḍ*, *Dhakhíra*, *Khuffí* and *Yádgár*) mentioned in the *Chahár Maqála*, and died at Merv in or about the year 531/1136–7.

The contents of the *Aghráḍu'ṭ-Ṭibb* ("Aims of Medicine"), composed for the Minister of Atsiz Khwárazmsháh (reigned A.D. 1127–1156), and the manuscripts of it existing in different libraries are fully described by Fonahn[8], as are the *Khuffí-i-'Alá'í*[9] (composed in A.D. 1113) and the *Yádgár-i-Ṭibb* ("Medical Memoranda")[10], which deals with Pharmaco-

[1] As already noted, the text was lithographed in India in 1309/1891–2, but is rare. Mr A. G. Ellis most kindly placed his copy at my disposal. Mírzá Muḥammad mentions two MSS. in the British Museum, *viz*. Add. 16,830 and Add. 16,659, ff. 258ᵇ–342ᵇ, and there is another, Or. 16,830. See Rieu's *Pers. Cat.*, pp. 433–434.

[2] *Ṭabaqátu'l-Aṭibbá*, ii, pp. 4–9

[3] Pp. 417–426 of Lippert's edition.

[4] In an old thirteenth century MS. of Books I–III of this work in my possession.

[5] *Zur Quellenkunde d. Pers. Med.*, p. 129.

[6] *Pers. Cat.*, p. 466.

[7] *Hist. de la Médecine Arabe*, vol. ii, pp. 18–20.

[8] *Op. cit.*, No. 16, pp. 11–13.

[9] *Ibid.*, No. 39, p. 35.

[10] *Ibid.*, No. 280, p. 105.

logy and Therapeutics. These I have not seen, and they are completely overshadowed by his *magnum opus* the *Dhakhíra-i-Khwárazmsháhí*, or "Thesaurus of Khwárazmsháh," of which I have collected several fine manuscripts and which I have studied with some care. Before speaking of in however, I must observe that the *Khuffí* was so called from *khuff*, a boots because it was written in two elongated narrow volumes, one of which the traveller could carry in each of his riding-boots, and that its name is not *Khafí* ("Hidden," "Secret"), as stated by Fonahn and Leclerc[1].

The general contents of the *Dhakhíra-i-Khwárazmsháhí* are pretty fully stated by Fonahn[2], and in particular the contents of Book IX, dealing with poisons and antidotes, bites and stings of animals, *etc.* He also enumerates the MSS. of the work, which has never been published in the original Persian, though an Urdú translation has been lithographed in India. The complete work, of which I possess one manuscript, while another, wanting only a few leaves, and bearing the class-mark **Mm. 2. 6**, is preserved in the Cambridge University Library, originally comprised 9 Books[3], 75 Discourses, 1107 chapters, and 450,000 words. I also possess three fine old MSS., transcribed in the thirteenth or fourteenth century, containing portions of the work, *viz.* (1) Books I, II and part of III; (2) Book III, Maqála iv, Bakhsh 1 to the end of Book V; (3) Book VI, Guftár xi to the end. I also possess a more modern MS. of the whole work, and another of the whole of Book VI, Guftárs i–xxi. I have discussed this book more fully in my FitzPatrick lectures, delivered before the Royal College of Physicians in November 1919 and 1920, which are now in the press, so that I need say no more of it in this place.

Note XXVIII.

Jámí's rhymed versions of Anecdotes XXXIV (Text, p. 73) and XXXVIII (Text, pp. 82–4) in the Silsilatu'dh-Dhahab.

(*The text is taken from a MS. dated* 997/1589 *in my own possession, and* **Or. 425**, ff. 75[b] *and* 76[a] *in the Cambridge University Library.*)

Anecdote XXXIV.

حکایت آن طبیب دانا که آفت زده*را بی وجود اسباب معالجه کرد
و بی دستیاری آلات و ادوات از تنگنای مرض بیرون آورد،

یکی از ملوکِ سامانی، داشت دوران طبیبی ارزانی،
در همه کارها باو همدم، در همه رازها باو محرم،
دادیش در حضورِ خود پیوست، نبضِ جمعی مخدّرات بدست،
روزی از گفت و گوی خلق خلاص، بود با او درونِ خلوتِ خاص،

[1] Mírzá Muḥammad has pointed out to me that, as we learn from Qifṭí (p. 80) and Ibn Abí Uṣaybi'a (i, p. 201), one of Isḥáq ibn Ḥunayn's works was similarly entitled *Kunnáshu'l-Khuff*, and that Sayyid Isma'íl probably got the idea from him.

[2] *Op. cit.*, No. 15, pp. 7–11.

[3] Book X on Compound Medicaments was subsequently added by the author.

پای نا محرمان از انجا پی، نامهٔ مجرمان از آنجا طی،
ناگه آمد کنیزکی چون ماه، خوان بکف پیشِ شاه گشت دوتاه،
تا نهد خوانِ خوردنی بزمین، ریخت خلطی بپُشتِ او ز کمین،
الفِ قامتش چو دال بماند، خم چو پیران دیرسال بماند،
کرد چندانکه زور راست نشد، پُشتِ او همچنانکه خواست نشد،
گفت با آن حکیم شاهِ کریم، کای شفا بخشِ هر مزاج سقیم،
هم درین دم گشای دستِ علاج، وا رهانش ازین فسادِ مزاج،
ماند حیران حکیم چون اسباب، بود بهر علاجِ او نایاب،
دست زد معجرش ز فرق کشید، جامه‌اش‌را ز پیش و پس بدرید،
از ازارش کشاد بندِ ازار، کرد بیرونش از سُرین شلوار،
غرقه شد زآن خجالت اندر خوی، خلط بگداخت در مفاصلِ وی،
قامتِ خود ز سروِ بستان راست، کرد و آزاد از زمین بر خاست،
در طبیبی چو نیك ماهر بود، پیشِ او سرِّ کار ظاهر بود،
چون بماند از علاجِ جسمانی، دست زد در علاج روحانی،

Anecdote XXXVIII.

معالجه کردنِ شیخ ابو علی سینا آن صاحب ماخولیارا که طبیبان از معالجهٔ وی عاجز بودند،

بود در عهد بو علی سینا، آن بکُنْهِ اصولِ طِب بینا،
ز آلِ بویه یکی ستوده خصال، شد ز ماخولیا پریشان حال،
بانگ میزد که کم بود در ده، هیچ گاوی بسانِ من فربه،
آشپز گر پزد هریسه ز من، گُرددش گنج سیم کیسه ز من،
زود باشید و حلقِ من بُرّید، بدکانِ هریسه پز سپرید،
صبح تا شام حالِ او این بود، با حریفان مقالِ او این بود،
نگذشتی ز روز و شب دانگی، که چو گاوان نبودیش بانگی،
که بزودی بکارد یا خنجر، بکُشیدم که می شوم لاغر،
تا بجائی رسید کو نه غذا، خوردی از دستِ هیچ کس نه دوا،
اهلِ طب راهِ عجز بسپردند، استغاثه ببو علی بردند،
گفت سویش قدم زنید ز راه، مژده گویان که بامداد پگاه،

میرسد بهر کُشتنت بشتاب، دشنه در دست خواجهٔ قصّاب،
رفت ازین مژده زو گرانیها، کرد اظهارِ شادمانیها،
بامدادان که بو علی بر خاست، شد سوی منزلش که گاو کجاست،
آمد و خُفت در میان سرای، که منم گاو هان و هان پیش آی،
بو علی دست و پاش سخت ببست، کارد بر کارد تیز کرد و نشست،
بُرد قصّاب وار دست سویش، دید هنجارِ پُشْت و پهلویش،
گفت کین گاو لاغرست هنوز، مصلحت نیست کُشْتنش امروز،
چند روزیش مهر علف بندید، یك زمانش گرسنه مپسندید،
تا چو فربه شود برانم تیغ، نبُوَد ذبحِ او فسوس و دریغ،
دست و پایش ز بند بگشادند، خوردنیهاش پیش بنهادند،
هرچه دادندشْ از غذا و دوا، همه‌را خورد بی خلاف و اِبا،
تا چو گاوان از آن شود فربه، شد خود او از خیالِ گاوی به،

Note XXIX. The Ma'múní Khwárazmsháhs.

(Text, p. 76; Persian notes, pp. 194 and 241–4.)

This older dynasty of Khwárazmsháhs was originally tributary to the Sámánids, but, during the interval (A.H. 380–407 = A.D. 990–1016) which separated the decay of these latter rulers from the final ascendency of the House of Ghazna, it enjoyed a quasi-independence. The following are those of its rulers whose names occur in history.

1. *Ma'mún ibn Muḥammad Khwárazmsháh.*

He was originally governor of Gurgánj (Jurjániyya), and in 385/995 captured and killed Abú 'Abdi'lláh Khwárazmsháh, the lord of Káth, and annexed his realms. He himself died in 387/997[1]. He was succeeded by his son—

2. *'Alí ibn Ma'mún ibn Muḥammad Khwárazmsháh,*

who succeeded his father in the year last mentioned and married the sister of Sulṭán Maḥmúd of Ghazna Avicenna came to Khwárazm during his reign, and met with much honour at his hands[2]. The date of his death is not exactly known. Abu'l-Ḥusayn Aḥmad ibn Muḥammad as-Suhaylí, a great patron of learning, to whom Avicenna dedicated at least two of his works[3], was Minister to him and afterwards to his brother and successor—

[1] Ibnu'l-Athír, vol. ix, pp. 76 and 93.

[2] Al-Qifṭí, p. 417.

[3] See p. ۲۴۲ of the Persian notes. He fled from Khwárazm to Baghdád in 404/1013–4 and died in 418/1027 at Surra-man-ra'a.

3. *Abu'l-'Abbás Ma'mún ibn Ma'mún ibn Muḥammad Khwárazmsháh,* the hero of Anecdote XXXVI, who was likewise a generous friend to men of learning, and, like his brother, was married to one of Sulṭán Maḥmúd's sisters. He continued for some time on friendly terms with this ambitious potentate, who, however, finally ordered him to recognize him as his over-lord and insert his name in the *khuṭba*. This Abu 'l-'Abbás Ma'mún consented to do, but after the departure of the envoy to Ghazna his nobles rose and murdered him in 407/1016–7 when he was only thirty-two years of age.

4. *Abu'l-Ḥárith Muḥammad ibn 'Alí ibn Ma'mún ibn Muḥammad Khwárazmsháh.*

He succeeded to the throne on the murder of his uncle, but no long while had elapsed when Sulṭán Maḥmúd, on the pretext of avenging his murdered brother-in-law, invaded and annexed Khwárazm and carried off as hostages or captives the survivors of the family. This happened in 408/1017–8, and the event was celebrated by 'Unṣurí in a *qaṣída* of which the opening lines are quoted by the editor[1]. The historian Abu 'l-Faḍl-i-Bayhaqí in his *Ta'ríkh-i-Mas'údí*[2] gives an account of these events based on a lost work of Abú Rayḥán al-Bírúní's on the "Notables of Khwárazm" (*Masháhír-i-Khwárazm*). From this it appears that al-Bírúní spent seven years (A.H. 400–407 = A.D. 1010–1017) at the Court of Abu'l-'Abbás, where he held various offices, and was conversant with all the circumstances which led up to his death.

In conclusion Mírzá Muḥammad observes that the Qáḍí Aḥmad-i-Ghaffárí, probably misled by the *Ta'ríkh-i-Guzída* (p. 389 of the Gibb *facsimile*), in his *Nusakh-i-Jahán-árá* confuses the dynasty discussed in this note with the Faríghúní family who acted as viceroys first for the Sámánids and then for the Ghaznawís in Júzján.

Note XXX. Sháhinsháh 'Alá'u'd-Dawla.

(Text, p. 82; Persian notes, p. 251.)

The Amír 'Alá'u'd-Dawla Ḥusámu'd-Dín Abú Ja'far Muḥammad ibn Dushmanziyár ruled over Iṣfahán and the adjacent districts from 398/1007–8 to 433/1041–2, in which latter year he died. His father Dushmanziyár was the maternal uncle of Sayyida, the spirited mother of Majdu'd-Dawla[3] ibn Fakhru'-Dawla, the Daylamí or Buwayhid prince, and since in the Daylamí dialect "*Kákú*," or "*Kákúya*" signifies "uncle," he is often called by this title, and his son 'Alá'u'd-Dawla by the title of "*Ibn Kákúya*," while the dynasty to which they belonged is called by S. Lane-Poole[4] "Kákwayhid."

[1] Persian notes, p. ٢٤٧.

[2] Ṭihrán lith. ed., pp. 663–677; Cairo ed. of 'Utbí's history with Maníní's commentary, p. 258. Yáqút in his "Dictionary of Learned Men" (vol. vi, p. 311 of the Gibb edition) mentions amongst al-Bírúní's works a *Kitábu'l-Musámara fí Akhbári Khwárazm*, which, as Mírzá Muḥammad points out, is probably identical with this work. He suggests, indeed, with great probability, that Bayhaqí's *Masháhír* (مشاهير) is probably a corrupt reading for *Musámara* (مسامره).

[3] See pp. 43–44 of my edition of Dawlatsháh.

[4] *Mohammadan Dynasties*, p. 145. See also the references at the foot of p. ٢٠١ of the Persian notes.

In this Anecdote (XXXVIII) two errors occur, for Avicenna acted as Minister to Shamsu'd-Dawla ibn Fakhru'd-Dawla (brother of the above-mentioned Majdu'd-Dawla) at Hamadán, not to 'Alá'u'd-Dawla, whom he never served in this capacity, and who, moreover, lived not at Ray but at Iṣfahán, whither Avicenna went to attach himself to his Court in 412/1021–2 on the death of Shamsu'd-Dawla and the accession of his son Samá'u'd-Dawla.

Note XXXI. The Shaykh 'Abdu'lláh Anṣárí.

(Text, p. 84; Persian notes, pp. 255–8.)

The Shaykhu'l-Islám Abú Isma'íl 'Abdu'lláh ibn Abí Manṣúr Muḥammad...al-Anṣárí al-Khazrají al-Hirawí traced his pedigree to Abú Ayyúb, a well-known companion of the Prophet. He was born on Sha'bán 2, 396 (May 4, 1006), and died towards the end of A.H. 481 (March, 1088). He was a notable traditionist and theologian, and, in spite of his fanatical attachment to the narrow and anthropomorphic doctrines of the Ḥanbalí school and his hatred of philosophers, who stood in terror of him, was accounted a leading Ṣúfí. In Persia he is generally known as Khwája 'Abdu'lláh Anṣárí. In his Persian poems and quatrains, which are highly esteemed and have been repeatedly lithographed in Persia, he calls himself Anṣárí, Pír-i-Anṣár, and Pír-i-Hirí. The prayers (*Munáját*) which he composed in Persian are also greatly admired. He used to lecture on the lives of the Saints, taking as his text the *Ṭabaqátu'ṣ-Ṣúfiyya* of as-Sulamí, and adding observations of his own. One of his disciples took down these lectures in the ancient language of Herát, and on this version Jámí based his well-known Hagiography the *Nafaḥátu'l-Uns*[1]. Of his numerous works there still exist, besides those already mentioned, a condemnation of Scholastic Philosophy (*Dhammu'l-Kalám*) in Arabic[2], a less rare treatise in the same language entitled *Manázilu's-Sá'irín ila'l-Ḥaqqi'l-Mubín*, and in Persian a tract entitled *Zádu'l-'Árifín*[3]; and another, of which extracts are preserved[4], called the "Book of Mysteries" (*Kitáb-i-Asrár*).

Mírzá Muḥammad gives, on the authority of the historian adh-Dhahabí, two narratives of attempts to discredit the Shaykh made by the philosophers whom he persecuted. On one occasion, when Sulṭán Alp Arslán the Saljúq and his great Minister Niẓámu'l-Mulk visited Herát, they asked him why he cursed Abu'l-Ḥasan al-Ash'arí, whose doctrines the Niẓámu'l-Mulk professed. After some hesitation he replied, "I do not recognize al-Ash'arí; him only I curse who does not believe that God is in Heaven." On another occasion they produced a little copper image, which, as they told the King, Anṣárí's anthropomorphism led him to worship, but he, being summoned and accused, so vehemently denied this calumny that the King, convinced of his innocence, dismissed him with honour and punished his detractors.

[1] See pp. 1–3 of Nassau Lees's edition of this work. Mírzá Muḥammad informs me that a MS. of these lectures in their ancient original form exists in the Núr-i-'Uthmániyya Library at Constantinople, and that M. Louis Massignon shewed him the copy he had made of the portion referring to the celebrated Ṣúfí al-Ḥalláj. I suppose that this is the MS. (No. 2500) to which M. Massignon refers in his striking work on the *Kitábu'ṭ-Ṭawásín* of al-Ḥalláj (Paris, 1913), p. 94, n. 4 *ad calc.*

[2] Add. 27,520 of the British Museum.

[3] Rieu's *Pers. Cat.*, p. 738.

[4] *Ibid.*, p. 774.

XXXII. Additional Note by Mr W. Gornold on the "Part of the Unseen" and other Astrological terms.

"It appears to me quite patent that all theories as to what the Part of the Unseen may be are dispelled by the text of your work which clearly gives the rule (p. 131 *supra*):

"'As for the Part of the Unseen, by day they compute it from the Moon and by night from the Sun, adding thereto the degree of the Ascendant, and subtracting thirty (for) each (whole sign) from the Ascendant, as before: then what remains over is the place of the Part of the Unseen.'

"In the case cited, 28 Ṣafar, A.H. 511 (1 July, A.D. 1117), the time of birth being New Moon (here shown to be at 5.32 p.m. local mean time) when both the luminaries were above the horizon, we have to deal with a day horoscope. Therefore we count from the Moon's place to that of the Sun, which is twelve whole Signs and nothing over. The Part of the Unseen must therefore be on the Ascendant, and this must be the case at the time of every New Moon, whether it happens by day or by night. Only we have to note that as the Moon separates from the Sun the Part of Fortune is carried from the Ascendant downward to the nadir, while the Part of the Unseen is carried upward towards the midheaven, and this converse motion goes forward in each case at the rate of about 12 degrees per day until they meet again, this time in *opposition* to the Ascendant, at the full of Moon.

"I had the pleasure of seeing Mr Shirley yesterday and conferred with him in regard to his use of the term 'Alcochoden' as synonymous with 'Hyleg' or *Hayláj*, and he informed me that he derived his information from Wilson's *Dictionary of Astrology*, a work of which I am extremely suspicious, as on many occasions I have found that he treats of subjects about which he has evidently no practical experience. But I think the matter must be settled by reference to some of the Arabic or Persian works in which the term is used. The context would undoubtedly give any astrological student the clue to interpretation. If, as I think, Alcochoden is Ruler of the 12th House then its influence would be associated in the text with enemies, capture, imprisonment, *etc.*, which would clearly indicate its evil repute, while Almuten, conversely, would be associated with friends and supporters, favours and wishes granted, *etc.*, indicating its beneficent influence. Probably you can turn up some reference in support, or otherwise, of this view. I hope so."

"P. 6, l. 4. 'The four subservient forces' appear to answer to mental as well as physical processes thus:

The 'Force Attractive' = Absorption = Perception,
" 'Force Retentive' = Circulation = Cogitation,
" 'Force Assimilative' = Secretion = Memory,
" 'Force Expulsive' = Excretion = Expression.

"P. 63, ll. 1 and 3. The *Almagest* of Claudius Ptolemy appears, from observations recorded by him, to have been compiled about the year A.D. 140, for it contains no account of observations made after the year A.D. 138. It was translated into Arabic in the ninth century by command of the Caliph Al-Ma'mún. Persian, Hebrew, and Greek versions are also mentioned. The best English translation is that of Achmand. Ptolemy's astrological work, the *Tetrabiblos*, or *Quadrapartite*, is standard work on the subject in general use among modern students. The *Almagest*, *Syntaxis* and *Tetrabiblos* are works of extreme interest to astronomers and students of astrology.

"P. 67, l. 23. The 'Part of Fortune,' depending on the elongation of the Moon referred to the Ascendant of the horoscope, would of course be on the Ascendant at the time of New Moon. At First Quarter it is on the nadir, at Full Moon on the descendant, at the Last Quarter on the midheaven. Some authors compute its place by longitude in the Zodiac and others by oblique ascension or descension. The rule of Ptolemy is that it corresponds with the place held by the Moon at the time of sunrise, but he does not say whether it is local or equatorial sunrise, nor whether the 'place' of the moon is to be taken by longitude, right ascension, or oblique ascension.

"P. 67, l. 21. July 1st, A.D. 1117 is equivalent to Ṣafar 28, A.H. 511. This appears evident from reference to other dates occurring in the course of your pages.

"This date, July 1st, is O.S. and corresponds with July 8th N.S.

"By adding 760 years (or 40 cycles of 19 years each) to the date 1117 we get equivalent year of cycle A.D. 1877, and to the date we must add two days due to the omission of leap year days in the 12th and 16th century-years, which brings us to July 10th, 1877, when it is seen that there was a New Moon. Hence the date is correctly taken.

"As to the 'Part of the Unseen,' this appears from the context to be derived from a reversal of the method employed for the 'Part of Fortune.' The former is counted from the Moon to the Sun, and the latter from the Sun to the Moon, and the distance in the Zodiac is set off from the Ascendant.

"Unlike all the planetary Points to which I have drawn your attention, and which are determined by their solar elongations, the 'Part of the Unseen' appears to be a lunar Point, determined from the Sun's elongation in respect of the Moon.

"The date of birth having been fixed, we are left to find the time of birth by the reference to the positions of the Sun and Moon, which it is said were so situated that there was no space at all between them. It is not presumed that this was an observation made at the time of birth, but one that was afterwards calculated and found to be correct. The New Moon of Ṣafar 28, A.H. 511, took place locally in longitude 68° E. at 5.32 p.m. (G.M.T. 1 o'clock) when the luminaries were in ecliptic conjunction in Cancer 15° 8′. The Moon was then only about 11° past the S. Node, and therefore had about 57′ of S. latitude. It was a partial eclipse of the Sun. The fact that this is not mentioned goes to prove that the calculation was retrogressive and that the observation was not made at the time of birth.

"The following is the horoscope set for lat. 35° N. and long. 68° E. The planets' places are put into the nearest whole degree. I do not know what symbol was used for the 'Part of the Unseen,' and if it occurs in any of the works to which you have access, I should be glad to have it. The others, belonging to the planets, I have put in according to their traditional use among the moderns. To these we have recently added the Lightning Flash, due to Uranus, and the Web or Grille due to Neptune. They are found in the same way as the others, by the planet's distance from the Sun in the order of the signs.

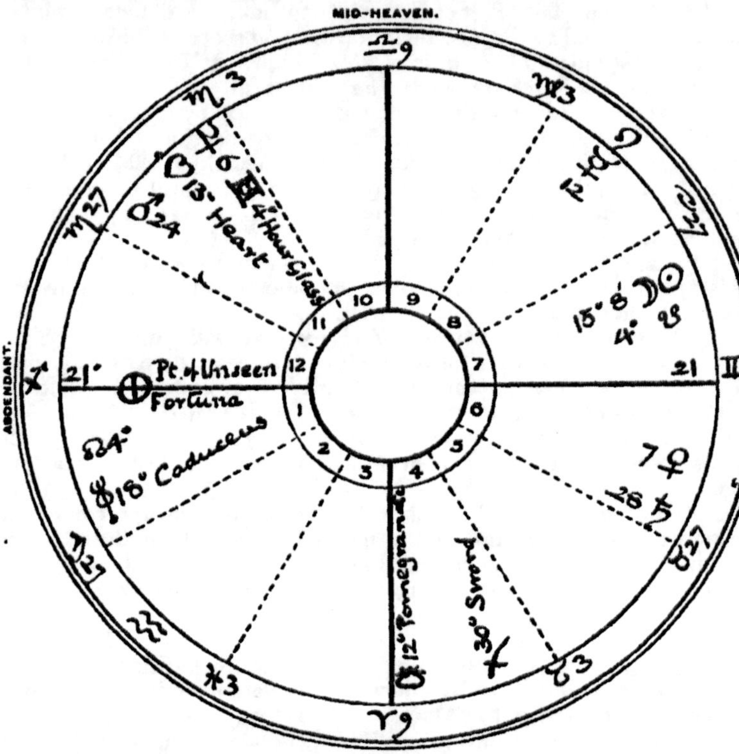

The Map of the Heavens

Date 1 July, A.D. 1117; Hour 5.32 p.m. (local); Long. 68° E., Lat. 35° N.

"The symbol for the 'Part of the Unseen,' when found, should be placed on the Ascendant with Fortuna, and the figure will then be complete. I do not think that it will be found very far out of the true, but I am of course relying on Lunation Tables which are not quite up to date. The secular equation due to these may be as much as 5 minutes for seven centuries, as they were constructed about A.D. 1800, and are here applied to a date about 700 years previous.

"P. 64, l. 22, and pp. 130–131. *Khaby* and *Ḍamir*—The Hindus have systems of horary astrology, called *Salyana* and *Arudha*, by which they are able to determine what is hidden and where lost property may be found. Things held in the hand concealed have often been well described to me by Indian *Jyoshis*.

"'Hyleg' or *Hayláj*—This term is in common use among astrological students, and the rules for finding it are contained in Ptolemy's work on Astrology, and also in Placidus de Titus'[1] 'Primum Mobile.' Both these authorities differ from the Arabic authors in their method of location.

"P. 132, l. 17. 'Exaltation.' The planets, also the Sun and Moon, are held to be 'exalted' in certain Signs, and especially in certain degrees of those signs. Thus the Sun is 'exalted' in the sign Aries and the 19th degree thereof. 'Altitude'[2] is an astronomical term which signifies distance above the horizon and should preferably not be used in this connection.

"The term *Almuten* refers to the Planet which has dominion in the 11th House, or the House of Friends and Allies. *Alchocoden* or *Alcochoden* (whichever may be the correct form) refers to the planet which has dominion in the 12th House, or House of Enemies. It has not any connection with the Hyleg, as Mr Shirley seems to think.

"The term *Kad-khudá* (Lord of the House) refers to the Planet which rules the Sign in which the Hyleg is found at birth. Thus if the Sun were so qualified as Hyleg and were in the sign Scorpio, then the planet Mars would be the *Kad-khudá*.

[1] Mr Gornold sends me the following note: "Of Placidus de Titus, who first rendered a studied version of Ptolemy's work on Astrology, we have very little information. It appears that he was known as Didacus Placidus, and was a native of Bologna, became a monk, and was appointed mathematician to the Archduke Leopold of Austria. He wrote in the early part of the seventeenth century a work entitled the "Primum Mobile," in which he gives a thorough digest of the teaching of Ptolemy. The best English translation is by Cooper. Placidus showed that Ptolemy recognized two sets of directions arising out of two sets of planetary positions, one in the Zodiac and the other in the World, *i.e.* in the prime vertical. To Placidus remains the credit of having elaborated that part of directional Astrology which has regard to all directions *in mundo*."

[2] I originally translated *Sharaf* by this term, but have corrected it according to Mr Gornold's suggestion.

GENERAL INDEX

In this Index I have followed the same plan as that adopted in my *Persian Literature under Tartar Dominion*. Where numerous references occur under one heading the more important are printed in **Clarendon** type, which is also used for the first entry under each letter of the alphabet, and for headings under which two or more homonymous persons are grouped together, either in chronological order, or in order of importance, or in classes (rulers, men of learning, poets, etc.). The letter **b.** between two names stands for **Ibn** ("Son of..."), and **n.** after the number of a page indicates a foot-note. The addition in parentheses of a number after a name, book, battle, or the like, indicates, if Roman, the century, if Arabic, the year of the Christian era in which the man was born (b.), flourished (fl.) or (d.) died, or in which the book was written or the battle fought. Prefixes like **Abú** ("Father of...") and **Ibn** ("Son of...") in Muhammadan, and **de, le, von** in European names are disregarded in the alphabetical arrangement, so that names like **Abú Sa'íd, Ibn Síná, le Strange, de Slane**, etc., must be sought under **S**, and **von Kremer** under **K**. Titles of books and foreign words are printed in *italics*, and an asterisk is prefixed to the former when they are quoted at any length in the translation or notes. A hyphen preceding a word indicates that the Arabic definite article **al-** should be prefixed to it.

INDEX OF TECHNICAL TERMS EXPLAINED OR DISCUSSED IN THE NOTES

ق

ك، گ

ل

م

ن

و، ه، ى

CAMBRIDGE: PRINTED BY J. B. PEACE, M.A., AT THE UNIVERSITY PRESS

Treasure of
Books
Under One Roof

Demand
Any Rare Book
at
www.facsimilepublisher.com

Demand Any Rare Book at:

www.facsimilepublisher.com

if not available, give information,
our team will search and update you.

Promote Knowledge:

If you have any rare book
which is not available at
www.facsimilepublisher.com,
offer it to other readers so that others can also be
benefitted with your cooperation.
The book will be printed with your courtesy.

Print & Publish:

If you wish to get your book printed or published,
we have the service for you.

Customization on Demand:

We offer customization of books
as per the demand of the customer.

Published by

Facsimile Publisher
Ashok Vihar, Delhi-110052 (India)
Website: www.facsimilepublisher.com

Distributed by

Gyan Books Pvt. Ltd.
5, Ansari Road, Daryaganj, New Delhi-110002 (India)
E-mail: books@gyanbooks.com, Website: www.gyanbooks.com

2 222000 010423